Child Psychiatry
in the
Soviet Union

Child Psychiatry
in the
Soviet Union

Preliminary
Observations

NANCY ROLLINS, M.D.

Harvard University Press
Cambridge, Massachusetts
1972

To Clifford F. Youse

Contents

Contents

III. Diagnosis   71

IV. General Treatment Methods   113

V. Special Psychotherapy   146

Contents

Tables

Foreword

Those of us who have been in Soviet studies for some time tend to develop two traits, one of which is laudable and the other less so. In the first, constant contact with Soviet materials, plus background reading, sometimes supplemented by travel to the USSR, gives us a "feel" about Soviet society that comes only from such long exposure and experience. After reading countless numbers of *Pravda* or *Izvestiia* editorial leaders, we could write one easily: the form has an invariable, almost liturgical structure. First comes praise about the great achievements of the Soviet people led by the Communist Party (and before 1953 by Comrade Stalin himself), followed by the critical shift introduced by a word such as "however" (*odnako*), and then a sermon on the inadequacies of certain comrades or institutions, the need to shape up, and so on. We learn to read between the lines; we discount such phrases as the "people" and translate it as the "Party leaders"; and we know where the information is, or where to start the search for it if it is available at all. In other words, we become experienced Sovietologists.

The other trait, however, is not so pleasant to recount: as we plow through the Soviet materials, we tend to become set in our ways. We acquire a rigid and static picture of Soviet society; we assume certain viewpoints and adopt certain stereotypes that fail to change as Soviet society itself changes. It is true that Sovietologists have been speaking of "models" of Soviet society, indicating that earlier conceptions such as "totalitarianism," "industrialism," or the "developmental" models are simply not adequate tools anymore to encompass changing Soviet reality. But although new approaches are needed, we often resist them because they require a major change in our thinking, and change is disturbing. In the light of these rigidities and stereotypes I, at least, welcome people who do not have a heavy investment in Soviet studies, and who come with a fresh new look to see things our jaded eyes do not.

The only trouble with such views is that they are often naïve as well as charming. The neophyte in the Soviet area simply does not know his way around the mine fields and far too often blunders badly because he has misinterpreted a clue, has been mistriggered by a stimulus, or simply lacks the historical and other background to understand what he sees and hears and place it in proper perspective. I suppose this is true of anyone who wanders into a strange society; for example, foreign interpretations of many aspects of American life often strike us as ludicrous. But the distorting effect tends to be heightened by the very nature of the Soviet political system, with its emphasis on secrecy and propaganda and its monopoly of mass communications.

Indeed, there is a tradition of well-meaning, highly motivated, often quite intelligent Western intellectuals who have trekked to the Soviet Union and come back to make fools of themselves by reporting a world of fantasy that conformed only to their own wishes, abetted by clever Soviet manipulation. Malcolm Muggeridge, in a review of a book on Western intellectuals' involvement with the Soviet Union, once noted "this strange aberration whereby the ostensibly most enlightened minds and feeling hearts of our civilization found it possible to adulate and justify [the Soviet regime]" and added that it would be possible "to make a collection of observations about the USSR by the flower of our Western intelligentsia compared with which the sayings of . . . Emily Post or . . . ex-President Eisenhower would seem like the very distillation of wisdom."

Dr. Nancy Rollins has not come back from the Soviet Union telling us that she has seen the future and that it works. Rather, what I find remarkable about her work and her experiences is that she has taken a fresh look at one aspect of Soviet society—child psychiatry, which is not well known in the West—and has done a conscientious and professional job of it. And, most importantly, she has made as sober an assessment as possible.

I first met Nancy Rollins several years ago at a meeting of the Association for the Advancement of Psychotherapy, where I had been asked to give a paper on certain aspects of Soviet psychiatry and its relationship to ideology and society. She expressed a strong interest in learning more about Soviet psychiatry, particularly child psychiatry (her own field of professional activity), an interest that had been sparked by a short trip to the USSR under the sponsorship of the Citizens' Exchange Corps. I encouraged her to follow that path and suggested she apply for support to the Public Health Service under the provisions of the US-USSR Cultural Exchange Agreement. She was accepted, but the Soviet occupation of Czechoslovakia in August 1968 delayed her trip until November 1968.

Few people in the West who have not themselves been through this kind of experience realize what it means to spend four months as a lone foreigner in the Soviet Union, particularly in the winter. Moscow or Leningrad, in contrast to European capitals, can hardly be called swinging. Soviet professional colleagues, generally, will not be able to extend much hospitality to a foreigner because of the cramped conditions under which they live (44 percent of Leningrad physicians, for example, live in communal apartments and share cooking and other facilities with other dwellers in the same apartment), and also because it is healthier not to make too close contact with a foreigner. Thus I can only admire her ability to stay in an atmosphere that is often lonesome and depressing, especially after work hours.

I think, furthermore, that her experience is almost without parallel. Indeed, the only other Western psychiatrist I know who has spent an extended period of work in psychiatric institutions and had a chance to observe clinical practice is Isidore Ziferstein, but his interest was not centrally in child psychiatry. Very few other American psychiatrists or social scientists have paid any systematic attention to psychiatry in the Soviet Union since Joseph Wortis, who published *Soviet Psychiatry* in 1950. It is true that a few have gone on a visit, written their impressions for their colleagues, and then got back to their daily practice. I have in mind such persons as Zigmund Lebensohn, Nathan Kline, Alex Kaplan, Alec Skolnick, J. Moreno, and Stanley Lesse. There is also the 1967 U.S. Mission on Mental Health, but here again we have a flying delegation which was shown the highlights, given handouts, and exposed to well-rehearsed presentations. Dr. Rollins, on the other hand, had more staying power: four months' worth. I believe she has succeeded in catching the flavor of child psychiatric clinical practices in large Soviet towns, and I assume that what she saw was fairly typical (if perhaps of a higher quality than the rest of the Soviet Union).

Dr. Rollins once stated to me what she called "Rollins' Law": that the degree of positiveness in American observations varies inversely with the length of the stay in the USSR (other factors remaining constant). I would amplify this as follows: an important element in one's reaction to the Soviet Union (particularly if one is not a Sovietologist) is the original set of attitudes one brings to the Soviet Union. Often people of a liberal persuasion expect to see socialism realized, or at least to see most problems that worry them at home resolved. For example, for many left-wing intellectuals in Western Europe it was inconceivable that there should exist a system of social stratification in a "socialist" society. Often such individuals (of whom André Gide was one of the first in 1936) are embittered and disappointed by what they see. On the other hand, the conservative businessman or congressman, fed on *Reader's Digest* stories about concentration camps and endless days in the lives of Ivan Denisoviches, find that people in Moscow and other cities laugh, the hotel has hot water, the caviar is good, the ballet splendid, the subways marvelous, the labor unions spineless, the secret police manifestly absent—and they come back impressed, even feeling that they might have been sold a bill of goods by those hostile to the Soviet Union.

I would agree with Dr. Rollins that a lengthy stay is apt to fray the visitor's nerves, for it is bound to show acutely the discrepancy between reality and propaganda. A fairly standard Soviet anecdote has a comrade listening to a lecture about the achievements of the Soviet regime, about this building, that new store, and so on. Finally, during the question period, he asks, "All that you said is well and good. But I go around town, and I do not see any of these great achievements you are talking about." To which the Party agitator replies sternly, "Comrade, you had better read your *Pravda* more carefully and look around a great deal less."

A short visit by a delegation probably does not produce the "Rollins' Law" effect—one hardly has the time to see *anything* in depth. And in some instances, the regime forbids certain types of visits for good reasons of its own. But it is my hope that as the propaganda picture and the reality begin to converge, the secretiveness, official prevarication, and deceptiveness will also decrease so that it will no longer be necessary to build Potemkin villages for foreign visitors. But isolation and parochialism are not a Soviet monopoly: we have plenty of that at home. Cultural exchanges are a two-way street in which each side, I am convinced, benefits.

This is an extraordinary book because it is an exploration of foreign territory, in more ways than one. By broadening our perspectives, by suggesting ideas that could be tried and adapted, even if not adopted

Foreword

in toto, Dr. Rollins enriches us (and I hope Soviet doctors too). If nothing else, Dr. Rollins demonstrates the usefulness of the comparative approach and breaches American insularity in this small corner of medicine and social policy.

Mark G. Field

Preface

The general aim of the present study is to expand our knowlcdge of the Soviet Union in one special area: the theory, diagnosis, and treatment of psychiatric disorders of children and adolescents. It is my hope that these pages will be of interest to a broad spectrum of English-speaking people concerned with education, children's services, and cultural study, as well as the medical audience, although many of the observations and discussions of clinical material have a medical character. I also sincerely hope that my Soviet colleagues will read this work and respond with constructive criticism, for the second broad aim of the study is to stimulate a professional dialogue. It should be helpful on both sides of the ocean to define more precisely what we agree about as well as what we disagree about.

The interest which led to this work stemmed from the larger problem of the existence of the two colossi, the Soviet Union and the United States, who still know relatively little of each other, yet possess the power of mutual destruction and the annihilation of civilization as we know it. A three-week trip to the Soviet Union in the summer of 1966, under the auspices of the Citizens' Exchange Corps (CEC), provided an introduction to the Soviet scene. CEC is an organization which tries to promote tolerance and understanding between Soviet and American citizens by a person-to-person exchange. Meetings between professional counterparts are an important feature of the program. I returned home determined to learn more Russian and to study the segment of Soviet professional life corresponding to my own field: child psychiatry.

The opportunity presented itself through the Medical Cultural Exchange, one part of the Cultural Exchange Agreement, negotiated every two years between the two countries. I worked in the Soviet Union for four months as an individual medical specialist during the winter of 1968–69. Traveling expenses were paid by the U.S. government, and the Soviet government paid a stipend for living expenses and made arrangements for hotel accommodations and professional visits. As a guest of the Soviet government, I found myself for the duration of the stay in the Soviet Union avoiding conclusions about the data I was collecting. During those months, however, certain aspects of American psychiatric practice took on a new perspective. When I returned to the United States, the perspective shifted and a long evaluation process of the Soviet experience began.

Readers should know that the places seen were restricted arbitrarily to those authorized by the Ministry of Health, USSR, for foreigners to visit. I was limited to Moscow, Leningrad and Kiev, although I made specific requests to visit Tbilisi, Kharkhov, and Tashkent. Permission to see important institutions in Moscow was withheld in spite of specific requests to observe in the Twelfth Psychoneurological Hospital (which had a Department for Adolescents, 16–18 years), the Fifteenth Psychoneurological Hospital (which specializes in psychotherapy), and the Serbski Institute (which kept general statistics on disorders of childhood and adolescence in addition to the investigation of problems of crime and delinquency). The Ministry of Health, USSR, through their representatives, Mikhail Victorovich Borisov and Alexander Alexandrovich Sazanov, evaded direct answers to many questions by giving a series of plausible excuses. After these ran out, they finally said I was asking to go to places where no foreigner had ever been! It was distressing to have these representatives frustrate efforts to gain a complete picture of the psychiatric scene. If increased communication and the establishment of a dialogue is up to the bureaucrats, the second broad objective of this study has a gloomy prognosis.

This criticism of the bureaucracy does not apply to the professional people. Professors G. E. Sukhareva, M. S. Vrono, and V. V. Kovalev in particular were most cordial and helpful. Their outstanding contributions are described in the clinical section. My warm regard and appreciation must also be extended to the many co-workers in the departments of these professors who spent much time talking with me and demonstrating clinical material. I would also like to express my thanks to colleagues at home who read parts of the manuscript, especially Amelia Blackwell, Ph.D.

A preliminary review of the American literature on Soviet psychiatry impressed me with the high degree of professional isolation which has enabled a psychiatric system to develop in the USSR independently of our system in the United States. Although both were influenced by nineteenth-century psychiatry in France, Germany, and England, the divergences seem far more important than the influences in common.

Relatively few previous American studies have been devoted to psychiatric services for children in the Soviet Union. Wortis published a book on Soviet psychiatry in 1950, with one chapter on child psychiatry (3). He outlined the development of the network of psychiatric services after the Revolution. They do not differ too much from the services described in Chapter II as I found them in 1969. Wortis stressed prophylaxis and showed how many children's problems were handled as educational rather than psychiatric. Child psychiatry proper was confined more strictly to medical problems.

It is also of interest that in Wortis' review, the writings of T. P. Simpson and G. E. Sukhareva stood out, as they still did 20 years later in my own observations.

Skolnick's report was based on a review of the Soviet literature and a month's visit in 1962 (2). The children's unit he described at Kashenko, a mental hospital in Moscow, has been replaced by a separate children's unit in a complex of buildings of its own. Other facilities he visited were in a hospital in Moscow, Solovev, Sanatorium Forest School No. 7 in Moscow, a children's militia room, and general child-care facilities in Uzbekistan. An interesting theoretical section traces the changes and development of Marxist-Leninist theory in a parallel time sequence with the evolution of Freudian theory. In spite of clashes, the two points of view arrive independently at a similar view of psychic determinism with limited freedom of will, placing on the individual responsibility for his choices and decisions.

Miller, traveling to the Soviet Union for a four-week visit in 1967 with an official delegation of Americans on the Medical Cultural Exchange, reported specifically on psychiatric facilities for children (1). He described the activity of the child psychiatrist in the polyclinic and the children's City Psychoneurological Dispensary and Hospital, which replaced the Kashenko Unit.

Many important questions were raised in my mind by these studies of children's psychiatric facilities and other studies concerned with broader questions of society and character formation. These observers, whose work is described later, were interested in assessing the success of the Soviet experiment of trying consciously and deliberately to create a new collectively oriented man. New Soviet Man is supposed to have a social conscience, enabling him to do what is good for society, with no coercion or resentment. In theory, he has internalized collective values and adjusted personal values so there is no sense of conflict between his individual needs and society's needs. I wondered whether there is a describable difference between the Soviet conscience and the American conscience, as it develops during the years of childhood and adolescence. What about problems of sexual identity in the two societies? Identity crises? Are Soviet citizens really more obedient and (paradoxically) more manipulative than Americans? Is there a real conflict between the school, the family, and the political organization in bringing up children? What characterizes Soviet thought with respect to psychiatric diagnosis, general treatment, and psychotherapy of the disorders of children and adolescence? How are Soviet child psychiatrists trained and what research problems do they investigate? Why have Soviet psychiatrists and educators remained so consistently anti-Freudian?

The general plan of this study is first to consider the history of the development of Soviet psychiatric thought, with the major influences shaping the direction of child psychiatry. Next, the social perspective is considered, with personal observations of Soviet culture and society. This chapter forms the background for my assessment of the society, the characteristics of the children it rears and the kind of psychiatric service it produces. The chapters on organization of psychiatric services, diagnosis, general treatment methods, special psychotherapy, training, and research are more strictly clinical. Throughout these pages, the reader will find comparisons with American psychiatry and areas of the Soviet experience which might be applicable to American problems. In a concluding section, broader problems are reexamined, along with some reflections on American child psychiatry in relation to the Soviet experience.

Frequent comparisons are made between Soviet and American child psychiatry. Since the United States is a pluralistic society, we have a multitude of professional viewpoints and foci of interest within our own field. It is really an oversimplification to speak of American child psychiatry. However, to delete all comparative statements in deference to the complexity of this problem would reduce the value of the work to the professional community. References to American child psychiatry should therefore be taken to reflect personal experience with common views and practice in the Boston area.

Much of the clinical material was gathered from conversations with doctors and educators. We talked mostly in Russian, without benefit of interpreter. My Russian colleagues were very considerate about talking slowly and repeating key concepts when I did not understand everything that was said. However, there may remain some undetected distortions due to idiom, nuances of meaning, and cultural differences. A complete list of the institutions visited in Moscow, Leningrad, and Kiev appears in Appendix I. I was allowed to see a rich variety of clinical case material, many examples of which appear in the clinical chapters and Appendix IV, disguised with pseudonyms. Many of these children were presented in conferences and consultations. The histories were given by the doctor treating the case. I saw nearly all of these children personally and occasionally questioned a child briefly, but the bulk of the interviewing was done in my presence by the consultant. Many clinical case presentations and interviews with patients were recorded on audio tape. I am grateful to my Soviet colleagues for their cooperation in allowing these recordings. Another source of data is the literature, published and unpublished. Soviet colleagues were more than kind about giving me articles and reprints. Bibliographies for each chapter appear in one section at the end. References to the bibliographies appear, throughout the text, in the form of numbers in parentheses. Where Russian sources are used, they are separated from sources in English. The titles of the former are translated into English. Supplementary sources are personal observations of Soviet life and some exposure to Soviet theater, movies, art, and other cultural material.

Child Psychiatry
in the
Soviet Union

I

Historical and Social Perspectives

Child psychiatry is a medical subspecialty highly sensitive to socio-political forces. Ideological factors alien to American thought must be considered in order to understand how Russians diagnose and treat patients and go about investigative work. Nineteenth-century socio-political theory, medicine, and neurophysiology form the cornerstones of Soviet child psychiatry. Child psychiatry as a separate specialty developed in Russia early in postrevolutionary times and was molded by historic decisions of the Soviet government in the twenties and thirties. Contributions to child psychiatry have been made by some leading Soviet thinkers, and post–World War II developments have also come about.

Cultural considerations include the problem of seeing the child in relation to his environment. The maladaptations of children and adolescents are affected by the kind of society in which they live and grow. Thus we must investigate child-rearing practices and aspects of Russian culture which may be relevant to character formation and psychiatric disorder. Finally, child psychiatry must be viewed as a reflection of the Soviet sociocultural system which it serves.

The Historical Perspective

The materialistic, monistic base of Russian psychiatry was established in the midnineteenth century when two manifestos appeared, one on physiology and the other on sociopolitical theory (20, p. 157). In 1847 Carl Ludwig, Emil Dubois-Raymond, and Herman von Helmholtz asserted that living processes must be understood in terms of the principles of physics and chemistry. The Communist Manifesto of Marx and Engels asserted in 1848 that social relationships were determined by concrete material acts of producing goods and the resulting economic relationships. It also established the dialectic principle of continuous change and class struggle.

Psychiatry in Russia first became distinct from medicine in 1845 under V. F. Sabler (39). Courses were offered, based on the teachings of Griesinger. Sabler must have been an intuitive thinker, for he was credited with viewing mental disease as a curative effort on the part of nature by sacrificing one part to save the whole. He was also aware of a defensive function of delusions in warding off depression (39).

One of the earliest Russian psychiatrists to concern himself with the problems of children was S. S. Korsakov, who became the first director of the Moscow University Psychiatric Clinic in 1887 (39). In his book, *The Psychology of the Microcephalic,* he ascribed the cause of this condition to damage to the brain in the intrauterine period of development. He also established a psychiatric school in Moscow (13, Intro.). Other early studies also dealt with gross disturbances producing mental retardation. The first institutions established for children's disorders treated epilepsy and retardation. S. N. Danillo wrote about childhood catanonia (now recognized as a form of schizophrenia) in 1892. O. B. Feltzman, one of the first to study lesser psychiatric disorders, wrote a book entitled *Nervous Children* (13, Intro.). V. M. Bekhterev established an important psychoneurological research institute in Leningrad for the study of child development and upbringing. This center had both educational and medical departments and still is a major focus of investigative work.

PREREVOLUTIONARY INFLUENCES

The impact of Marxist theory, later elaborated by Lenin, on child psychiatry is complex and can only be touched upon in this study. That Soviet psychiatrists themselves consider it important is evident in the lecture time devoted to Marxism-Leninism in the training program for psychoneurologists. However, the subject was not discussed in any of my visits to clinics and institutions. The influence of Marxism operates on many different levels: an underlying philosophy and epistemology stressing monistic materialism and the dependence of psychic activity and consciousness on the material substratum; a particular view of reality and of scientific investigation of reality; a morality stressing the need to integrate personal values with collective values; a theory of economics and of the impact of economic relationships on human relationships, character formation, health and illness, both physical and psychic; a political theory, the ideological base of the Communist Party, to mention only a few. In addition, the changes and development of the theory must not be underestimated.

Basic principles of Marx and Engels forming the epistemological and philosophical base for Soviet psychiatry were summarized by Wortis (41, pp. 2–3) as follows:

1. The world is material.
2. Mind is an objective function or reflection of matter.
3. The objective world is knowable.
4. No phenomenon is isolated. Everything is interrelated.
5. All nature is in constant motion, in a continuous process of development and disintegration.
6. Quantitative changes are converted into qualitative changes at a higher level of organization.
7. Opposing forces are always found in any single phenomenon.

This materialistic monistic base is one cornerstone of Soviet psychiatry. Psychic phenomena in this view are aspects of matter. However, the principle that quantitative changes may be converted into qualitative differences means psychic phenomena cannot be reduced to physiological phenomena. It also means the whole cannot be considered only the sum of its parts. The principle that the objective world is knowable fosters the development of scientific method. The concept of interrelationships paves the way for the elaboration of the role of the social milieu and interpersonal relationships in personality formation. The dynamic element of struggle and change is related to the view of nature as in constant motion and to the principle of opposing forces, the principle of the dialectic.

Moving to the economic level, Marx and Engels saw consciousness as a social product (34, p. 94). They asserted that economic relationships determine the quality of interpersonal relations: "The main force in the system of the material life of society, responsible for all aspects of the life of the society, is the means of production of material wealth" (34, p. 98). The social implications of economic relationships form the Marxist base for a theory of personality and deviations. Language is closely linked with consciousness, both arising from men's dealings with each other in the daily process of producing goods. Basic needs for food and shelter are modified as they are satisfied, giving rise to secondary needs.

From the basic ideas of capitalist exploitation of the working class set forth in the Communist Manifesto, there arose a set of moral principles which came to dominate all aspects of Soviet life. Communist morality influences all Soviet medical writing, as well as educational and therapeutic approaches to neurosis and personality deviation. Economic exploitation of one class by another makes man only an object, a thing to be used. As V. N. Myasishchev said, "Man as a means, as a commodity, as the object of exploitation in the system of attitudes of a capitalistic society may be contrasted with man as a purpose, the highest value, as a subject in the system of attitudes in a communist society" (34, p. 98). Economic exploitation was held to account for a broad spectrum of physical illnesses, mental disorders, and personality deviations.

One aspect of Marxist theory least understood by Western readers is important in understanding Soviet criticism of Western psychiatric literature. This pertains to the Soviet rejection of eclecticism. The Soviet psychiatrist Myasishchev contrasted the eclectic and his dialectic approach. As he explains the dialectic view of nature, it is not to be taken as a "mechanical agglomeration of unconnected objects but as a single continuously developing entity in which the separate objects are all interrelated and dependent on each other in many ways" (34, p. 92). In presenting his interpretation of Lenin's views, Myasishchev said, objects must be studied "firstly, in their comprehensive relationships, secondly, in their development, thirdly, on the basis of practice, and fourthly, with consideration of those aspects and relationships which are inherent in the concrete conditions and aims of the study" (34, p. 92).

If the object is a child, the first dialectic principle requires that he be studied in relation to his surroundings. The principle of the whole transcending the sum of its parts requires that the child-in-his-environment be taken as the unit of study. So eclecticism in the sense of outside influences acting on the system would become an absurdity. Secondly, the child must be studied in his development, both his developmental stages and his concrete history. Finally, "on the basis of practice" means the child must be studied as he actually functions under concrete conditions.

The unity of theory and practice is very important: the unity of action and contemplation, idea and reality allows for no separation between what ought to be and what actually is. From an American point of view, this leads to a confusion between an ideal to be striven for and actual conditions.

Nineteenth-century medicine, too, left its imprint on Soviet child psychiatry, particularly the medical model of psychiatric disease developed in Germany by Wilhelm Griesinger. His monistic view led him to an extreme somatic position in the controversy between the mind and the body, perhaps as a reaction against romanticism, mysticism, and speculative philosophy. Psychiatry was to be identified with neuropathology. As Zilborg said, "Diagnoses were to be made only on the basis of causes and causes were always physiological. He [referring to Griesinger] saw no difference between organic and functional disorders" (42, p. 436). Zilborg considered Griesinger the forerunner of V. M. Bekhterev, I. P. Pavlov, and the school of behaviorism in the United States. For Griesinger, each new mental symptom was not a new disease, but each phenomenon was to be described as clearly as possible. Compare A. V. Snezhnevski's discussion of the unitary versus multiple etiology of schizophrenia in a contemporary text (3, pp. 131–132). Though conceding the etiology of schizophrenia is still a subject of controversy in Soviet psychiatry, Snezhnevski adds that the usual way of defining a disease entity is first by clinical description and only later by etiology, pathogenesis, and pathological anatomy. He cites the example of progressive paralysis, first defined as a clinical syndrome and only years later as a form of syphilis. I met Soviet child psychiatrists associated with Snezhnevski's group who closely adhere to the hope of establishing a unitary etiology for schizophrenia (M. S. Vrono) in conformity with Griesinger's midnineteenth-century ideal.

A Soviet writer, V. M. Morozov, saw in Griesinger not only the equation of psychiatric disease with brain disease but also the beginnings of an interest in the study of localization and, curiously enough, a precursor, through the detailed study of case histories, of the study of depth psychology in the Freudian tradition (32, p. 663).

The equation of mental disease with brain disease and precise description of mental symptoms paved the way in German psychiatry for the classification of psychiatric disorders by Emil Kraepelin. Through careful observation of the course of psychiatric illness, Kraepelin delineated the manic depressive psychosis and dementia praecox. Kraepelin has been criticized for equating prognosis with diagnosis, for in his formulation all patients who do not recover have dementia praecox, while all those who do, have a form of manic depressive psychosis (42, p. 456). In a less extreme form, the Kraepelinian interest in an accurate description of the extended course of an illness has carried over into Russian psychiatry and is evident in the kinds of research conducted by Soviet psychiatrists in childhood epilepsy and schizophrenia. The emphasis in Soviet child psychiatry on diagnosis and classification left an overwhelming impression on me as I listened to case consultations and training sessions.

A third cornerstone of Soviet child psychiatry is neurophysiology, established in Russia by I. M. Sechenov after his exposure to Dubois-Raymond and Ludwig in Germany and Claude Bernard in France (20, pp. 139–140). Sechenov's classic essay, *Reflexes of the Brain,* contained the basic assertion which became the starting point of I. P. Pavlov's work. Sechenov conceived of higher nervous activity in three sectors: the sensory or afferent inflow, a central process, and an efferent outflow resulting in a muscular response. The whole process was explainable in physical terms. Subjective emotions were essentially muscular responses. He thought of the central portion as modifying the sensory input either by excitation or inhibition.

V. Ya Danilevski continued the tradition by showing that the cerebral cortex regulates visceral function. He studied hypnosis and related this state to Sechenov's idea of inhibitory activity. Further, in 1876, he independently discovered the electroencephalogram but failed to report it until 1890, attributing the waves to an artifact (20, pp. 152–154). Even to present times, these trends are evident in Russian psychiatry.

The work of Pavlov spanned prerevolutionary times and the early Soviet era. Later he extended his investigations to the study of higher nervous activity, with applications to human psychopathology. The broad areas of Pavlov's thought most relevant to understanding contemporary Soviet child psychiatry concern his theory of neurosis and the theory of treatment derived from his ideas, in regard to psychopharmacology, general regime, and psychotherapy. His influence is also evident in the Soviet approach to psychosomatic problems and the study of language.

Pavlov introduced experimental neuroses in dogs by creating a conflict between a conditioned response and a conditioned inhibition to stimuli too similar for the animal to differentiate. In studying experimental neuroses, he observed differences in the responses of his laboratory animals that led him to postulate a typology of the nervous system (35). He found characteristic reaction patterns in different dogs to the same injurious influences and concluded that the duration and severity of the disorder induced was determined by the type of nervous system of the animal. He proposed a tentative classification based on the ancient typology of human temperaments:

1. Sanguine: His laboratory dogs of this type were energetic, active, and responsive under ordinary conditions but became drowsy, unresponsive, and difficult to condition when they were brought into the laboratory and subjected to monotonous stimuli.
2. Melancholic: These dogs, in contrast, were highly reactive to change or new stimuli, with a predominance of stable conditioned inhibitory reflexes.
3. Phlegmatic: These animals were characterized by a high threshold of reactivity and stability of responsiveness.
4. Choleric: These were excitable animals with a diminished stability of conditioned inhibitory reflexes.

The existence of types of nervous systems in animals determining varying degrees of susceptibility to experimental neuroses suggested there might be many applications to the human condition. As Pavlov said in 1934, in a lecture delivered to physicians in Leningrad, "The nervous activity, as all physicians are aware, consists of two mechanisms or two processes—excitatory and inhibitory. With regard to these processes, we distinguish three fundamental elements, namely the strength of both the excitatory and inhibitory nervous processes, the mobility of these processes—their inertness and lability—and finally, the equilibrium between these processes" (36). Pavlov maintained that a nerve cell could be weakened, that is, its work capacity could be decreased in three ways: by excessive excitation, by excessive inhibition, or by excessive mobility (collision between excitation and inhibition). A weakened nerve cell would sometimes enter a paradoxical phase in which a weak stimulus would elicit the expected response, but a strong stimulus elicited no response. Finally, there was an ultraparadoxical phase in which the weakened cell would no longer respond to a positive stimulus, and a stimulus usually eliciting inhibition would give rise instead to a positive effect.

While the ancient terminology (sanguine, melancholic, phlegmatic, and choleric) was not retained in Soviet psychiatry, the idea of temperaments based on types of nervous system remained. Myasishchev wrote an article in 1954 entitled "The Problem of Psychological Type in the Light of Pavlov's Teaching" (33). He described the four basic temperaments in more modern terminology (33, pp. 125–126):

1. Weak
2. Strong and unbalanced (unrestrained)
3. Strong, balanced, and mobile and
4. Strong, balanced and sluggish or inert.

The following terms pertaining to higher nervous activity are in everyday usage in Soviet psychiatry. American psychiatrists may appreciate definitions, from Myasishchev's work:

1. *Strength-weakness:* "Endurance, capacity for work, and ability to solve difficult problems. Weakness is characterized by lack of endurance, fatigue, timidity, cowardice" (33, p. 133).
2. *Excitability-inhibitability:* "Excitability is characterized by ease of manifestation and strength of reactions, inhibitability by easy development of inhibition . . . The correct evaluation of excitability is thus determined by the significance of the motive for the reaction and by the situation existing at the time, inhibiting the reaction or facilitating its manifestation" (33, p. 134).
3. *Mobility-inertia:* "Inability to become adapted quickly to new demands and to solve new problems characterizes inertia; the opposite qualities characterize mobility" (33, p. 134).

Although Pavlov's major contribution was to experimental animal neurophysiology, he made many efforts to extend his concepts and to test their applicability to human psychopathological states. The specifically human condition is characterized in his terminology by the second signal system, where language operates in the formation of complex conditioned responses. The word becomes a powerful conditioned stimulus. The first signal system, excluding language, is common to men and animals. It consists of stimuli transmitted and sorted by the various analyzers (sensory apparatus, afferent nerve fibers, and their cell bodies in the central nervous system).

Pavlov's observations in his laboratory laid the foundation for the Soviet theory of neurosis and approach to psychopharmacology (36). Experimental neuroses induced in animals, he claimed, have a human counterpart where the psychopathological state is induced by a conflict between excitatory and inhibitory processes. However, he added, there are specifically human neuroses as well. Hysteria and psychasthenia cannot exist in animals, because these conditions depend on language development. Pavlov supplemented his observations on dogs with direct observation of psychiatric patients and discussion with neuropathologists.

In experiments alleviating a previously induced neurosis in dogs, Pavlov demonstrated that extremely small doses of bromides would facilitate inhibitory processes in animals with a weak type of nervous system, rather than reduce excitatory processes. But large doses were injurious. He found the same paradoxical response to bromides in neurotic patients. The effect of rest was comparable to the reinforcement of inhibitory processes obtained with bromides.

Pavlov further demonstrated that isolated pathological points can be established in the cerebral cortex and that the pathological point can be modified pharmacologically. In one neurotic dog subjected to a collision of inhibitory and excitatory processes in response to cutaneous stimuli, the symptoms of neurosis were alleviated by giving a combination of bromide (to reinforce inhibition) and caffeine (as a cortical stimulant). The animal's violent reaction to the positive and negative stimuli completely vanished. Another dog with an experimental neurosis showed no improvement when treated with bromides alone, but improved when given a combination of bromide and caffeine. This medication came to be called "Pavlov's mixture" in Soviet psychiatry and has been extensively used in sanatoria for neurotic children. It is curious that amphetamines have not been used for their calming and inhibiting effect on hyperactive distractable children as they have in American psychiatry: the principle is exactly the same—facilitation of cortical inhibition.

While the influence of Pavlov's work on Soviet psychiatry has been both pervasive and lasting, its influence has limits. I saw no efforts to apply conditioning principles to the development of a behavior therapy as was attempted in the 1960's in the United States. Nor was there in the Soviet literature of the same period a great number of investigations utilizing the conditioning methods of studying higher nervous activity.

THE EARLY POSTREVOLUTIONARY PERIOD

Following the Revolution came a short period of permissiveness and experimentation. The favored position children were to be given in the society was evident in this letter, written in 1918 at the time of the formation of the Department of Maternal and Child Welfare: "Children, as future citizens, from the first days of their lives are the subject of concern for the proletariat state and must be reared in circumstances providing a wide possibility for the many-sided development of their physical and spiritual powers" (1, Intro.). Children receive priority in Soviet society because they are future builders of communism. They are also genuinely loved; one has only to walk around in parks and play areas to sense this.

At the beginning of the Revolution in 1918, a special institution was created in Leningrad called the Educational-Clinical Institute for Nervous Children, named for Academician V. M. Bekhterev. After the Revolution there were many homeless, unsupervised children, uneducable in ordinary schools, and in 1926 this residential center had 75 beds for boys and girls (10). About half were clearly neurological problems, and the remainder were various types of neuroses and infantilism. The educational program included three years of regular school, supplemented by political education through the Pioneer and Komsomol Soviet youth organizations. Work therapy, physical therapy, and self-help were stressed. A staff of 27 people, 11 with technical training, tended the children. Each child was studied from the medical point of view. The description of this institution in the article appearing in 1926 shows the pattern already established for schools and sanatoria (see Chap. IV below).

Further evidence of the early concern of the regime for the needs of children was the establishment of a new governmental department of psychopathology for children in 1919, at a time when the country had been rocked by world war, revolution, and the establishment of the Bolshevik government. A wall chart in the Psychoneurological Dispensary for Children and Adolescents in Moscow showed the beginnings of Soviet child psychiatry. The first institutions were an observation point, a treatment school, and several types of sanatoria, including one for "nervous children." Child psychiatry as an emerging specialty was also influenced by the discipline of "defectology," which developed methods of studying abnormalities of childhood and special schools more from the educational and psychological points of view. Psychoneurological offices began to appear in the polyclinics of Moscow by 1920, and in 1924 psychoneurological consultations were made available to pre-school children. The focus right from the start was on preventive psychiatry.

In the exhilarating atmosphere of freedom and experimentation of the early twenties, L. S. Vigotsky did some highly original work relating language, thought, and consciousness to the social environment of the developing child. K. N. Kornilov's work in the twenties centered on reconciling psychology with Marxism. A. R. Luriya worked on many problems, including psychoanalytic concepts; the relationship of language development to the social environment and activity patterns of the child has been a continuing focus of Luriya's contributions.

Initially, psychoanalysis and its postulates about the unconscious were accepted. A Leningrad psychiatrist, Elias Perepel, described the all-but-forgotten movement in the early postrevolutionary days (37). In Moscow, the Russian Psychoanalytic Society was formed and met regularly. Analysts were also practicing in Leningrad, Kiev, and Odessa. Freud's works were published in Russian in 1923, edited by I. D. Ermakov. In 1924, the second all-Russian Psychoneurological Congress in Leningrad gave sanction, though with reservations, to the practice of psychoanalysis. After the structural theory of the id, ego, and superego appeared in 1925, there was growing criticism. Early attempts to reconcile Marxism and psychoanalysis, including the work of A. R. Luriya, were eventually abandoned (41, pp. 72–73).

However, the breath of fresh air was short-lived. In 1928 came the first five-year plan and Stalin's decision to develop the country's industrial base, at the same time enforcing the collectivization of agriculture. Socialism was to be achieved with active suppression of all dissent and indefinite postponement of individual consumer needs. In the philosophical dispute between mechanistic and dialectic Marxism, revolutionary activism, representing the dialectic position, won. Things don't just happen. Stalin would make them happen. The profound consequences were felt with gradually increasing intensity in the thirties and perhaps are still operating to this day.

Another major influence on child psychiatry in the postrevolutionary period was the thinking of A. S. Makarenko. Following the sequence of World War I, the Bolshevik Revolution, and the Civil War, conditions in the new socialist state were chaotic. The hardships of war had left many children and youths homeless. Some banded together in groups and roamed the streets, fending for themselves. Crime and delinquency rose under these conditions. Makarenko, an educator loyal to the communist regime, established colonies for these young people and wrote for parents and educators about child rearing and character formation (31). The character of the growing child was seen as the precipitate of the child's relationships with people in his surroundings. This concept of character is derived from the Marxist idea that consciousness is a social product.

The distinctive emphasis in Makarenko's thinking was the role of the *collective* in character formation. The collective is the social group surrounding the individual. The family is the first collective, an important one (but not as important in Makarenko's scheme as the family in Western thought). The other major collectives are various peer groups and the school. According to Makarenko, collectives outside the family begin to influence the Soviet child even in preschool years. The child experiences a social humanitarian orientation which teaches him that his interests as an individual are one with the interests of the collective. Makarenko's anecdotal approach in his advice to parents shows that he valued warmth in personal relationships; he emphasized both cooperation and competition. While Makarenko placed the responsibility squarely on the parents for the child's upbringing, he stated that experience in other collectives and Soviet life in general make a decisive contribution as well (31, p. 21). However important the family, there is no doubt that in Makarenko's thinking the state comes first: "I am a great admirer of optimism and very fond of young lads who trust the Soviet rule to such an extent that they are carried away and will not even trust their own mothers" (31, p. 49). In the twenties, one child, Pavlik Morozov, informed on his father and testified against him in court. He became a hero of the Young Pioneers and his picture was still preserved in a poster illustrating the Pioneer pledge, reproduced in Bronfenbrenner's recent book (21, pp. 37, 45). This extreme example illustrates Makarenko's position that the child's first loyalty should be to the state; parents come second. My observations of family life did not include such circumstances.

There is no question that the influence of Makarenko was a lasting one. His ideas have been consistently carried into psychiatry with its aim of bringing the sick person into harmony with the collective and restoring his capacity to work. In psychiatric treatment, work therapy and collective therapy complement other approaches. These measures are also applied to some extent in the treatment of older children and adolescents. The optimistic view of man as educable and adaptable strongly opposes the view of illness as static and unchangeable.

THE THIRTIES: DECADE OF TERRORISM

The Stalinist insistence on the unity of theory and practice and a rigorous application of Lenin's reflection theory led to increasing party control over all scientific investigation. R. A. Bauer quoted I. Zalkind's speech in 1930 at the First All Union Congress on Human Behavior, which set the keynote of the new psychology that was to study man as the instrument of socialist reconstruction (18, chap. VIII). Zalkind indicated the need for a tractable kind of man, open to social influences, adaptable to collective life. He must be trained politically and ideologically. Yet he must be capable of independence. The works of A. R. Luriya, Vigotsky, and Kornilov were criticized, and Vigotsky's book was suppressed by the Stalin regime. Social control in general was also tightened.

For a time, the momentum in the development of child psychiatry continued with the opening in 1930 of a sanatorium at Sokolniki, in Moscow, for neurotic children (see Chap. IV below). In 1932, under P. D. Pevzner and M. B. Pevzner, a day hospital for children was started at the Psychoneurological Dispensary in the Oktyabraskaya District of Moscow. Special groups were formed for ill children in infant and preschool day-care centers. In 1934, E. A. Osipova created a scientific methodological center, later reorganized.

Here, the entries on the wall chart of the psychoneurological dispensary ended. Is this coincidence, or was the development of child psychiatry really brought to a halt in the midthirties because of the political situation? I had no opportunity to discuss this with Soviet child psychiatrists.

The climax of the crisis for psychology and education came with the Communist Party Decree in 1936, "On Pedological Perversions in the System of the People's Commissariat of Education" (41, pp. 242–245). The decree abolished testing, because the defects exposed by tests were falsely supposed by pedologists to be immutable and the emphasis was to be shifted to training and corrective measures. The teaching of pedology as a special science was to be abolished. The pedologist until then occupied a powerful position in schools. He made up classes, determined causes of the lack of progress of students, transferred children to special remedial schools, controlled political opinions, conducted experimental and test programs (18, chap. X).

A little-known part of this decree criticized the schools for "difficult children" for their poorly qualified, irresponsible personnel and a poor quality of instruction. Teachers in regular schools were criticized for the high rate of grade repeaters: 15 percent in the first seven grades in 1935–36 (18, chap. X). Most of the problem children were to be transferred back to the regular educational system. The burden of responsibility for deviance and school failure was to be borne by the teacher. The decree must have profoundly inhibited the development of special schools and special educational programs. In psychology, the hereditary-environment theory was replaced by a quadripartite theory: heredity, environment, training, and self-training. Psychology was to stop experimenting and evaluating and concentrate on training techniques for building "New Soviet Man."

The impact of the decree was no less profound for the infant discipline of child psychiatry. Ideological errors in this field were summarized by G. E. Sukhareva (13, pp. 14–17):

1. Theories of etiology emphasizing constitutional and hereditary factors (with insufficient attention to modifiable environmental factors).
2. The "reactionary theories of Kretchmer" (a typology implying immutability?).
3. The "reactionary theories of Freud," with his emphasis on the role of the sexual instinct in character formation: "He denied the historic evolution of the human psyche under the influence of the conditions of the social milieu, first of all, work activity" (13, p. 15).
4. The theories of Jaspers; Sukhareva felt they pointed to dualism.
5. Ignorance of the theories of Pavlov.
6. Separation of child psychiatry from general psychiatry.

It is probable these criticisms of Sukhareva were also influenced by the genetic controversy which began in the Soviet Union in the early thirties. T. D. Lysenko advocated a revival of the Lamarckian theory, asserting that hereditary characteristics could be modified by environmental factors, basing his claims on the work of I. V. Michurin. The need of the state at the time was best served by a scientific theory which emphasized the modifiability of the environment and man's control over nature. In child psychiatry, genetic and unmodifiable constitutional factors were played down in the study of psychopathic personality deviations, epilepsy, and schizophrenia. Much emphasis was placed instead on preventable organic factors in the intrauterine, perinatal, and early postnatal periods of child development.

The political atmosphere of the thirties also dealt the death blow to the psychoanalytic movement in the Soviet Union. Freud was criticized for too much emphasis on sexuality and unconscious motivation, for dwelling on the past at the expense of consciousness and modifiable cultural factors in the present. The Soviet State publishing office stopped printing psychoanalytic books, although for a while some literature on the subject appeared through private printing (37). The Russian Psychoanalytic Institute was closed in 1936; for some time after that, a group of 15 psychiatrists continued to meet in Moscow (41, pp. 72–75). As Perepel pointed out, the resistance to psychoanalysis in the Soviet Union was not of the same order as that in other countries at the time of the rise of fascism (37).

POST–WORLD WAR II AND THE CONTEMPORARY SCENE

The influence of the war years led in psychiatry to studies of the effects of head injuries and psychic phenomena of reactive states induced by war conditions. The whole issue of the relationship of psychic trauma to predisposing factors came under scrutiny. Interest continued in the effects of various infections, both systemic and of the central nervous system, on the psychic apparatus. The network of psychiatric services for children had to be rebuilt.

In 1950 under Stalin's initiative there was a reaffirmation of the principles of Pavlov in all fields of medicine (13, pp. 15–16, 30). As we have seen, the basic concepts of inhibition and excitation and their relative balance were claimed to underlie all physiological processes, normal and pathological. The manifestations of disease were to be analyzed with respect to the predominance of the first or second signal system. Also, a symptom should be evaluated as part of the primary disease process or of the organism's attempt to defend itself and achieve adaptation—the physician had to distinguish between a defensive failure and a protective process and plan his therapeutic program accordingly. Neurophysiological adaptive mechanisms (more than the hormonal defensive and adaptive mechanisms elaborated by Selye) are greatly emphasized in Soviet psychiatry. The relationships between a neurophysiological adaptive mechanism and psychopathological symptom formation was considered by Sukhareva in an introductory chapter of her textbook on child psychiatry (13, pp. 23–38). While she conceded the relationship is close, she claimed a definite line of demarcation between a symptom caused by a primary pathogenic agent and adaptive mechanisms evoked in the organism's response to the pathogen.

Pavlovian theory is confining in some respects. Stalin's directive resulted in some indiscriminate applications of the theories regarding higher nervous activity in various branches of medicine. In a discussion of Russian neurophysiology, the tendency to generalize easily was noted by Magoun as a characteristic of Russian scientific thought (20, p. 160). In particular, the regulatory role of the central nervous system was overemphasized at the expense of other factors. However, Pavlovian theory did provide the framework for the development in several fruitful directions. Sukhareva noted the shift from anatomical localization of disease process in the central nervous system to an emphasis on physiological centers and systems and the dynamic interaction of cortical and subcortical processes (13, p. 16). Pavlovian concepts of adaptation and defense have recently been extended to the regulatory function of the reticular activating system on the cerebral cortex and to studies of the unconditioned orienting reflex to various environmental stimuli. The traditional Russian interest in the conditioning properties of the vegetative nervous system, along with the monistic orientation to mind-body interrelationships, has resulted in increasing interest in psychosomatic problems. Pavlovian concepts of first- and second-order conditioning are utilized in explanations of symptom formation in the psychosomatic sphere, for example, in the psychogenic vomiting and anorexia commonly seen in early childhood (12, pp. 25–36).

N. I. Krasnogorski was the first to apply the secretory–motor conditioning method to the study of higher nervous activity in children with physical and psychiatric illnesses. A. G. Ivanov-Smolenski carried on, utilizing the method of motor–speech reinforcement, in studies of higher nervous activity of psychiatric patients in childhood and adolescence (27). He studied patients with mental retardation, schizophrenia, acute infectious diseases, and neuroses. He reported differences in the interaction, strength, and equilibrium of cortical processes and disturbances in the conditioned and unconditioned vegetative reactivity, as well as disturbed interrelationships of the two signal systems (27, pp. 280–294). Studies utilizing the method of Ivanov-Smolenski appear in Soviet textbooks of child psychiatry (12).

The interest in the second signal system has led to further studies of language and speech. The more recent work of A. R. Luriya includes the role of language and speech in child development and disturbances of language in various types of brain damage (29, pp. 359–423). Luriya credited Vigotsky with recognition of the role of the verbal relation between mother and child in the developing mental organization of the child. In his own contributions, he showed experimentally the regulating and controlling function of speech and the process of interiorization of control in children two and one-half to five years of age. He concluded there is an important turning point in child development between the ages of four and five years when speech becomes truly interiorized (29, p. 382).

The concepts of first and second signal system have been elaborated by K. I. Platonov into a theory of suggestive psychotherapy (38). The word is viewed as a powerful conditioned stimulus and therefore as a potent influence on physiological functions. Hypnosis, a therapeutic tool utilized more in Soviet psychiatry than in American practice, is conceived as a state of practical cortical inhibition, with a wakeful portion selectively attending the stimuli that come from the hypnotizer.

Contributions of V. N. Myasishchev relevant to child psychiatry are reviewed here in some detail to show the influence of the "Leningrad school" and to illustrate how one Soviet psychiatrist has blended ideas from Marxism-Leninism, Bekhterev, and Pavlov into his own theory of personality, neurosis, and psychotherapy (2, 7, 8, 9). Born in 1893, Myasishchev completed his medical training and has spent his whole career at the Bekhterev Psychoneurological Institute. His first work in 1920 was a "Report on the Difficult Upbringing of Children with Nervous Illness." In 1921 followed a report on the need for an inter-disciplinary approach to the problems of work. One ramification was the concept of work therapy in psychiatry.

Myasishchev defined personality as a system of social attitudes reflecting external reality, especially relationships with other people. Elements of a reflection theory were already present in Marxist thought and later elaborated by Lenin. Some of Lenin's statements relevant to personality theory are quoted by Myasishchev as follows:

"Concepts (and their relationships, transitions, and conflicts) are shown to be reflections of the objective world. The dialectics of material objects creates the dialectics of ideas, and not vice versa" (34, pp. 92–93).

"Man, as a subject, reflects not only the objective world facing him and outside him, but also his own state and his own attitude toward the world" (34, p. 105).

"Human consciousness not only reflects the objective world, but also creates it" (34, p. 104).

Myasishchev stressed that a human being is at once an object and a subject. A human being simultaneously reflects objective reality and acts on, molds, and changes external reality. There is a hierarchical arrangement of attitudes, with some in a leading position and others subordinate. Some of these attitudes are personal and others are social. Temperament, as in Pavlovian thought, is seen as a function of cortical processes and cortical-subcortical relationships, forming the substratum of personality. At a higher plane are qualitative aspects of personality with particular stress on the degree to which conduct is regulated by principles, the dimension of "collectivism-individualism." Always, Myasishchev emphasized the importance of the historical dimension. Development is conceived of as a dynamic process of struggle, in which the individual is reorganized by his social experience, not losing in this process his individuality but gaining a new socialized character. A person is conceived of as a complex developing unity influenced on many different levels, from the biological and physiological to the social. The dialectic principle that development entails an element of conflict and struggle is evident. "Blind instincts" of the organism are converted in this developmental process to conscious demands.

For Myasishchev, the roles of early childhood, family relationships, and the school years are important but, in contrast to psychoanalytic views, later stages of development, molded by what has gone before, are also considered decisive. How otherwise bring about therapeutic change if subsequent experience is not important? On this basis, Myasishchev criticized both Freud and Adler for placing in a decisive position the role of early childhood trauma. There is no recognition, in Myasishchev's discussion, of the *development* of Freud's thinking and the profound alteration in the direction of psychoanalytic thought which came about when Freud realized all of his hysterical patients could *not* have experienced sexual traumata.

Developmental stages in the child's relationship to reality are considered important in their own right and also in terms of the age characteristics they imprint on various forms of psychopathology. In infancy, the child experiences spontaneous, pleasure-seeking organic drives. At the next stage, the child experiences spontaneous, impulsive affective reactions, evoked by objects and people. Next appear specific attitudes toward reality which still remain spontaneous, emotional, concrete, personal. Later in childhood, awareness of necessity is formed along with the capacity and willingness to subordinate affective stimuli, wishes, and emotions. At the highest level appear social attitudes, abstract thought, and conscious motivation of behavior. At this stage, external demands are perceived as necessity and behavior is motivated by internal principals.

No less decisive for Myasishchev is the role of acquired experience. Since the personality is molded by the social experiences of the individual, he believed class considerations are extremely important. Under capitalistic conditions, "a person is a wolf to another person." Under socialism, everyone can be friends and brothers. There is no need for the distortions of human relationships which arise from exploitation. Real independence is only possible to achieve within the framework of the collective, where some synthesis is forged between personal and collective attitudes so that the individual experiences them as mutually supportive rather than conflicting.

The Marxist-Leninist orientation of Myasishchev's thinking has remained firm throughout his career. In discussing personality as a biosocial unity, Myasishchev conceded that "bourgeois" psychology shows an awareness of the social significance of the problem of personality. But the Westerner's point of view could never be as free of bias as the Marxist-Leninist. For, said Myasishchev, the bourgeois psychologist is either trying to free himself from ideological political considerations or masking his dependence on them. He criticized Western authors for empiricism and eclecticism, for a denial of personality which reduces man to a robot or at the opposite extreme, for personalism or the "cult of personality," and the associated evil consequences of thinking in terms of superman. He objected to Freud's "biologizing personality." Although the superego is a social product, social factors are underplayed because the superego and ego gain their energy from the id. Yet Freudian theory was taken seriously enough to be the subject of the "Conference of the Academy of Medical Sciences, RSFSR, on Questions of Freudianism" in 1962 and "Philosophical Questions about Higher Nervous Activity and Psychology" in 1963.

Myasishchev defined neurosis as an illness of personality characterized by disturbed relationships to reality, a product of the social historical environment and of individual development. Neurosis results from conflict with the environment of several different types:

1. Wishes versus reality.
2. Conflicting emotional attitudes; for example, love versus hate.
3. Principles versus concrete personal attitudes.
4. Ethical demands versus sexuality. Freud mistook his case material for having universal significance.

5. Demands of reality versus opportunity to fulfill them; the neurosis of attitudinal insufficiency.
6. Self-assertion versus social demands.

Conflict alone is not sufficient to produce neurosis. Conflict must generate tension for which there is no outlet or possibility of resolution. Neurosis in turn may cause a change in the structure of personality. Traumatic experiences per se are not necessarily decisive. Even where trauma occurs as early as five years, the modifying effects of subsequent experiences must always be considered and are the justification for therapeutic intervention. Further, traumata do not always mean the same thing to every individual.

Myasishchev also considered neurotic predisposition in the form of constitutional neuropathy an important factor, especially in children. The child with a constitutional neuropathy shows a disproportion between his emotional reactions and the external circumstances. He is prone to excitement, prolonged severe reactions, unmotivated mood fluctuations, fatigability, disturbances of sleep and appetite. Somatic symptoms of the skin, cardiovascular system, and gastrointestinal systems are also characteristic.

The other major factor in producing neurotic symptoms and character distortions is incorrect handling of the child, described in Myasishchev's terms as pedagogical errors or ineptitude. He nevertheless felt it possible to distinguish in relatively pure cases between inadequate upbringing or education and "psychoneurosis." The former type is characterized by the picture of antisocial traits, lack of positive interests, hostility toward school, authority, and the child collective (peer group). The disturbed psychic functions of these children, consequences of the child's poor attitudes and habits, include rudeness, impulsiveness, cruelty, short attention span, and poor capacity for self-observation. In contrast, the latter type (psychoneurosis) is characterized by the presence of conflicts as previously described (for example, ambivalence), volitional and affective disturbances, and poor habits arising from disturbed psychic functions.

Myasishchev's theory of psychotherapy follows from his concept of personality as a system of social attitudes and from his conception of neurosis as an illness of personality with distorted relationships to reality. His theory of psychotherapy is based on the teachings of Pavlov concerning higher nervous activity, on historical materialism and materialistic psychology. Pavlov himself recognized the importance of psychology; since man is both object and subject, questions of psychogenesis and of psychotherapy will never be resolved by a study of only the physiology of higher nervous activity without considering psychology.

For Myasishchev, the Pavlovian concepts most relevant to the understanding of psychotherapy are the second signal system and the role of the word as a powerful conditioned stimulus. Man is distinct from other animals also by virtue of possessing a developed second signal system. Emotions are categorized as unconditioned subcortical responses. The higher ethical and moral conflicts specific to man must be studied and understood in their social-historical context. In man, too, the role of past experience often outweighs the role of the present. Therefore, the meaning of psychic insults such as loss of an important person, slight or offense in human relationships, is not the same for everyone and depends for effect on the relationship of one person to another.

Another concept Myasishchev adopted from Pavlovian thought is the pathogenic or weak point. This is understood as a point of pathological sensitivity and excessive irritability, leading to neurotic predisposition, and is also studied in its genetic and historic aspects, through the methods of objective and subjective anamnesis. In some instances, there is an irradiation from the original pathogenetic point with involvement of other systems.

What are the effective factors in psychotherapy? How does the "word" gain such power as to remove serious external and internal conflicts? First, said Myasishchev, psychotherapy is not only a speech process: the influence of one person on another is transmitted also through pantomine and mimicry. The major effective factors in psychotherapy are suggestion and persuasion. Suggestion acts on irrational, emotional factors, while persuasion is a rational process, requiring a high degree of internal tension and capacity for critical analysis.

Suggestive therapy, most highly developed in hypnosis, may be used in two ways. First, the hypnotist in the role of a super-powerful being influences the subject. Second, hypnosis may be used to induce a state of peace, calm, and relaxation. Soviet psychiatrists refer to suggestive psychotherapy as representative of the thinking of the "Moscow School," or the "Kharkhov School," where there are chairs of psychotherapy connected with institutes for graduate study for physicians.

Pathogenetic therapy, in contrast, is associated more with the name of Myasishchev and the "Leningrad School." To continue with Myasishchev's own presentation, he claimed pathogenetic therapy is based on the Pavlovian concept of neurosis as a disorder of self-regulatory mechanisms, including disturbances of self-control, self-observation, and self-direction. Though the neurophysiology of pathogenetic psychotherapy is not known, a leading role is played by the second signal system. The psychotherapist becomes very important to the patient, whose previous experiences have brought failure and frustration. As Myasishchev said, the patient turns to the therapist as a "teacher of life." Initially, in pathogenetic therapy, the efforts to uncover the cause of the illness may lead to exacerbation because contact is made with the pathogenetic point. Later, however, the symptoms gradually disappear, as the therapeutic process of becoming conscious of the associative connections with automaticisms and other pathological formations continues. For Myasishchev, analysis of the past is necessary insofar as it relates to the understanding of the present illness. Where pathological character traits are present, the therapeutic task is more complex.

Myasishchev suggested specific indications for each form of therapy. Acute neurotic states and functional illnesses with somatic symptomatology (e.g., cardiovascular, gastrointestinal, or skin symptoms) respond better to hypnosis. Character distortions are an indication for pathogenetic psychotherapy with emphasis on reeducation and reorientation of pathological attitudes. Bekhterev's method of diversion, rechanneling interest and energy into healthier activities, is also utilized.

Collective psychotherapy has an established place in Myasishchev's thought, but it does not replace individual treatment. It may be used to supplement and strengthen the processes initiated in individual psychotherapy. Soviet group therapy may take one of several forms: discussion of the general aspects of psychic illness; discussion of a specific case of psychic illness; investigation with a patient of the history of his illness and how it formed in the presence of other patients.

Although Myasishchev's thought has undoubtedly been a major contribution to Soviet psychiatry, it was curious and disturbing to me to find how isolated his thinking is from the main stream of child psychiatry. Even in his own institute, the child department seemed largely preoccupied with the investigation of epilepsy and other problems at the level of organic central nervous system pathology. (One notable exception is described below in Chapter V.) There was no effort that I could discern to apply the concepts of Myasishchev to the problems of childhood. In major centers of Moscow, too, Myasishchev's ideas about child development, personality, and neurosis have had far greater influence on the development of a psychotherapeutic approach to adult neurotics than they have on the understanding of childhood neuroses and character distortions, their prevention and treatment.

To conclude the historical survey, some developments since the death of Stalin are noteworthy. With the shift away from the extreme Lamarckian position in the understanding of genetic factors in illness, there has been renewed interest in the genetic study of schizophrenia, epilepsy, and rare syndromes which accompany chromosomal abnormalities. The increased flexibility in scientific investigation has also made it possible to recognize that the conditions of life in the socialist state have far from abolished mental illness. The general polyclinics are filled with adults and children who have functional disturbances. Belatedly recognizing this fact, Soviet doctors began developing the field of psychotherapy, but the Soviet anti-Freudian position has, if anything, hardened.

In child psychiatry, the quality of family life and of education are blamed for functional disturbances, but the aftermath of trauma and infection are considered important too. Expanded training programs for psychoneurologists working in polyclinics and new chairs of child psychiatry outside Moscow were important developments of the sixties. However, in 1969 it still seemed to me that insufficient attention was paid to training these specialists in the skills of psychotherapy.

SOME TRENDS AND PARADOXES

This review of the history of child psychiatry in the Soviet Union reveals some conflicting trends and paradoxes. The German medical model of Griesinger and Kraepelin fosters a kind of fatalistic attitude toward disease as leaving an immutable defect—either through genetic etiology or early acquired cerebral damage in intrauterine or postnatal life. But the therapeutic nihilism such thinking encourages clashes with the Soviet view of man as a tabula rasa who can be infinitely modified by training and self-training. How do Soviet psychiatrists reconcile these conflicting opposites? I saw far more interest than I had expected in genetic problems. The genetic factor is described as a predisposition, which can be made more or less manifest by favorable or unfavorable external factors, operating later in development. So therapeutic nihilism is avoided and man remains modifiable. But this leads immediately to another error which Sukhareva complains about—the need for multiple causality (predisposing factors and later external precipitating environmental factors) conflicts with the need to see a disease as an entity with one definite etiology. The recognition of multiple factors in the causation of an illness leads to an unacceptable eclecticism.

Again, the obsessional German interest in description and classification which has carried over into all aspects of Soviet psychiatry clashes with the warmth, intuitiveness, and subjective understanding which characterize the Soviet doctor at his best in his dealings with his patients. This curious combination of obsessional hair-splitting and compassion and intuition seemed to me to be peculiarly Russian. I found myself wondering why the Russians tended to accept German influence, in view of the devastations of World War II, which are still active memories in the consciousness of the people.

At a different level, I have been impressed with the Marxian principle that qualitative changes appear at a higher level of organization as a result of quantitative changes. This must mean that phenomena at a complex level cannot be understood only in terms of principles applying to the organization of matter at a simpler level. Translated into psychiatric terms, this must mean that psychiatric disease is not only brain disease. Russians themselves acknowledge the error of reductionism and are careful to say, as Myasishchev does, that psychology is necessary as well as physiology to understand personality and its illnesses. But in actual practice, much Soviet diagnostic thinking I observed seemed to me to suffer precisely from the error of reductionism.

On the other hand, to allow too much focus on psychology leads in the Soviet view to the error of idealism, again the reaction of nineteenth-century materialism against speculative philosophy and theology. Much American psychiatric thinking appears to Soviet critics to suffer from the error of idealism. But the wish to avoid this error may have had serious consequences in the form of delaying the development of the speciality of psychotherapy.

In comparing Soviet and American child psychiatry, it is interesting to note certain parallel trends. The mechanistic emphasis in the twenties appeared in the psychology of both countries: in Watsonian behaviorism and in the theories of Pavlov and Bekhterev. Then it became more appropriate to study consciousness. The development of Freudian theory in the West and Marxism-Leninism in the East led, as Skolnick showed, to a similar philosophical position regarding freedom of will and man's responsibility for his acts (40). In both lands, limited freedom of choice is recognized and man himself is held responsible for his behavior. In both countries, the importance of infancy and early childhood is recognized for the formation of the personality, though Soviet psychiatrists would emphasize intrauterine and early postnatal damage, while Americans would highlight incorrect handling and upbringing as they are mediated through disturbed parent-child relationships. Both American and Soviet psychiatrists recognize the importance of functional disturbances and a psychotherapeutic approach, though belatedly on the Soviet side.

Russians and Americans share a cultural heritage of materialism and an optimistic belief in the perfectibility of man, as well as a humanistic commitment to the value of man. If two systems of thought converge as points and see segments of reality in the same way, perhaps the convergent points represent some fundamental truths. I thus consider it important to see where we agree with Soviet psychiatrists, though I have no wish to overlook our deep persisting differences.

The Social
Perspective

Transcultural comparisons have the twofold aim of helping us to know another culture and of knowing ourselves better. We all have unconscious value systems which make it difficult to take stock of our own culture and its impact on social science. Transcultural studies present us with the opportunity to become aware of our own values and to gain new perspective.

THE SOVIET CHILD AND HIS ENVIRONMENT

In Soviet thinking, the family plays a decisive role as the first collective. A contemporary Russian psychologist wrote (5, p. 94):

> The first knowledge about right and wrong, about good and evil, the child receives within the family. The family is the first social formation, the first collective in his life. This is why it is very important in the earliest years when thought and character are in the process of formation that the little one find himself in an atmosphere of friendliness, understanding; that the members of the family have concern for each other, help one another. After all, the child is not born either an egoist, an individualist or a collectivist. He becomes one or the other, depending on the environment in which he lives and certainly chiefly depending on upbringing.

Several American observers of the Soviet scene have been interested in the problem of the relationship of society and child rearing to the problem of character formation. Alt and Alt described a variety of children's services, based on a three-week trip in 1956 (15). They were critical of the way Soviet society raises its children. While they recognized the important position children occupy in the communist society, they objected to the tendency to submerge the individual in the collective and to the use of public reprimand for social control. After a second visit in 1959, the Alts reported a conflict between the role of the family and the role of the state in child rearing (16). The Alts believed problems in the society could no longer be blamed on bourgeois capitalism. They felt Soviet achievements in education, mental health, and general well-being were at the price of conformity achieved by coercion. They also concluded that there were "core problems in the development of the personality of the Soviet child: the duality of values which characterizes the dominant ideology and the conflict between the family, the school and the political organizations in the child rearing responsibility assigned to them" (16, p. 289).

In 1966 I found the Russians themselves beginning to study the family as a social institution. A new department of sociology had been formed at the Institute of Philosophy in Moscow under A. G. Kharchev. The problem under investigation at the time was the effect of mothers working outside the home on children and the family. In his book, published in 1964, Kharchev decried the "bourgeois legend of the enmity of Marxists towards the family" (4, p. 4). There is some truth in this allegation, that westerners do not perceive accurately the role of the family under socialist conditions. The American stereotype of the communist child separated from his family, brought up in a completely institutionalized environment, is overly simplistic.

Bronfenbrenner, whose observations extended throughout the sixties, reviewed how Soviet educators, sociologists, and psychologists treated the controversial issue of the withering away of the family as the society turns toward communism. The trend in 1970 was to reaffirm the importance of the family, consistent with my observations of the Soviet scene (21, pp. 83–84). He described how the Soviet public protested about an essay by economic planner Stanislav Strumilin, published in 1960, predicting that facilities for communal living would become so superior that the family, reduced to a couple, would be absorbed into a social commune (22, pp. 112–113). Champions of the preservation of the family appeared, among them Kharchev and the psychologist V. N. Kolbanovski, who asserted that the party never intended for the family to be supplanted; the child's need for love is best satisfied within the family (22, pp. 113–114). The commitment of the Russian people to family life should not be underestimated. It is palpable when one is talking to Russians.

My observations were limited to the Soviet child growing up under urban conditions, since I was denied permission to go to rural areas. Neither was it possible to take into consideration the various non-Russian cultures of the Eastern republics, or differences between highly privileged and less privileged segments of the society. Urban conditions were quite similar in Moscow, Leningrad, and Kiev and I would assume in other large centers.

Soviet urban families are typically small, with one or two children. There is less concern than in the United States about the only child. When I gave a set of Flagg dolls, used in play therapy by American child psychiatrists, to a Soviet colleague, she exclaimed over what a large family this was. The set consisted of a mother, a father, a brother, a sister, and two babies. There are many reasons for the smaller families. Many Soviet women hold jobs outside the home to supplement the family income. In Field's opinion, economic need is the main reason for the high percentage of women in the labor force (22, pp. 13–14). However, many women, particularly those in the professions, want to work outside the home. A tradition of valuing education and intellectual achievement dating from the prerevolutionary era has been reinforced by the communist teaching that it is good to work and to contribute to the building of communism. One Soviet colleague in Kiev said that many women deliberately limit the size of their families, as she had, in order to be free to pursue their intellectual interests.

Since children are highly valued and families are small, there is danger of overprotection. A chance observation on New Year's Day illustrates this. I took a *troika* ride (a sleigh drawn by three horses) with a Russian family: a young man and woman with a little girl, about three, all done up in fur. We were comfortably buried under a fur blanket, feeling very cheerful, but the mother cupped her hands in front of the child's face, fearing that the cold air rushing past us as we sped through a wooded park might be harmful. She kept obstructing the youngster's view and talked about the need to shield and protect her. The child remained content during the half-hour ride, but I wondered about the long-term effects of such anxious hovering. A case of school phobia in a girl who was the focus of anxious concern of both parents is given in Chapter III. Bronfenbrenner reported warmth and solicitousness as major characteristics of the mother-child relationship (21, p. 8).

Forces that weaken the family structure were evident in Russian psychiatric case material. Marital conflicts were extremely common, and the divorce rate was continuing to rise. Frequent mention was made of family conflicts centering around the introduction of a stepfather into the home and the inability of the child to accept the situation. Male alcoholism was a pressing social problem, readily acknowledged by Soviet child psychiatrists as taking a toll on the emotional health of children. There was much dislocation and disruption of families during World War II. The sociologists at the Institute of Philosophy in Moscow mentioned the problems created for children of that era who had been separated from their families. Particularly difficult situations arose when these children were adopted and subsequently reunited with natural parents who had been missing or were believed dead. After the war, family disruption was fostered because training and job opportunities in distant cities frequently resulted in prolonged separations of husband and wife. This may be diminishing. After the breadwinners find definitive jobs, there appears to be less moving around than there is in the United States.

The problem of unwanted children may be less critical in the Soviet Union than in the United States. There is no strong religious tradition, at least in the Russian culture, which opposes birth control measures and abortion. Although abortion is not encouraged, it has been legal since 1955, when the law was changed because so many women were resorting to harmful illegal abortions. There seems less censure of the unmarried mother who wishes to keep her child. There is far less social pressure to marry early and to have large families.

An additional factor, less negative in its social effects, still tends to loosen family ties: children are trained to relate to the wider collective and to gain major satisfactions outside the family circle from the toddler stage on. American observers have been largely divided between positive and negative evaluations of Russian child care centers. Families are encouraged to use the nurseries without as much concern as in the United States about the harmful effects of separation from the child during the day. Bronfenbrenner reported in 1970 that 10 percent of all children under two years and 20 percent of children three to five years were in nursery or kindergarten day care centers (21, p. 15). This seemed to me a small percentage in view of the value set by the society on collectives other than the home in character formation. My overall impression was of the enduring Russian belief in the family as the basic and essential social unit.

I visited a nursery in Kiev for infants and children two or three months of age to three years. One of the doctors who accompanied me on the visit had an eleven-month-old girl of her own whom she told me was home with a nanny. After we left, she said the nursery personnel had convinced her that her daughter would be better off in a nursery than at home. At the nursery, the children were divided into three groups: infants up to one year old, the one- to two-year-olders, and the two- to three-year-olders. There is a current trend to combine the nurseries with the kindergartens which take children from three to seven, since it is considered that better continuity of care can be provided. This particular nursery was run by a kindly staff of doctors, up-bringers, and administrators. The city educator visited to supervise the work of the upbringers. The children were taught colors, how to count, how to pronounce consonants correctly, and the upbringers were given a specific daily regime to follow in organizing the activities of the children—music, learning simple verses, fairy tales, puppet shows, celebration of holidays.

The attitude of the personnel was that the nursery is better for the child than remaining at home because the collective is so important. There was awareness that a child is not ready to play with other children before he is three years old. However, the specialized knowledge of the upbringers was considered superior to the knowledge of a parent. Up-bringers receive training similar to that of nurses: after eight years of regular school the upbringer takes a two-year course devoted to medical and educational subjects. Soviet professionals also value an orderly regime and feel this can be provided better in the nursery than it can under home conditions. The younger the children come, the easier the separation from mother, so they like to receive the children at three or four months of age. Working mothers receive pay after the birth of the child until he is four months old, and after that their job is kept open for them until the child's third birthday, so the mother does have some real choice about whether to stay at home with her child or to use the nurseries.

Many of the Russian children who do stay home in the preschool years are in the care of a grandmother (*babushka*). Many Russian children become very attached to their grandmothers, and this is a recurrent theme in many case histories. The babushka frequently represents old values which the society would just as soon erase in its desperate effort to urbanize and industrialize at a rapid pace. On the other hand, the role of the babushka as someone who is needed in the society may have positive value for retired people accustomed to a lifetime of hard work. Sociologists at the Institute of Philosophy in Moscow mentioned both positive and negative effects on the child of spending the early years with a babushka. The warm, close ties between the child and the grandparent formed a needed bridge between the generations. But the permissiveness of the babushka often conflicted with the values of the mother's generation. They also said there were cases in which a struggle arose over who was boss.

I noted certain consistent child-rearing practices in conversations with various doctors, observations in the nursery, and books for parents. Soviet parents make a serious effort to follow recommendations made by authoritative professionals. During the newborn and infancy periods, breast feeding is encouraged. There is an awareness that the mother's mood is important in helping the child to achieve a pleasant, satisfying feeding experience. Swaddling is now discouraged, though formerly it was common among the uneducated in rural areas. I did notice that in the cold Russian winters the children are wrapped up tightly and taken outdoors to be wheeled around in carriages while they are asleep, but free motor activity is also encouraged. In conformity with the Soviet attitude of conscious direction and control, the child is actively helped to sit, to stand, to hold objects, and to walk. Sensory stimulation with a variety of attractive toys is stressed, and parents are advised to talk constantly and freely to their young infants. Intellectual and speech development are not left to chance but are systematically cultivated in the child.

My several sources consistently advocated early toilet training based on conditioning principles. The urge to defecate is conditioned to sitting on the pot and the sound "ahah" starting at six months of age. They consider it definitely wrong to wait until after one year. Enuresis is a common problem, and occasionally children are encountered who soil, but I have no idea whether the frequency is about the same as it is in the United States or not.

The psychologists advocate a regular regime of feeding, sleeping, and waking, describing in considerable detail what can be expected at various age levels. In infancy they expect a child will be fed at least seven times a day. In describing the approach to an infant, E. A. Shumilin, recognizing the parents' wish to avoid spoiling, advised "the attitude toward the child should be attentive, caring, tender and along with that demanding" (5, p. 47). This is an excellent description of the attitude of Soviet parents, educators, and upbringers toward children up through the early school years. In discussing what to do with a screaming baby,

Shumilin advised not to yield to the impulse to hold him all the time but to try other measures first. It is acknowledged that it is important to hold the baby and to have a close warm relationship, but only when he is calm and happy. In other words, the baby is rewarded for calmness. It is not considered good practice to condition a child to expect to be carried around constantly or rocked to sleep. This combination of warmth and strictness agrees well with observations reported by Bronfenbrenner (21). There is, further, a kind of flexibility and readiness to recognize and accept a child's individual characteristics in spite of the emphasis on the collective (23). Praise is used lavishly and punishment sparingly. Physical punishment is definitely frowned upon. Bronfenbrenner described withholding of love, a hurt look, an attitude of coldness as the main method of Soviet discipline and the decisive factor in achieving obedience and a high degree of acceptance of adult standards (21, pp. 13–14). In short, the Soviet preschool child is a special person and receives every consideration.

The transition to the school years must seem very abrupt to a Soviet child who has been the center of attention at home with a doting babushka or who has received warm, kindly care in a nursery-kindergarten. I visited one Soviet school, #739 of the Leningrad district of Moscow, which has been shown to many foreigners. The school was described in the report of the US Mission on Mental Health to the USSR (25, pp. 145–146). It is difficult to judge how typical it is. There were 800 boys and girls in school #739 in classes (grades) one to ten when I visited. Soviet children do not usually begin school until they are seven. Classes are large, usually about 40 children. Some schools have double sessions. At the time of my visit, 36 of the children, or 4.5 percent, were attending the school of the prolonged day, i.e., they remained in school after classes were over for recreation and study until 6:00 in the evening because both parents were working. (Bronfenbrenner reported in 1970 that 5 percent of Soviet children attend boarding schools or schools of the prolonged day [21, p. 15].) Again, this percentage seemed small to me for a society in which so many women work. The atmosphere in this large, barren school was one of drabness, regimentation, and firm discipline in the classroom. In the halls, however, the children who were getting ready to go home seemed lively and normal. A couple of boys, catapulting themselves like rockets, were reprimanded by the principal. These children seemed far more childlike and natural than the subdued children who were under treatment for neuroses at a sanatorium. Psychiatric consultation was available to this school through the Regional Psychoneurological Dispensary. I have no idea how often it was used.

The curriculum in all Soviet schools is centralized. Eight years of school were required in 1969, with a projected increase to ten years. Although one curriculum is planned for use in schools throughout the country, the Moscow schools have higher academic standards than schools in remote regions. This question came up in the case of a boy who had developed symptoms when he moved from Siberia to Moscow and found the school program much more demanding. There is very little choice of subjects in the Soviet schools beyond the foreign language introduced in the fifth grade; there is no guidance department. The curriculum emphasizes foreign language, mathematics, and science.

The Soviet school I visited seemed to me to carry with it pressures which might lead to conflict and ultimately contribute to psychiatric disturbance: the formal atmosphere, the demand for conformity, the large classes and lack of individual instruction. Transitional growth crises or points when Soviet psychiatrists feel that a child is particularly vulnerable to psychiatric stress include the seven to eight-year-old period of the child's introduction to school (see Chap. III below). During the later years, there is sharp competition for admission to various institutes of advanced training and universities.

The question of the Soviet attitude toward creativity has been of great interest to American observers of child rearing. In principle, educators are aware that the vitality and strength of the society depend on fostering creativity in individual members. There is also a belief that creativity, like motor, sensory, and intellectual development, must be trained rather than allowed to unfold. This is in conformity with the Soviet value of conscious control and direction over all aspects of individual development as well as national life as a whole. At the nursery and kindergarten level I would agree with Cole and Cole, who report that creativity is recognized as desirable but considered less important than other values (23). At the school level it is stifled by the rigidity of the curriculum and the formality of the classroom. In higher education there is a serious conflict between creativity with the atmosphere of intellectual freedom it requires and the ideological political requirements of the regime.

Aside from the formal educational system, there is an organization for young people which plans after-school activities and a summer camp program called the Young Pioneers. Nearly all children in the age range 9–13 years belong. (Although some of its aims may be equivalent to our Scout organizations, I was told in Czechoslovakia, where both Scouts and Pioneers exist, that the Scouts are forbidden in the USSR.) For children of kindergarten age, there is an organization called the Octobrists. Teenagers when they reach 15 may join the Komsomol where they prepare to become members of the communist party. I have the impression that many young people choose not to be Komsomols, or else they join and drop out after secondary school. If so, this suggests conflict with official policy which, since World War II, has aimed at universal party membership and is concerned with apathy and indifference on the part of working and peasant youth (28, pp. 123–125). Bronfenbrenner, who has published the most recent figures on membership, said over half of the eligible population in the 15–28-year age range are enrolled, but that the percentage of active Komsomols in the later years of school is higher, implying that the percentage of young adults is lower (21, p. 36). Resistance to the Komsomol may be a convert form of youth rebellion in the Soviet Union, where there is no tolerance of competing youth groups.

The purpose of all of these organizations is education for communist morality. Two versions of the Pioneer pledge learned by nine-year-olds have been published in English: one by Alt and Alt in 1959 and the second by Bronfenbrenner in 1970. The differences between the two show changes in the teaching of communist morality (15, p. 87; 21, pp. 39–48). The names of Lenin and Stalin have been deleted, in line with the policy of playing down the cult of personality. One might wonder how heroic models for identification can be used without references to personalities. I saw many Lenin rooms and corners in classrooms which continued to make of this national hero something more than human. Other deletions are references to hatred. New inclusions are various forms of altruism: friendship with other nations, care and concern for others, for animals and nature. The overall impression is of a shift away from militancy towards a more love-oriented collective conscience.

The values of Soviet communism with respect to work and achievement impressed me as strikingly similar to conservative Yankee values and the values of the Jewish middle class in the United States. There is a communist saying with a biblical ring to it that he who does not work shall not eat. At the present stage of socialist development, the benefits of the society are distributed to people according to their contributions. This means that inequality is tolerated. There is still the ideal for the future of distributing the benefits of the society according to needs when a state of pure communism is achieved. The communist morality transmitted by the Pioneer Organization appeared to me to lack revolutionary zeal, basically perpetuating the interests of the establishment.

Another aspect of communist morality emphasizes the obligation of the individual, within the collective, to help one's neighbor, so that the achievement level of the group as a whole will be raised. Thus, on the one hand, mutual assistance is encouraged. In school, the more gifted students are expected to help the less gifted. On the other hand, mutual criticism is introduced, even in the early school years. Children are first taught to criticize each other, later to anticipate group criticism with self-evaluation. The Pioneers are organized with small groups or links competing against each other for rewards and recognition. So the structure of the Pioneer Organization fosters the communist values of mutual aid and mutual regulation. The value and aims of the Pioneer Organization are also carried into the programs of forest schools and sanatoria which treat children with psychiatric problems.

There was too little opportunity to talk with teenagers still in school and young adults in institutes and universities. The following material is in the category of broad impressions. I felt that there was a clear mandate operating within the family, the educational system, and the broader society to accept authority from infancy through all stages of life. My impression was corroborated by studies reported by Bronfenbrenner of readiness to engage in morally unacceptable behavior. Twelve-year-old Soviet children were presented with a series of ten moral dilemmas such as whether to cheat on a test, or whether to deny having destroyed property. One group was told their answers would be made available only to scientists. A second group was told their answers would be made available to parents and teachers. A third group was told their answers would be known only to other children. In comparison with 12-year-old children in West Germany, the United States, and England, the Soviet children were significantly less willing to indulge in these unacceptable acts. It was of special interest that the Soviet children were influenced in the direction of conformity and the United States children in the direction of delinquency when the expectation was that other children would learn of their behavior (21, pp. 77–78). Rebelliousness among Soviet young people does not take extreme forms. Further, I sensed a more general acceptance of dependence in the Soviet Union, since life in the collective is valued so highly. However, free-loading is definitely frowned on, and one frequently sees popular articles about the sin of "parasitism."

Many American observers have written about the state control of
dissent, especially criticisms of the Soviet regime. I only mention it
here as one palpable and important factor in the Soviet culture at large
which must profoundly influence those going through the adolescent
years. While there appeared to be no hippies at the time I visited the
Soviet Union, there was awareness of them and even envy, as a case
given in Appendix IV shows. Some young people were spending their
vacations camping out in the wooded areas around the city or in more
remote regions. They were called "tourists" and were said to follow the
type of life they imagine hippies might lead in the United States.

Adolescent problems in the Soviet Union, as far as I could observe,
did not include widespread use of drugs. Soviet psychiatrists conceded
problems with alcoholism in older adolescents and young adults and,
to a very small degree, addiction to heroin and experimentation with
hashish. They all denied the existence of marijuana or LSD in the
country. They also denied the widespread identity crises which occupy
psychiatrists in America dealing with adolescents. In a discussion with
me, Professor Kovalev said he considered adolescent problems centering around the issue of finding oneself not the business of psychiatry
but of psychology. These problems, he said, are not disease but aspects
of normal development. I was left wondering whether there was a real
difference between Soviet and American youth with regard to the
appearance of extreme forms of the identity crisis. I am not sure, because for ill-defined reasons I was not permitted to observe the mental
hospital facilities for older adolescents between 16 and 18. Further
exploration and dialogue in this area are clearly needed.

Perhaps the identity crises are less flamboyant and less visible in
Soviet young people simply because they have less freedom. There are
fewer choices to be made and a shorter moratorium. This term is used
in Erikson's sense as a time during which one is protected from making
a definite commitment (24). I met the 16-year-old daughter of a doctor
in Kiev. This young woman was very attractive, conscious of her femininity, and gave the impression of great stability and maturity. In fact,
she seemed to me more like an 18-year-old. She was in the tenth class
in school and had already made the decision to become a psychologist.
The following year she expected to enroll in the Institute of Philosophy
at Kiev, which had a department of psychology. It seemed to me that
her moratorium had already ended and she had made firm commitments
which would affect the direction of her future. I wondered whether
many Soviet youth are not subjected to a premature crystallization of
their character as a result of this early closure. Rebellion goes on in a

more covert form, I would have no doubt, but I was not in a position to observe it.

What about the question of male and female roles in Soviet society? I feel that certain broad differences exist between Russians and Americans in this regard. There were many indications that the traditional supremacy of the male remains in the background of Soviet attitudes. During my visit to the Pioneer camp in Sochi, a program of song, dance, and general entertainment was put on for us. One dance was done by a little group of five-year-old girls and one masterful little boy in the center of the circle holding a whip. He would crack the whip, and the little girls would do his bidding. Perhaps masculine supremacy remains only an ideal in the social consciousness of the people, because there has been many a fatherless family as the result of disruptions of war. More recently, widespread male alcoholism has perhaps too frequently prevented the father from taking his traditional dominant role within the family. On the other hand, Field emphasized the persistence of male supremacy. As he pointed out, a woman may have equality in a legal and ideological sense and work side by side with men, but she must also assume the full burden of domestic duties and child rearing (22, p. 8). Further, women are poorly represented in the top echelons of management, in executive positions, and in the higher ranks of the communist party (22, pp. 14–15).

The problem of feminine identity in the Soviet Union was of considerable interest to me in comparison with the United States. Intellectual pursuits and hard physical labor, both of which become associated with masculinity in American thinking, traditionally were characteristic of Russian women in prerevolutionary times. In those days, upper-class women belonging to the intelligentsia pursued literary or artistic interests. Peasant women toiled in the fields, but there never seemed to be a question in either case of the woman surrendering her femininity because of her work role. The same pattern has been carried into Soviet times. There is said currently to be a preponderance of women in universities, and it is well known that the majority of Soviet doctors are women. Many women enter the hard sciences, and there seems no concern about whether intellectual careers make a woman less feminine. I happened to go to a fashion exhibit in Kiev offered for the women in a society of chemists. Women in the sciences do not experience their feminine interests as in conflict with their scientific interests, and at lower educational levels they are still employed in hard physical labor. Masculine and feminine identities, Russian style, must be constructed along other lines. Work and achievement are values embraced by the communist society as a whole. Soviet adolescents are somewhat freer than Americans to make vocational choices in line with their real capabilities and motivation to achieve. A Soviet woman can feel feminine and still be a chemist or a Cosmonaut, and a Soviet male can be an internist or a psychiatrist and not feel less of a man because most of his colleagues are women.

The Soviet attitude toward sexuality is characterized by shyness, a complex attitude not directly comparable with Victorian prudishness. Psychiatric histories show concern about overt adolescent expressions of sexuality, heterosexual or perverse. A case in Appendix IV shows how restrictive a Soviet family became with their early adolescent daughter to prevent her from meeting with boys in unsupervised situations. The case also shows how the physicians in a way agreed with the family because they accepted the girl first for hospitalization and later for sanatorium care. However, Russians do not deny sexuality as an inner feeling state or even as a factor in the etiology of some psychiatric conditions. Under crowded living conditions, children must witness adult sexual acts, but I have no knowledge about the degree to which this is recognized as a factor in psychiatric disturbances. There is a growing realistic attitude about giving children sexual information. Old-fashioned practices of telling children stories about the stork, and so forth, are yielding to the modern practice, advised by Soviet doctors, of telling children the truth.

Certain broad aspects of Soviet culture may have a profound impact on the growing child and youth. The first group of these has to do with basic dimensions: the use of time, the use of space, attitudes toward inner reality, and the treatment of outer reality or "truth."

While Soviet and American people are future oriented in the sense of emphasizing achievement, education, and an advanced technology, there is a curious inconsistency in the way in which Russians handle time. There is a willingness to tolerate inefficiency which would be exasperating to the American to whom "time is money." Side by side with the procrastination and ability to tolerate endless delay is a paradoxical, tumultuous sense of rushing. People nearly knock each other down in an effort to run to a subway train even though the next one will come in three minutes. There seemed to be in December a precipitous year-end rush to get reports written and plans fulfilled. Some of the frustrations of Soviet life stem from this ambivalent attitude toward time. I wonder whether the paradox of endless delays and precipitous rushing might reflect superimposed cultural layers: the basic timelessness of the rural peasant persisting in the urbanized population upon whom the hurry and bustle necessitated by rapid industrialization have been superimposed.

My very first impressions had to do with the use of space. Flying over Russian territory, I was struck with the vast empty reaches of the country, contrasted with dense, compact little villages and crowded, huge cities. I later learned that there is a long history of crowding together in little places in that vast land. This peculiar Russian use of space has persisted into Soviet times and is reflected in the construction of new housing. There is no significant suburban development such as one sees around American cities. People live in either an urban atmosphere or a rural village atmosphere. Cities tend to become larger and larger but rows of apartment houses, city streets, and trolley lines end abruptly at the forest. Soviet children in urban centers grow up in crowded conditions amidst the bustle of a modern city. Even resort areas tend to be crowded. Perhaps there is more Russian tolerance for crowding and more comfort in a restricted living space than an American would experience. Along with this, however, is a deep Russian reverence for nature, reflected in Soviet planning of residential mental health facilities for children.

With respect to the problem of dealing with inner reality, there is an attitude of tolerance and acceptance of inner emotional states: an inner emotional freedom. However, it is definitely accompanied by rather rigid restrictions on external behavior. Typically, Russians seem to be more ready than Americans to acknowledge a variety of positive feelings: tenderness, romance, longing, love of country, ecstasy, and even states of devoutness. The traditional Russian capacity for suffering seemed to me to be a reality. Perhaps there is not more masochism but more artistry in dealing with it. There is less tolerance of hostile feelings. Children raised in this atmosphere of emotional warmth and strictness tend to be well behaved, inhibited with strangers but self-aware, well-developed in verbal capacities. Some may be outwardly conforming but inwardly rebellious. The Soviet child is free to experience his feelings but not to act upon them. American observations, including my own, have pointed to the good, well-disciplined behavior of Soviet children, at least in public places and in conditions of the collective.

With respect to dealing with outer reality, there is a profound difference between the Soviet and the American attitude toward "truth" and its place in the hierarchy of social values. The Soviet attitude appears to be that those aspects of external reality will be studied, elaborated, and made generally available to the public only if they serve the col-

lective aims of the State as it represents the interests of society. The
corollary is that inconvenient aspects of reality which clash with over-
riding social values will be suppressed. However, the corollary to this
corollary goes as follows: These suppressed segments of reality can
be revived at any time that the value of the wider society demands it.
This means that history can be written and then rewritten as the example of the question of Stalinism shows.

Aronson and Field have pointed out another dimension of the problem of Soviet attitudes toward truth and reality (17): according to
Marxist doctrine, social reality is constantly changing with segments
diminishing and disappearing and other parts becoming more dominant.
Russians confuse what actually is with what ideally ought to be in the
future. There is a tendency to deny or underplay inconvenient aspects
of reality which represent uncomfortable truths. The general Soviet
reluctance to say a definite no is very real and may be related to this
question of dealing with reality. This peculiar inability to be frank must
lead to unbelievable frustrations for the Soviet people when they apply
for jobs, permission to travel, and other privileges. With respect to
bringing up children, this general attitude means that they should not
be confronted with unpleasant truths about their origin or situation,
but rather protected from such truths. A case is presented in Chapter V
in which a child was protected from knowledge of her adoption.

The typical Russian way of handling the problem of separation is
unlike the usual American way. Since Russia has been racked by wars
and social upheaval, traumatic separations have been an important
feature of the external reality each individual has had to confront. Russian literature abounds with separation themes. So frequently there are
trains departing in the snowy wastes with one lone figure left behind, a
tiny speck in a vast, silent land. The longing, sadness, and grief en-
gendered by these descriptions are fully understood and sensitively
described. But the tendency is to protect people from knowing that they
will have to face a separation. It is easier, as we noted in discussing
the nursery, to expose an infant of three months to separation from his
mother because he does not yet know sufficiently how to differentiate
his mother from others. American professionals, trained to feel a child
must actively work through the separation experience, tend to be
shocked by this practice.

Perhaps what we overlook is that these early separations, before the
infant has differentiated mother from grandmother or nurse, may not
be experienced traumatically. Instead, they may foster the building of
a "collective mother image." This term is used as Phyllis Greenacre did.

She introduced the term "collective alternates," defined as the "range of extended experience which may surround or become attached to the main focus of object relationships" (26, p. 57). A particularly sensitive infant, she believed, might experience more deeply and broadly the relationship with the mother in the personal sphere and at the same time enter into a "love affair with the world" which would "occupy varying relationships with individual love relationships, sometimes the one being at the expense of the other; at other times, or in other individuals appearing as quite separate or as complementary attachments. But generally the more powerfully demanding one is that of the world. Further it is possible that in the libidinal phases of development of the infantile years, the presence of such collective alternate relationships permits diminution of the effect of critical situations involving the individual object relationships" (26, p. 58). Although Greenacre did not elaborate on the implications of the collective alternate for the tolerance of separation experiences, the concept might be relevant in understanding the role of the collective in early child development in socialist countries. The collective preschool experience of Soviet children may provide an opportunity for formation of collective alternates not present in more individualistic societies. The implications are profound for ego development, identification patterns, and the development of self-perceptions, as well as handling separation experiences and the capacity to sublimate or accept substitute gratification. In Soviet society, everyone is to a degree mother, father, or big brother. This could be a very real source of comfort and reassurance to a little one temporarily or permanently separated from his mother.

A second cluster of Soviet attitudes relevant to the environment surrounding the growing child has to do with religion and antireligion. Is religion a living institution on the Soviet scene? Certainly the official answer would be that religion is tolerated but is slowly dying out. The state forbids the religious instruction of children. Intuitively, however, I sensed that religious concerns remained a living issue and were for some young people a means of protest against the establishment.

The Soviet attitude toward the exposure of children to religion is revealed in an article in *Pravda* entitled "A Singular Case" (6). A ten-year-old girl had written to the newspaper that she had been visiting a Baptist church and had found there some young people praying who told her "only relationships to God can bring happiness." This child's rebellion against Soviet society's antireligious bias stimulated some soul searchings. The correspondent looked into the girl's background to find where things had gone wrong in her upbringing to make her resort to this crutch. He found her to be a lonely, withdrawn child, reacting to the separation of her parents. Neither the Komsomol nor the school nor her grandmother with whom she was living had done anything to ease the situation. The child was quick to deny any acceptance of the Baptist beliefs. She had, she claimed, written *Pravda* only to affirm her belief in atheism!

The Soviet child is brought up in a society which highly values all of the arts. By way of contrast, there is a general drabness in daily living conditions. The problem of adequate living space recurred in case history after case history. Frequently situations would be described in which three families were living in one three-room apartment. Although the Soviet people may be able to tolerate crowding better than Americans, the Soviet psychiatrist is aware of the adverse effects of crowding on patients and in some cases may even arrange for an individual patient to have separate living space. The relative scarcity, high cost, and indifferent quality of consumer goods were still problems in 1969. Although there has been a gradual improvement in this area, there was still a mad scramble for scarce goods and services. Though materialistic, the society seems to have infinite patience in the sense of a capacity to delay gratification in order to achieve broader social aims. For young people growing up in the present, these conditions mean there is still a great deal of emphasis on obtaining personal possessions and the manipulations necessary to attain them, with implications for character formation.

Another aspect of daily living conditions is the bureaucratic superstructure, so frustrating to Soviet citizens as well as foreigners. The dehumanizing influence of urbanization and industrialization is as evident in Moscow as it is in New York. However, in the Soviet case, economic arrangements have not made courteous, efficient service particularly rewarding. Gogol's play "The Inspector-General" shows that the problem of paying off the bureaucracy predated the Soviet regime. Somehow, the play seems much funnier in Moscow than it does in Boston. I began to wonder whether these aspects of the Soviet environment encourage traits of manipulativeness and exploitativeness in the growing child's character in order to survive. One Soviet story dealt with the elaborate machinations of a family to help the daughter who was applying to one of the institutes for advanced study (11). In the end all the manipulative activities of the family were ridiculed. The young woman earned her place at the institute simply by studying for the examination.

I have included this section about day-to-day living in order to give American readers some broad impression of the environment in which a sensitive child, vulnerable to psychiatric disorder, lives and grows.

CHILD PSYCHIATRY AND SOVIET CULTURE

What can be said about the field of child psychiatry viewed as a product of a sociocultural system? Some of the values already enumerated in earlier sections bear directly on one or more of the following aspects of child psychiatry:

1. Ideological base.
2. Organization of psychiatric services.
3. Diagnostic problems.
4. Philosophy of treatment.

The present discussion is a preliminary attempt to relate selected cultural values to characteristics of child psychiatry. After the clinical material has been presented, we will return to these broader issues.

We have seen how important collectivism is to Soviet society along with the commitment to building communism. Together, these values tend to combine to produce a society which tolerates a rather high degree of dependence and submission to authority in its individual members. The building of communism requires a dedicated youth, devoted to work and achievement. The aim of treatment when psychic decompensation occurs is to restore as fully as possible the child's adaptation to a productive life within the collective and his ability to participate constructively in the building of communism.

The value of submission to authority has as a corollary low tolerance for uncontrolled behavior of either a sexual or aggressive kind. However, as we have tried to indicate in the discussion of "inner reality," there is a certain emotional freedom to experience inner affective states. I would agree with Aronson and Field, who reported that Russians are more tolerant of deviant emotional states, even the extremes of psychotic behavior (17). This seemed to be a curious inconsistency in a totalitarian state.

What kind of treatment practices are fostered by this curious combination of values? We should not be surprised to find widespread use of drugs and other physical measures to induce a state of outward tranquility. Concomitantly, there is a deemphasis of the subjective emotional experience of the patient in diagnostic thinking and a playing

down of emotional expression in psychotherapeutic methods. This
seems to me not so much a denial of inner emotional states as a hands-
off attitude which implicitly says: "I respect your inner freedom. I do
not equate inner emotional turmoil and suffering with psychiatric disease. As a physician, I treat your disease and leave you your soul." I
could not help contrasting these attitudes toward affective states with
the widespread American difficulty of acknowledging tender feelings.
(Compare Erikson's discussion of the problem of intimacy, 24, pp.
167–169.) The task the American psychotherapist faces of helping
people to acknowledge their love feelings and to take them seriously
may be far less of a problem for the Soviet psychotherapist. Perhaps it
is appropriate to notice in this connection that Russian psychiatrists
have never developed play therapy techniques. This is not because of a
lack of empathy with children or a lack of interest in making fascinat-
ing, innovative toys.

Traditional Russian warmth and kindliness have been consistently
reported by American observers of Soviet psychiatrists in their everyday
handling of their patients. This sensitivity for people has been in the
best Russian humanitarian tradition. My own observations in psychiatric hospitals and clinics fully confirm this point. Russian doctors typically combine sensitivity with a protective attitude, shielding children
from unpleasant truths about their conditions or life situation. To
illustrate: Children with chronic physical diseases rarely receive much,
if any, explanation of their illness or what to expect in the future.

The cluster of Soviet attitudes which have to do with faith in the
(Marxist-Leninist) scientific method, materialism, and the monistic
position with regard to the mind-body question encourage a physiologically based psychiatry, which, although lacking many testable scientific
hypotheses, stresses descriptive classification. A related ideal of conscious control and planning everything is expressed in a centralized
system of psychiatric services for children (see Chap. II below). Most
American observers concede that Soviet psychiatrists are justified in
being proud of their rationally based system, organized on the basis of
human needs. This is one area where the unity of theory and practice
is illustrated at its best.

Finally, the traditional isolation of Russian culture has extended
into the Soviet era, compounded by the distrust of the regime for foreign
ideas. The state of mutual ignorance that this has created in the psychiatric field has already been referred to as the starting point of this
present inquiry.

IMPLICATIONS FOR MENTAL HEALTH AND ILLNESS

The family is still valued as the basic unit of Soviet society and the first collective, although there are contemporary forces common to other industrialized societies which tend to weaken family ties. Over the years of Soviet power, there have been shifts in the relationship of the family to other collectives in the task of child rearing. The most recent trend I noted was to reaffirm the importance of the family. There is potentiality for conflict in child rearing between the mother and other mother figures. In particular, conflicts between old and new values, the old embodied in the person of the babushka, enter into character formation and character distortions in growing children.

Children are very special in the Soviet Union and get top priority. They are genuinely loved and are considered the future for Soviet power and the building of communism. Child-rearing practices are characterized by warmth, protectiveness, insistence on controlled behavior, and diffusion of parental roles into the wider society. Early toilet training is consistent with crowded, difficult living conditions, but may also be related to some of the bureaucratic rigidity, obsessive concern for detail, and concrete compartmentalization of thinking which characterize the adult members of the society. The abrupt transition between the warmth and individualized attention of the preschool years and the demands of early schooling may form a vulnerable point for the onset of psychiatric disturbances.

There is a basic difference between Russian and American attitudes toward the problem of parent-child separation, which to my knowledge has not been described by other American observers. Perhaps Russia's long history of wars and other upheavals leading to traumatic separations has fostered the tradition of collectivism with diffusion of parental roles. The formation of collective alternates early in life has profound implications for the formation of object relations, identification patterns, and capacity for sublimation. To the degree to which this factor operates to increase a child's feeling of security, it should be extremely important in promoting mental health.

Although both the Soviet Union and the United States have in common the conflicts in identity formation associated with urbanization and industrialization, the problem of sexual identification is different in the two societies. The American obsession with maleness and femaleness seems not nearly so prevalent among Soviet young people. Perhaps this affliction is one price of increasing self-awareness, just around the corner for Soviet youth. I thought it important that intellectual striving is not sex-linked to nearly the degree it is in the United States. As matters stood in 1969, Soviet young people were freer than their American counterparts to select an occupation consistent with real capability. This freedom could conceivably reduce neurotic conflict stemming from wishes culturally attributed to the opposite sex. The Russian acceptance of inner emotional states has been noted by previous American observers, but the role such acceptance may play in fostering healthy intrapsychic development has not been sufficiently stressed.

Differences described between Russian and American handling of basic dimensions of time, space, internal, and external reality seem to me to be fundamental in attempting to appreciate broad cultural divergences between the American and Russian people. There are also implications for the development of character, both normal and pathological.

II

The Organization
of Psychiatric
Services

The leading child psychiatrist in the Soviet Union, G. E. Sukhareva, wrote in 1958 on the question of how to construct a network of psychiatric services in accordance with age characteristics of psychiatric illness in childhood (4). In order to answer this question and the related one of evaluating the effectiveness of existing services, Sukhareva asked, first, what are the predominant forms of psychiatric illness in childhood? From figures gathered in 1931 in Moscow, Sukhareva concluded that 70 percent of childhood psychiatric disturbances were mild enough not to require hospital care. Therefore, the focus of the psychiatric care system should be on extramural help, with emphasis on prevention, since later development is so crucially affected by early pathology. Close cooperation was needed between the educational system and the psychiatric care system. Furthermore, Sukhareva maintained that a psychiatrist treating children should know neurology, because it is difficult to separate the two fields in childhood disorders.

In addition to full psychiatric hospitals for children and adolescents, Sukhareva cited the need for day hospitals, which could provide special remedial educational work, night hospitals for patients whose home conditions were unfavorable, and separate night hospitals for adolescents that could provide continued treatment for patients discharged from the hospital. Besides psychiatric facilities, special education was needed in 69.5 percent of the surveyed children. These needs would be met by several types of institutions under the Ministry of Education: schools and kindergartens for the retarded, sanatorium-schools and kindergartens for nervous children, and school-*internats* (boarding schools) for children with behavior difficulties whose management required a special regime.

Sukhareva's second question was, what are the age characteristics of psychiatric illness in childhood and how does the symptomatology change with age? What is needed in a hospital service to meet these requirements? In the birth to four-year age range, Sukhareva considered a small unit in a pediatric hospital to be the most suitable, since the most frequent psychiatric illnesses at this age were infections, intoxications, and traumata of the central nervous system. In the kindergarten and school-age children the commonest syndromes were neurotic-like and psychopathic-like states, epileptiform phenomena, fears, and motor restlessness. Psychotic phenomena were relatively rare. Requirements for admission of this age group should not be danger to oneself or others, as in adulthood, but need for precise diagnostic study or special treatment. The hospital she thought suitable for such patients was a psychiatric facility. In such a hospital the role of the educator would be important in contributing observations to the diagnostic process, as well as in therapy. Finally, because adolescents had a higher percentage of psychotic disorders, the most suitable hospital for them would be a department in an adult psychiatric hospital.

The final question Sukhareva raised was, what are the age characteristics of the course of psychiatric illness in childhood and what does this say about the percentage of hospital beds and the percentage of colony (chronic) beds needed? In the birth to four-year range, she found a more serious course of illness and developmental failure, and therefore the percentage of colony beds required exceeded the percentage of hospital beds. In older school-age children and adolescents, psychiatric disorders usually ran a less malignant course, which meant the number of sanatorium beds and hospital beds should be equal.

Sukhareva concluded that the network of services in 1958 was lacking in several respects. Sanatorium-schools for nervous children and schools with a special regime for children difficult to educate and to rear were needed. Such facilities only existed in the large centers. Treatment-educational hospitals for four- to seven-year-olds were also lacking. The network of psychoneurological offices with all supporting services in polyclinics still needed expansion. Workshops and day hospitals were lacking in the majority of institutions. The needs of chronic patients were not being met, as there were too few colony and sanatorium beds. Too many of these patients were remaining in hospitals.

The Russian psychiatric care system for children and adolescents is described in the following sections as I actually observed it in 1968–69. A complete list of the institutions visited appears in Appendix I. How well has the unity of theory and practice been achieved with respect to psychiatric care? Has Sukhareva realized her ideal, the unity of organizational and clinical considerations? The central concept of prevention is in actuality the focus of the whole system, shaping the organizational structure.

Child psychiatry in the Soviet Union is closely tied both with pediatrics and neurology. The child psychiatrist in outpatient practice is called a psychoneurologist and in accordance with this title sees both psychiatric and neurological case material. (The psychoneurologist only functions in children's clinics.) The Soviet psychoneurologist in common with his American counterpart sees psychosis, personality disorders, neurosis, and developmental crises. Some psychiatric problems extremely common in American clinics are not so definitely included in the Soviet field. For example, many school disciplinary problems may be handled by educators. The emotional aspects of physical disorders receive less stress in Soviet clinics, because psychiatric departments for the most part still do not exist in general pediatric hospitals. This may be one of the general weaknesses in the Soviet system. On the other hand, the Soviet psychoneurologist sees a variety of neurological problems. These include the sequelae of brain trauma and infection, the management of epilepsy, and diagnostic problems in mental retardation. In Soviet psychiatry, too, the whole field of speech disorders is much more closely tied with psychiatry than it is in the United States.

General Structure of Children's Psychiatric Services

Children's psychiatric services fall under the Ministry of Health, the Ministry of Education, and the Ministry of Social Welfare. Each of these exists at the national level and in each republic where local programs are administered. There are also regional and city health departments. Table 1 summarizes psychiatric services administered by the ministries of health, education, and social welfare.

Under the Ministry of Health are children's psychiatric hospitals and departments for acute and chronic psychotic patients, neurological de-

Ministry of Education	Ministry of Health	Ministry of Social Welfare
I. Specialized schools	Hospital service	1. Child invalids' home for severely retarded
1. Sanatorium-forest school for nervous and weakened children	1. a. Child department of psychiatric hospital	2. Home for children with physical defects
2. School for retarded children (with boarding, without boarding)	b. Child psychoneurological hospital	
3. Specialized boarding school with particular regime	2. a. Child department of psychiatric hospital for chronic psychic illnesses	
4. School for children with speech disturbances	b. Child psychoneurological hospital for chronic psychic illnesses	
a. Various forms of alalia	3. Neurological department of children's hospital	
b. Stuttering	4. Department for children with speech disturbances in a children's somatic or psychoneurological hospital	
5. School for children with sequelae of poliomyelitis		
6. School for children with spastic paralysis	Outpatient services and sanatoria	
	1. a. Department for children and adolescents of the psychoneurological dispensary with day hospital and speech office	
II. Specialized children's homes and kindergartens	b. Child-adolescent psychoneurological office in psychoneuro-dispensary	
1. Groups and kindergartens for children with speech disturbances	2. Psychoneurological office in children's polyclinic: psychoneurologist, speech therapist, nurse	
2. Children's homes for the retarded	3. Child psychoneurological sanatorium	
	a. School-age children	
	b. Preschool children	
	4. Sanatorium department of children's polyclinic	
	5. Adolescent groups in therapeutic workshops of psychoneurological dispensary	
	6. Home for children with sequelae of organic damage to the central nervous system	
	7. Nursery for children with sequelae of organic damage to the central nervous system	
	8. Nursery-kindergarten for children with sequelae of organic damage to the central nervous system	
	9. Nursery for children with speech disturbances	

Source: Adapted from wall chart at the City Psychoneurological Dispensary for Children and Adolescents, Moscow.

partments of general children's hospitals, and speech departments in both psychiatric and general pediatric hospitals. Ambulatory services include adolescent departments in psychoneurological clinics and psychoneurological offices in children's polyclinics. There are some workshops for children and adolescents connected with the psychoneurological clinics. Other services under the Ministry of Health are sanatoria, residential nurseries, and kindergartens.

Services administered by the Ministry of Education include schools for neurotic children, boarding schools for mildly retarded children, schools with special regimes for children with disciplinary problems, and schools for children with speech disorders. Special schools are also provided for children who are disabled with neurological sequelae. There are homes and kindergartens for preschool children with speech problems or retardation.

The Ministry of Social Welfare is responsible for homes for children with severe degrees of retardation who are considered trainable but not educable. There are also homes for idiots and homes for children with physical defects.

Special services not listed in Table 1 include a short-term observation center at the Institute of Defectology, sanatoria under the administration of trade unions, emergency children's psychiatric services, and private consultation. The observation center at the Institute of Defectology is a special research laboratory described by A. A. Smirnova in her discussion of the organization of health services for retarded children (3).

Psychiatric service for children, as for adults in the Soviet Union, is organized on a regional basis with emphasis on ambulatory care and a deemphasis on prolonged hospitalization or other forms of long-term residential care. The region (*raion*) is defined by size. For example, the Leningrad region of Moscow contains a total population of about 500,-000. Of these, children 0–18 years of age number 120,000: 96,000 are 0–14 years old and 24,000 14–18 years old. Regions in other cities may be somewhat smaller. The First US Mission report described the size of a raion as 300,000–400,000 (5, p. 26). I was told the Pecherski region in Kiev had 30,000 children. For each region, there is a psychoneurological dispensary.

The regional organization of child and adolescent services is summarized in Table 2. The adolescent service for a whole region includes the adolescent office in the dispensary where ambulatory patients are received. In addition, there may be adolescent workshops administered by the psychoneurological dispensary. The children's service for the

Table 2. Structure of the Regional Organization of Psychoneurological Service for Children and Adolescents

Organizational-Methodological-Guidance		Administrative Guidance
Central Psychoneurological Dispensary	Child-Adolescent Department at the Neuropsychiatric Dispensary	Regional Health Department
	Day Hospital Therapeutic Workshops	Regional Department of Public Education
	Speech Practice Therapeutic Workshops	
Regional Executive Commission		
Commission for Affairs of Minor Children	Organizational-Methodological Guidance offered by Senior Psychiatrist for Adolescents in a Region	Regional Social Welfare Department
	Psychoneurological Office in Polyclinics	
Structure of the Work of the Office		**Association with institutions**
Records of work		Speech groups in kindergartens
Preventive work, referral; sanatoria: professional work		Nurseries for children with organic disturbances of the central nervous system
Ambulatory treatment		Homes for children with organic disturbances
Hospitalization		Schools for nervous children
Speech service		Schools for retarded children

Source: Adapted from the wall chart at the City Psychoneurological Dispensary for Children and Adolescents, Moscow.

region varies in different cities. In Leningrad, the children's office is in the psychoneurological dispensary. In Moscow and Kiev, there are no psychoneurological offices for children in the psychoneurological dispensary but there is one such office in each children's polyclinic, several to a region. In the Leningrad region of Moscow, for example, the psychoneurological dispensary provides consultative and supervisory services to psychoneurologists, one of whom works in each of ten children's polyclinics. The senior child psychiatrist in the psychoneurological dispensary supervises the work of the psychoneurologists, and he also treats adolescent patients from the whole region.

The clinical personnel for children in each psychoneurological dispensary includes one psychoneurologist per 10,000–15,000 children and a patronage nurse who visits the homes of patients, carries out treatment, and assists in case finding and the assessment of social conditions in family life and at work. She may also assist in educating populations in matters of mental hygiene. The medical nurse works with the doctors in the clinic much as she does in the United States. Finally, most psychoneurological dispensaries have a speech therapist and educators to help with language and school disabilities.

Services for children and adolescents in a typical psychoneurological dispensary are quite varied. The doctor is concerned with primary prevention and early detection of psychiatric disturbance. There is a stress on active case-finding, even to the point of holding conversations with people in the community who may have observed somebody who is sick and in need of help.

Secondly, the doctor is concerned with follow-up. One dispensary had a system of automatic recall of patients:

1. Patients in acute states are to be seen once every three days. These are people who may be in imminent need of hospitalization or who have been recently discharged from the hospital.
2. Patients in partial remission are seen at least once every two weeks. These are patients who continue to require medication and close supervision.
3. Patients in full but unstable remission are seen once a month. They may still be on small maintenance doses of medication.
4. Patients with stable remission are seen once every three months.
5. Certain residual states and patients with oligophrenia (the Russian term for mental retardation) are seen once every six months.

6. Patients in the hospital are temporarily away from the administration of the dispensary, and not on regular recall.

The report of the First US Mission on Mental Health describes a slightly different grouping based on five categories, but the principle is the same (5, p. 29).

The treatment functions of the psychoneurological dispensary stress preventative factors. Every effort is made to keep the patient ambulatory. Home visiting is done by both doctors and nurses. Day hospital facilities are used, though less frequently for children than adults. The aim is to avoid prolonged institutionalization.

Secondary preventative measures supplement the clinical treatment procedures in the psychoneurological dispensary. These include legal assistance in cases where it is necessary to determine questions of responsibility. Some patients are assisted financially, others are provided more suitable housing arrangements. Social assistance is given with the aim of improving both working conditions and home conditions. Teaching social adaptation to psychiatric patients and helping them reintegrate into life in the collective are considered important aims in Soviet treatment. Work with the family is carried out mainly through visits from the doctors who also conduct lectures for parent and teacher groups.

Consultative services are an important part of the psychiatric system. As we have already seen, the regional psychoneurological dispensary provides a consultation service to the psychoneurologist working in the children's polyclinics. In addition, there are central-city polyclinics attached to research institutions and hospitals and also central-city psychoneurological dispensaries. The Moscow City Psychoneurological Dispensary for Children and Adolescents, for example, offered outpatient consultation to the polyclinics in Moscow for difficult psychiatric problems. There were several specialized offices: epilepsy, preschool diagnostic problems, and assessment of patients who may need hospitalization. There were services for the follow-up of adolescents who have been in the hospital and special ambulatory psychotherapeutic programs. This Moscow city dispensary served as a general clearinghouse where patients were selected for specialized services, such as hospitalization or sanatorium care.

Another type of central polyclinic was the one associated with the Specialized Clinical Children's Hospital in Kiev. The psychoneurological office of this polyclinic provided consultative services for the poly-

clinics in the various regions of Kiev and was used particularly for
neurological problems. Another central polyclinic was attached to the
Children's Psychoneurological Hospital in Leningrad. The dispensaries
and polyclinics of these large centers frequently have psychiatric commissions responsible for the placement of children in special sanatoria
and educational facilities. Children who are thought to be in need of
residential care are referred to these commissions, which consist of a
psychoneurologist, an educator, and perhaps the director of the special
school under consideration.

The Psychoneurologist
in Ambulatory Practice

A psychoneurologist has many functions:

1. Examination of the newborn if birth trauma is suspected.
2. Two prophylactic examinations in the first year of life.
3. Examination of all children entering kindergarten and school.
   Only a small percentage of children examined are considered ill,
   although no statistics were available.
4. Diagnosis of children with psychiatric and neurological symptoms including head trauma and epilepsy.
5. Observation and systematic follow-up of children with known
   schizophrenia, oligophrenia, or other chronic conditions.
6. Visits to nurseries, kindergartens, and schools of the region.
   Consultations with teachers and upbringers are frequently held.
   Problem cases first uncovered in this way may then be referred
   to the polyclinic for further study. The psychoneurologist also
   frequently holds conferences concerning children known to be
   schizophrenic.
7. Treatment. Heavy emphasis is placed on medication.
8. Visits to parents at home or at work.

The psychoneurologist works five days a week: four days on clinical
work and one day on home visiting, lecturing, and other preventative
activities. Each psychoneurologist is supposed to see an average of
two and one-half patients an hour; one of these doctors told me that
she saw eighteen to twenty patients a day! The rate of five patients per

hour reported by the First US Mission is even more hectic: 12 minutes per patient (5, p. 137).

Clinical records take the form of a small folder started for each patient shortly after birth (Appendix II). These records emphasize physical developmental data and medical history; social and environmental factors are included very briefly. The record on a patient moving from his district is sent with him to the new polyclinic. Statistical data are collected on each individual patient and sent every year to the scientific statistical center at the Serbsky Institute. The clinic must fill out a card for each patient with name, birth date, sex, address, diagnosis, educational level, and profession. If he is under some form of guardianship, this must be noted. Any history of antisocial activity is also recorded. These cards, therefore, provide a highly centralized record of the psychiatric and delinquent history of the whole population. I asked to visit the Serbsky Institute to learn about delinquency and statistics on psychiatric disorders, information previously unobtainable in the West, but my request was denied. Other American observers have also been critical of the absence of publicly available statistics. These records at the Serbsky Institute could, of course, be used for two purposes: to collect valuable data on the incidence of psychiatric disturbances, their course and natural history, or to exercise various forms of social control distasteful to Americans.

This general description of psychoneurological dispensaries and the children's polyclinics over which they exert supervisory and consultative control shows that child psychiatry is associated intimately, on the one hand, with pediatrics, because the polyclinics all have the whole spectrum of medical services for children. On the other hand, child psychiatry is closely associated with the administration of general psychiatry and with special educational programs.

I observed outpatient practice in three psychoneurological offices associated with polyclinics in Kiev and Moscow. One formed part of the specialized children's hospital in Kiev. Altogether, I saw twenty-six patients in these centers. Eleven were clearly neurological cases and ten were psychiatric cases. The remaining five could be considered in American terms either neurological or psychiatric. Two of the latter were prophylactic examinations of infants where questions of developmental slowness had arisen; another two patients were clearly retarded, and one was an adolescent girl with fainting spells.

Among the neurological cases, the focal issue of the consultation frequently had psychiatric implications. The withdrawn, listless behavior of an imbecile girl after her return home from a sanatorium seemed related to her mother's inability to accept her retardation. A boy with a history of severe fits after head trauma was not supposed to know that he had seizures. His mother had given up working and devoted most of her life to taking care of the boy. One fourteen-year-old girl with spastic cerebral palsy was having difficulty accepting her physical state. Her intellect was intact, but she had become withdrawn and cried frequently. A consultation was recommended with the psychoneurological dispensary, because psychiatric aspects were recognized. The doctor prescribed librium and agreed it would be important to find out more about the girl's interests and to encourage her to reestablish contact with the collective.

Among the psychiatric problems was a thirteen-year-old boy with a history of truancy, psychomotor restlessness, and rebellious behavior, diagnosed "psychopathy." His mother felt that she was unable to control the boy and cried when the doctor praised his interest in radio mechanics. The boy was free of anxiety and indifferent to his problems. He was treated with phenobarbital and chlorpromazine to control his restlessness. He was also given dehydrating therapy with magnesium sulfate; Soviet psychiatrists frequently diagnose "compensated hydrocephalus."

There was a case of neurodermatitis in a ten-year-old girl recognized as a psychiatric problem. The child was irritable and cried easily. No psychotherapy was recommended, however. One mother brought her eleven-year-old daughter with the complaint that the child was nervous, cried readily, and was irritable. The doctor sent the child out of the room so the mother could give the history. Two children, mother, and father all lived in one room. The mother described in an excited way many marital difficulties with the father, who drank and resorted to violence against her. When the child was seen, she acknowledged that she cried and felt frightened when her father drank and hit her mother. She said he then would become apologetic and promise that he would not drink again, but in spite of this he broke his promises. The doctor agreed to talk with the child's father at work and to see the patient again in 14 days. The highly charged emotional material in this case was discussed informally with several doctors present: two from the polyclinic we were visiting, one who accompanied me on the visit, and myself.

Finally, a seven-and-one-half-year-old girl in the first grade was brought in by her grandmother, who complained that the child was overactive, overtalkative, restless, and argumentative. The child repeatedly interrupted her grandmother as she tried to give the history.

One of the doctors in our group tried to control and correct the child. It was agreed that the problem centered around the child's tendency to play the mother against the grandmother. The next step would be to talk with the patient's mother.

Most striking in these visits was the flexibility with which the Soviet psychoneurologist approached her cases. In some there was heavy reliance on medication, and in others the family was actively engaged, even seen at work.

Psychiatric Hospitals

Five hospitals were visited during the course of my stay. The largest was the Psychoneurological Hospital in Moscow for Children and Adolescents, a part of the Moscow Psychoneurological Dispensary. This institution, with 535 beds and at least 14 departments, was located on the outskirts of the city. It had connections with two research psychiatric institutes and one "institute for the increased qualification of physicians" which trained child psychiatrists (see Chap. VI below). The buildings were rather shabby, resembling old American state hospital buildings. However, the spacious grounds contained gardens, play areas, and a small animal park. I spent considerable time making observations in 10 departments there. Preschool psychotic boys and girls 4 to 7 years of age were placed together in one department. Boys and girls 7 to 11 were in different departments, as were adolescent boys and girls 12–16. Then there was a department for adolescent boys 12–16 with difficult behavior who required more supervision. In addition, there were specialized departments: one for genetic and degenerative diseases, two for speech therapy of school-age boys and girls, and one new 50-bed unit for adolescent boys and girls specializing in suggestive psychotherapy.

The Children's Psychoneurological Hospital in Leningrad was smaller, with about 200 beds, and was located in a pleasant prerevolutionary building next to one of Leningrad's many waterways. This hospital, too, was associated with a central psychiatric polyclinic and with a pediatric research institute. There was also a training center for child psychiatrists. My observations here were limited to two days. The organization of the hospital appeared to be similar to that described above. A second facility in Leningrad was the children's department of the Psychoneurological Scientific Research Institute named for Bekhterev. The 50-bed unit in this hospital received children mostly from the Leningrad area, but also from other parts of the country according to the research interests of the institution.

The most attractive physical surroundings were found in two hospitals in Kiev. One was the neurology department and the polyclinic of the Specialized Clinical Hospital for Children. This was the only facility I saw where a general hospital for children admitted psychoneurological cases and had an outpatient clinic. The ward received many preschool and school-age children with neurotic problems, although the emphasis was on neurological cases. At the time of my visit, there were cases of tics, enuresis, hyperkinesis, and behavior problems. Also in Kiev, the Psychoneurological Hospital named for Pavlov was visited. This was a large hospital with a small children's department. It was located in a wooded hilly area with many yellow buildings and pleasant surroundings.

The children's wards in these institutions were clean and Spartan. They were well staffed by kindly personnel who showed genuine interest in the patients. Food was plentiful and attractive, and the children had many opportunities to use the outdoor recreation areas. Many wards were locked. On each ward, a large office was shared by doctors and educators. There was much less concern with the need for privacy than there is in the United States. There were classrooms for school-age children and also gymnasiums where physical culture was conducted. I was surprised not to see any workshops, considering the emphasis on work therapy in Soviet psychiatry. While there were cases of neurosis, character disorders and psychopathy, the major focus was on epilepsy, schizophrenia, and other psychoses.

At the preschool department of the Children's Psychoneurological Hospital in Moscow, I observed severely disturbed children, some of whom seemed autistic. Daytime care was given in small groups or individually by dedicated special educators, in some cases quite gifted. Pasha, a seven-year-old boy, was working individually with one teacher. He had had the acute onset of hallucinations shortly after he began school three months before. He had become increasingly fearful, excitable, and restless. He was obviously bright and had produced a series of complete drawings full of bombers, airplanes, ships, and black empty space. The drawings showed a perfectionistic preoccupation with details. They also betrayed a loosening of associations and confabulations. Pasha showed mounting anxiety when the teacher confronted him with one of his most disturbed drawings which he had done previously.

A few days later, we watched Pasha making another elaborate drawing: an enormous tall building with many floors. He kept emphasizing the height, making the buildings blacker and blacker. His mounting anxiety and excitement nearly disrupted his play activity as he added a second projection. His obsession with phallic objects had also been evident in the drawing of a clown with two noses, one of which was extremely long and curved downward. Next to the building he also made a long train which he said was carrying earth to make beaches. It was clear Pasha was using his individual relationship with his teacher to express through drawing (at which he was very gifted) many of his anxieties and conflicted feelings. However, neither the teacher nor the psychiatrist took note of the cathartic expressive process or of the dynamic content of the drawings. At one point, Pasha was requested to copy pictures of fruit. He complied for a while, with much obsessive attention to the black spot at one end of an apple.

In the Soviet mental hospital, much psychotherapy is done by special educators who have the most intimate daily contact with the children. The atmosphere is warm and friendly; the children are respected in their individuality and encouraged to participate as much as they are able in group activities. There is no attempt to formalize the psychotherapeutic process except in one hospital program for adolescents.

Special
Services

There is a variety of psychiatric services for specialized problems. Sanatoria and forest schools for the treatment of neurotic children are discussed in Chapter IV, and a special psychotherapeutic program for adolescents is described in Chapter V. The present discussion considers some other special services: services for retarded children, special schooling for children with central nervous system damage, and psychiatric aspects of the handling of children who commit antisocial and delinquent acts.

SERVICES FOR RETARDED CHILDREN

The organization of services for retarded children is described by A. A. Smirnova (3). As with psychiatric services, three ministries are involved. Under the Ministry of Health, the psychoneurological hospitals admit retarded children if they present diagnostic problems or

acutely decompensated states. Chronic psychiatric hospitals care for
retarded children who are chronically disturbed. Specialized homes
exist for children with central nervous system damage, as well as special
residential kindergartens where prolonged observation assists in diagnosis and where corrective education of a specialized nature can be
offered. Extramural help is offered at psychoneurological dispensaries
for adolescents or in children's polyclinics. Some children are placed in
workshops under the administration of psychoneurological dispensaries. A workshop receiving patients with deep retardation is described
in the discussion of work therapy.

Under the Ministry of Education, there are schools for children with
retardation, central nervous system damage, and schizophrenia without
severe symptoms. There are special boarding schools for educable children. Smirnova stated that day kindergartens are needed for retarded
children. I was told in Kiev that they exist for children three to seven
years old in the Ukrainian Republic. Smirnova also indicated that forest
schools and sanatoria are needed for children with temporary intellectual disturbances. There was in 1969 much interest among Soviet psychiatrists and educators in the problem of "delays and inhibitions in
intellectual development of a reversible nature," which Americans call
neurotic learning inhibitions. Some Soviet work on this problem is
reviewed in Chapter VII.

Under the Ministry of Social Welfare, there are boarding schools
with workshops for adolescent imbeciles. There are also boarding
schools for low-grade imbeciles and idiots. In the Russian Republic
these two categories of patients are placed together, while in the
Ukraine they are separated. Such institutions provide treatment for fits
and periods of excitement and can offer close supervision. They stress
training and self-help. Other kinds of facilities include homes and workshops for imbeciles eighteen to twenty years old who are capable of
doing agricultural work and special sheltered workshop sections in
factories.

A special psychiatric commission decides which children may be admitted to facilities for the retarded. The commission consists of the
director of the particular school for the retarded, a school inspector
from the Department of Public Education, a school doctor, a school
psychiatrist, a teacher in the school where the child is presently located,
and perhaps an educational representative of the special school for
which admission is being sought. Sometimes speech therapists and psychologists sit on this commission, according to Smirnova, but they

were never mentioned as being members of the commissions I actually
heard about.

I visited Kindergarten No. 468 in Moscow, a residential institution
under the Ministry of Health for children with retardation and central
nervous system damage. Two hundred children three to eight years of
age were cared for here, spending six days a week at school. For this
service, parents paid a fee of 4–15 rubles a month. The kindergarten
was housed in a new low building in an outlying district with row after
row of prefabricated apartments. Next door was a day kindergarten for
normal children. The two schools had adjacent play areas. The staff
was generous: 147 adults cared for 200 children. There were 56 educators, 3 child psychiatrists, 1 pediatrician, 8 nurses, and 45 aides.
Wards of about 24 beds each appeared crowded and regimented, but
the play areas were cheerful, full of beautiful, very neatly arranged
toys. One group of four-year-olds was observed during a music lesson.
The children were clapping, singing, reciting verses, and rehearsing for
the New Year's holiday festival. One schizophrenic was included in this
group. The child was first quite excited and later was allowed to lie on
the lap of one of the aides (upbringers), who responded to this child's
need to retreat temporarily from the overly stimulating group activity.
Many educators were working with individuals in offices, especially on
speech development. One speech therapist was massaging the tongue of
an apparently retarded child who finally announced, quite sensibly, I
thought, that her tongue was tired! The incident typifies the energy and
persistent individual and group attention given to children with special
needs.

Special Boarding School (*Internat*) No. 103 in Moscow provided
education for the mildly retarded. One hundred forty children (two-
thirds of whom were boys) 8–16 years of age attended this school five
days a week. The educational program was divided into classes I–VIII,
with 15–17 children in a class. After school, larger groups of about 20
children were taken care of by one upbringer. The parents paid a fee
depending upon their income; about half of the families paid no fee at
all. Referrals were made to the school through the commission by the
psychoneurologist of the local polyclinic or by the teacher in the child's
regular school. The personnel included a nonmedical director, a psychoneurologist, one nurse, and teachers with special training in defectology. The director told me they had graduated 13 students the previous year, of whom 12 were working.

Several classes were observed. In the second class studying Russian, the teacher was stern, old-fashioned, with a no-nonsense attitude. The children were haltingly reading little stories and verses about squirrels, bears, and Russian winter. A seventh-grade class in Russian was studying the poet Nekrasov. The children read aloud one poem about Russian winter and one about the Volga River. The teacher seemed very polished in her technique. After the children read the poems, she directed a discussion, comparing Nekrasov's poem with another poem on the Volga. I thought the whole performance was pretty good for retarded 13- and 14-year-olds. In a sewing class for early adolescent girls, a small group of six was working on simple cotton garments. One girl appeared and acted completely normal. She had swift, skilled movements, was capable of a high degree of concentration and a purposeful activity. Later at the Pioneer weekly "lineup," she received a prize for her group's performance. The atmosphere in this school was warm and relaxed, though physically the place was icy cold. When it was time to leave, the director, who had been very cordial, asked one of the boys to accompany me and show me where the trolley stop was. He was on his way home.

A comparable boarding school, Internat No. 1 of the Oktyabraskaya Region of Kiev, was visited. This school contained 314 educably retarded boys and girls. At the time, there were 4 such schools in Kiev and 140 in the Ukrainian Republic, although the others were smaller than this one. The curriculum was comparable to that in the Moscow school, except that Ukrainian was studied and there was no attempt to teach Russian. There were three workshops for boys, in woodworking and in making books, and there were sewing workshops for girls. Here, too, I was told by the director that 99 percent of the children are able to work after graduation. The psychoneurologist was studying neurotic and psychopathic behavior syndromes among the retarded. She described hysteriform states, speech disturbances, and enuresis. She considered pubertal crisis more severe in the retarded children than in normal children and recognized the presence of many sexual disturbances. She also found the adolescents sensitive to their defects. They would try to hide the fact that they were attending special school. The diagnosis "psychopathy" is avoided, since the intellect is not normal; however, among the psychopathic-like states, she specifically mentioned hysteroid states or emotional instability and sexual deviations, including sadism. Masturbation was considered common. She had observed only two cases of schizophrenia in this school in six years.

The curriculum at both of these special schools resembles that summarized in Table 3. The goal of special school education is to reduce

Table 3. Curriculum: Schools for the Retarded

School subject	Class, number of hours per week							
	I	II	III	IV	V	VI	VII	VIII
Russian	12	12	12	12	10	8	8	8
Arithmetic	6	6	6	6	6	6	6	6
Natural science					2	2	2	
Geography					2	2	2	
Episodes from history and Constitution of USSR						1	2	3
Singing	1	1	1	1	1	1	1	1
Drawing	1	1	1	1	1	1		
Mechanical drawing					1	1	1	2
Physical culture	2	2	2	2	2	2	2	2
Handwork	2	2	2					
Preparation for vocational work				8	10	12	12	14
Individual speech and language study	3	3	3	3	2	2	2	
Total per week	27	27	27	33	37	38	38	36

Duration of school year: September 1–May 31: 4 quarters, 35 weeks
      Fall vacation: November 5–9
      Winter vacation: December 30–January 10
      Spring vacation: March 24–31

Additional vocational practice
      Classes V, VI, and VII   2 weeks June 1–14
      Class V   3 hours a day
      Class VI, VII   4 hours a day
      Class VIII   4 weeks June 1–25
                  4 hours a day
                  Examination

Source: Programmy vspomogatelnoi shkoly: obshcheobrazovatelnye predmety (Programs of Schools for the Retarded: General Educational Subjects). Moscow: Izdatelstvo "Prosveshchenie," 1965, pp. 4–5.

the intellectual defect as much as possible and to train the children to earn an independent living. Programs at these schools provide the equivalent of five years of regular education in an eight-year period. Language is stressed. Classes I–IV have 12 hours a week of Russian to provide drill on correct reading and writing. Supplementary individual lessons are given where indicated by a speech therapist who works with general language skills as well as spoken speech. These children are made aware that they are preparing for a vocational future, starting in the fourth class. Vocational training groups are small, usually eight to ten children. Another feature of particular interest is the summer vocational training program introduced in the fifth class. This provides two weeks of intensive vocational instruction right after school closes. In classes VI and VII, a month is offered. Some degree of political indoctrination is introduced in the sixth class: the Great October Revolution and the revolutionary tradition; the construction of socialism in the USSR; the great socialist war of the Soviet people against the Fascist aggressors and the role of the communist party; decisions of the Twenty-second Congress of the Central Committee of the Communist Party. Guidelines are also provided for the teaching of Russian, arithmetic, and other basic subjects. The program provides mildly retarded children with a protected environment during the week to develop their potentialities away from normal children with whom constant comparison might be painful. But they are allowed to maintain contact with home and the world through the policy of spending weekends at home. It makes sense to use maximum resources for children who can become independent with special help.

The Darnitski Children's Home in Kiev was a residence for 200 imbecile girls 6–16 years old. Some remained until they were 18. The classes contained 10–12 girls each, and the upbringing groups after school were about 20 each. Girls were referred to the school by the psychiatric commission. The parents paid no fee. In nine years of education, the girls learned the equivalent of class I and part of class II in regular school. Epileptics were accepted if their fits were not too common. The program included school work, general upbringing, and vocational work. The school was housed in a nondescript brick building across the Dnieper River from the center of the city, close to a pine forest. As usual, everything was spotless and well organized inside. The girls wore red or brown dresses and were very neat, with bows in their hair. The visit was arranged so that I could not make prolonged observations of the children. One group of five was being supervised by an upbringer. Another group was observed in a sewing workshop. They were doing an excellent job and seemed to be even better at sewing than the girls of milder retardation observed in Moscow. For these girls, sewing started at 12 years of age. The children were considered very good at simple routine tasks of this kind. Another group of four girls was observed working with a speech therapist on correct pronunciation of "sh." One first class was learning the process of counting to three, a second class was learning how to write numbers, and a fifth class was learning simple subtraction with the abacus. This school had a modern audiovisual room for movies and special television, many play areas, and a gymnasium. The dormitories were small with six beds each. The staff included educators, upbringers, work instructors, a nonmedical director, a pediatrician, nurses, and assistants. There were far more men on the staff than other institutions I visited. The director was a dynamic little man full of Marxism-Leninism who asserted that retardation existed in only 1½ percent of the population! I told him we considered retardation to be present in 3 percent of the population. The doctor's role at this school was limited to a purely medical one. Tranquilizers and glutamic acid were occasionally used. The graduates of this school go to an adult home for invalids or live at home and work in sheltered workshops. Rarely, one may work in a factory, but the director would not tell me how often this occurs.

A SERVICE FOR CHILDREN WITH
CENTRAL NERVOUS SYSTEM DISEASE

I observed one boarding school (Internat No. 31 in Moscow) for children with normal intelligence who were suffering from crippling neurological disease. Children were accepted from the Moscow area if they were physically disabled so that they could not attend regular school. There were 325 boys and girls in classes I–X. Some younger children with intellectual abnormalities were admitted for diagnostic evaluation. The staff included 35 medical personnel. A psychoneurologist did neurological workups. He impressed me as warm and sensitive to emotional factors in the children's condition. A psychologist did examinations to assist the teacher in developing an educational approach to the child. The school had a camp session in Odessa, on the Black Sea. The winter recreational program included sessions at the large swimming pool in the center of Moscow. Older adolescents were permitted to go to Komsomol meetings in another part of the city. The atmosphere was warm, and the staff were all interested in showing me the kinds of children they dealt with. They asked many questions about what we do in the United States. The school was a gold mine of complex diagnostic problems with an interplay of neurological and emotional components. There were several muscular dystrophy syndromes in children with intact intelligence. Although the children were supposed not to be aware of the progressive nature of some of their disorders, it was common practice to discuss the disability in front of them.

One ten-year-old boy in the first class had been admitted to the school when he was eight and one-half years old. He had a complex history of brain trauma and birth asphyxia followed by febrile convulsions. As if this were not enough, he suffered tuberculous meningitis at five months and at two years was hospitalized with hydrocephalus. He was four years old before he began to say single words and he did not say phrases until he was five. On admission, the child was excitable, restless, and had a poor memory. He concentrated poorly. On neurological examination, his head was noted to be hydrocephalic, and there were eye movement disturbances. There was a left facial weakness and a spastic gait. When we saw the child, he was obviously in contact with reality. At first he seemed under great tension, but later relaxed, smiled, and answered questions with a sense of humor, although with lisping speech. The child fatigued rapidly, becoming increasingly restless during the brief interview. The diagnosis was postnatal brain damage, asphyxia, tuberculous meningo-encephalitis; hydrocephalus and spastic paralysis secondary to trauma and infection. The staff did not think oligophrenia was present, but I felt that the child must be somewhat retarded.

The teaching part of the program was interesting, too. The first class was observed while they were taking a reading lesson. This group, like others at the same time of year, was studying Russian winter and was able to read as well or better (as one would expect) than the retardates I had observed in the second class of Internat No. 3. We also watched a speech therapist working individually with one child who had dysarthria. This was a ten-year-old girl, undersized for her age, with a diagnosis of diffuse subcortical brain damage, diencephalic syndrome, and endocrine disturbances manifested by gross inhibition and pseudomyxedema. (I did not see the evidence of the latter.)

A SERVICE FOR CHILDREN
WITH ANTISOCIAL BEHAVIOR

The aspect of service for delinquent children which I was permitted to see was the children's militia room, a branch of the city police department where children and adolescents up to 18 years may be brought for a variety of behavioral deviations. The emphasis is on prevention, and children may be referred by the school, the family, or even a neighborhood group, before any definite legal violation has been committed. I was shown the work of the psychiatric commission. A referral is made if a general study suggests the offensive behavior is due to illness or to intellectual retardation. After a medical workup, the child and parent appear before the commission for a psychiatric evaluation. Particular attention is paid to home conditions. Specially mentioned were excessive drinking on the part of the father, crowded living conditions, separation of parents, psychiatric illness of parents.

The first case was a 13-year-old boy with chronic behavior problems. He had a very poor relationship with his father, who had been diagnosed schizophrenic but was still living at home. The mother, who accompanied the boy, worked as a nurse. She appeared careworn and prematurely old. She said the father had refused medical help. The boy was shabby, disheveled, with an impassive face and ptosis of both eyelids, conveying the impression of indifference. He answered questions tersely in a hollow monotone. The answers he did give were relevant, with no bizarre ideation. The Commission tentatively diagnosed schizophrenia and recommended hospitalization. The mother seemed almost relieved.

Next, a school-age boy was brought in by neighbors. He had no behavior problems and was doing well in school but was in need of financial help to continue his education. The youngster was living with an old grandmother because his mother was schizophrenic. The Commission decided the problem should be handled through the social assistance program of the psychoneurological dispensary.

A burly 17-year-old lad was seen because for the last four years, after completing the sixth class, he had been refusing to go to school or to work. His mother worked nights in a Moscow restaurant; his father worked, also at night, in the buffet at a theater. The boy was completely idle. When we saw him, he was surly, with slow thought processes. To me, he seemed intellectually limited, with a deep-seated pervasive personality disorder. He had no insight into the problem he was creating for his family and society. The Commission did not make the diagnosis of oligophrenia, but rather considered him a primitive personality, the product of simple, uneducated people. The special disciplinary school was recommended. I asked whether the Commission could insist against the boy's wishes and was told the boy would be obliged to comply.

Finally, a boy was brought in who had been seen before for chronic stealing. The psychiatrist first chatted with the youngster, establishing a friendly relationship, then confronted him with his stealing. The child tried to avoid acknowledging that his behavior should be called stealing. The doctor made him read aloud from a book of regulations. I am not sure what the disposition was. Evidently, some cases are followed over a period of time, if they are considered corrigible, with some attempt at supportive psychotherapy. They did not, however, talk about their work in these terms.

The work of the militia rooms was extremely interesting to me. The cases show one way referrals to educational resources, the psychoneurological clinic, and the hospital system originate.

Some Aspects
of Prevention

The Soviet psychiatric system is constructed to discourage long-term hospitalization. The basic unit of care is the regional psychoneurological dispensary and its connections with the general children's polyclinics. This emphasis on caring for disturbed people in the community may be a big factor in the prevention of the massive psychotic regressions seen in patients hospitalized early in life and retained in institutions for chronic care. Unfortunately, the day hospital is less available in the Soviet Union for children than it is for adults. One exists for children in the Oktyabraskaya region of Moscow. If chronic hospitalization is to be prevented, this type of care needs to be much more extensively developed, in our own country as well as in the Soviet Union.

The preventive functions of the adolescent office of the psychoneurological dispensaries and the psychoneurological offices in the children's polyclinics include routine prophylactic examinations. The psychoneurologist may even be called to the maternity home in the first few days of life if there has been a question of asphyxia or birth trauma. The screening examinations offered to children entering kindergarten and the first class of school present another opportunity for early detection of serious disorders. I am not sure how thorough these examinations are, as there is a danger of becoming insensitive when carrying out routinized procedures. The system of record keeping potentially provides the opportunity to keep longitudinal records and to study the epidemiology of various illnesses.

The regular automatic follow-up system has great potential in the handling of known psychotic patients. The recall system tends to prevent relapses which frequently occur when patients become careless about continuing their medication. The fact that most of the schizophrenic children in a given area are known and identified also enables the psychoneurologist to hold school consultations concerning the best educational approach to these sensitive children.

Active case-finding methods which take the psychoneurologist and the nurse into the community enhance the possibility of early detection of illness. The practice of holding conversations with neighbors in apartment blocks may not be compatible with the value Americans place on privacy, but this does seem consistent with the Soviet value of "collective parenthood." Certain children may therefore be referred to professional help earlier than in the United States, where everybody is supposed to mind his own business.

Ambulatory practice also includes work with parents, both in the office and in the community. This work, on the one hand, centers around individual cases: gathering information and giving advice on how to handle a child more effectively. Since there is no profession of social work, this responsibility falls to the psychoneurologist and to some degree to the patronage nurse. The other major type of work with parents is described as "medical propaganda." The doctor gives lectures to parent groups. In the various clinics one frequently sees wall charts and other displays illustrating points about mental health.

Books are also available giving information about mental hygiene. In one of these, mothers are warned about the dangers of trying to abort pregnancy with quinine and of ingesting alcohol during pregnancy (2). Prospective parents are told that the first five years of life are extremely important for the education and character formation of the child and that even the earliest months of life are vital from the educational point of view. "Correct" toilet-training procedures are outlined. Parents are warned that physical punishment and forced feeding are ineffective. They are cautioned to avoid overexcitement, overfatigue, and spoiling in young children. Since alcohol is a tremendous social problem, parents are warned against giving children even weak wine at holiday celebrations. The book concludes with the admonition that reeducation to correct defects is much harder and more prolonged than education which was correct in the first place.

The social and legal assistance offered by the psychoneurological dispensary serves a valuable preventive function. Finally, school consultations facilitate handling behavior problems in a reversible stage, before they become internalized as deep-seated personality disorders.

Workshops associated with psychoneurological dispensaries prevent the chronic institutional care of many imbeciles and other severely disturbed persons. The fact that a simple routine of work and self-care is expected may prevent them from deteriorating into a vegetative state. But this effort to keep disturbed people in the community may turn out to be a considerable burden to the families involved.

The preventive functions of the children's militia rooms are of great interest. The system is designed so that delinquency must frequently be checked before serious crimes are committed. The case described of the boy who was brought in by neighbors for material and financial help illustrates a point previously made—that separation experiences may be less disruptive for a child growing up in a society which diffuses the parental role to include the wider collective. This in itself may be a huge preventive factor built into the culture as a whole.

The special facilities also serve preventive functions. Special forest schools for neurotic children provide a protected atmosphere for youngsters particularly vulnerable to stress. The opportunity to spend a year in such protected surroundings may prevent decompensation to frankly psychotic states in some cases. The vigorous attack on speech problems may prevent secondary educational handicaps and neurotic overlay. The stress on early vocational training for the mildly retarded helps these children to form a positive identity as workers contributing to society. The system seems well designed to prevent excessive dependence, behavior problems, and crime.

In conclusion, I join with previous American observers in admiration of the preventive potentials of the Soviet psychiatric system as it applies to children and adolescents. There is no doubt that centralized planning permits the development of a system along rational lines and that a socialized system of psychiatric care insures the delivery of services on the basis of need rather than the ability to pay. However, I would not go so far in my praise of the system as the First US Mission on Mental Health report, which said, "Certainly the Russian children's polyclinic, strongly reinforced by the children's department of the N-P dispensary, is superior to the American child guidance clinic program" (5, p. 61). My reservations have to do with qualitative factors and the intensity of psychiatric care possible at the stage of development I saw in 1969. In terms of the standards set by the Russians themselves, day hospital facilities and workshops were still lacking and in outpatient practice little can be accomplished if the psychoneurologist must see two and one-half to five patients an hour.

III

Diagnosis

Diagnostic considerations occupy a more focal point in Russian child psychiatry than they do in the United States, so the role of consultation is a key one in the major psychiatric institutions. After initial study of a patient, the case is brought to the attention of a senior consultant, frequently a professor. A typical case study includes the following:

1. Family history, hereditary predisposition.
2. Pregnancy and birth.
3. Developmental history, medical and psychiatric history of the preschool years.
4. Childhood and adolescence: school history, peer relations, onset of psychiatric symptoms.
5. Present illness, including previous treatment and hospitalizations.
6. Mental status at the time of hospitalization.
7. Course of illness during hospitalization and treatment; reports of educators.
8. Physical examination; neurological examination.
9. Laboratory studies; psychological investigation.

The report is presented by the attending doctor in a conference attended by staff doctors and trainees. Then the consultant interviews the patient and sometimes the parents. A partial physical examination may be included. There seems to be no concern about interviewing in a group. The presenting doctor summarizes the case, including statements about:

1. The leading syndrome.
2. Associated symptomatology.
3. Dynamics.
4. Differential diagnosis.
5. Diagnosis.

In Soviet diagnostic thinking, the leading syndrome along with associated symptomatology is an intermediary step between the concrete anamnestic data and the more abstract diagnostic statement. Common adolescent syndromes are *dysmorphophobia,* or unduly critical and anxiety-laden preoccupation with the body, and "philosophical intoxication," or an excessive concern with the big unanswerable questions of life. These may indicate early schizophrenia, but are also recognized as characteristic of adolescence. In school-age children, psychopathic-like and neurotic-like behavior, are recognized as part of a schizophrenic process, a personality disorder, or a transitional growth crisis.

Following the leading syndrome and symptoms, much attention is paid to the "dynamics," meaning the onset and course of the illness: the age of onset, the acuteness of onset, and an assessment of whether the symptoms appeared in reaction to identifiable situations or appeared without adequate reason. There is little consideration of hidden or unconscious motivation. Diffuse fears, unattached to specific precipitating events, are regarded as a diagnostic sign of schizophrenia. The dynamics also include detailed attention to the course of the illness and to the clinical picture between episodes. This kind of analysis helps to differentiate between a *state* and a *process,* a key Soviet distinction with prognostic implications regarding the difference between a fixed state and a progressive, degenerative illness. There is also sensitivity to the diagnostic value of repeated observations over a period of time.

The doctor's summary ends with a differential diagnosis and a diagnosis, after discussion and sometimes lively disagreement from the group. The consultant's final diagnostic opinion, prognostic considerations, and recommendations for treatment are entered in the record of the patient.

In the following section, the most recognized diagnostic classification of psychiatric disorders of children is described. Subsequent sections describe Soviet diagnostic concepts which differ most strikingly from those widely used in the United States. Case illustrations are used frequently; the longer case histories may be found in Appendix IV.

Classification

Soviet child psychiatrists, especially in Moscow, tend to follow the grouping of their beloved teacher, Grunya Efimovna Sukhareva, who is practically unknown in the West. The privilege of knowing her was perhaps the most valuable experience I had in the Soviet Union. In November 1968, Grunya Efimovna was already in her seventies. She was short in stature, rather stout, indifferent to external appearances. The qualities I saw in her of warmth, compassion, and wisdom made an enduring impression. The first two were evident in the way in which she handled patients and in the devotion she inspired in her staff, trainees, and former trainees I met in other parts of the country. Her wisdom included intellectual clarity, though perhaps not great originality. Her psychiatric interests have been extremely broad. She has made contributions to the organization of psychiatric services, research in schizophrenia and epilepsy, and the training and teaching of child psychiatrists and psychoneurologists.

Grunya Efimovna's diagnostic grouping of psychiatric disorders of children and adolescents appears in English translation in Table 4. The table is taken from her letter to me of September 1969. A longer version, based on her three-volume text of child psychiatry (14, 15, 16), is found in Appendix III.

A comparison of Table 4 and the longer version shows a few differences. Both have three broad divisions: major psychiatric disturbances, and oligophrenia. The first is an etiological grouping that includes the major endogenous and exogenous psychoses and other psychic disturbances secondary to known organic causes. Systemic infections causing symptomatic psychoses are listed in Appendix III but separated in Table 4 into acute and chronic infections. In the later version of Table 4, intoxications, for example with alcohol and hashish, have been added as another cause of symptomatic psychoses. Perhaps this addition reflects the increasing Soviet awareness and acceptance of the problem they call narcomania, even in the adolescent age group. Infections involving the central nervous system are the second major subgrouping. Both versions give syphilis a separate listing. On

Table 4. Grouping of Psychiatric Disorders of Children and Adolescents, Based on Etiology and Pathogenesis

I. Basic endogenous and exogenous psychic illnesses in children and adolescents
   A. Psychoses and other disturbances in:
      1. Acute infections (grippe, malaria, measles, scarlet fever, diphtheria, pneumonia, enteritis, etc.)
      2. Acute intoxications (including alcohol, hashish and other narcomanias)
   B. Psychic disturbances in chronic infections (rheumatic fever, brucellosis, etc.)
   C. Psychic disturbances in acute brain infections (meningitis, encephalitis, etc.)
   D. Psychic disturbances in chronic encephalitis, leukoencephalitis, demyelinating brain diseases
   E. Psychic disturbances in syphilis of the brain and juvenile progressive paresis
   F. Psychic disturbances associated with brain trauma
   G. Epilepsy
   H. Schizophrenia
   I. Manic-depressive psychosis
   J. Periodic psychoses of an organic nature

II. Borderline forms of psychic disturbances
   A. Psychogenic reactions (internal conflict and external psychic traumata)
      1. Clinical forms
         a. Acute or subacute shock (continuing frequently as a twilight state)
         b. Reactive depression
         c. Neurasthenia
         d. Reactive paranoia
         e. Neurosis of fear (anxiety)
         f. Hysterical reaction
      2. Age specific psychogenic reactions
         a. Youngest children: monosymptomatic neuroses (chiefly vegetative somatic symptoms)
            i. Anorexia
            ii. Habitual vomiting
            iii. Enuresis
            iv. Encopresis
         b. Preschool and school ages
            i. Speech and motor disturbances (functional tics)
            ii. Special reactions of protest
            iii. Pathological changes in character and behavior (influ-

ence of unfavorable family circumstances and incorrect
upbringing)
   3. Transitional phases of development
      a. First transitional phase (unmotivated stubbornness, day and
      night fears, aggressive reactions, jealousy, etc.)
      b. Second transitional phase (psychopathic-like states)
      c. Third transitional phase (anorexia nervosa, hypochondriasis,
      dysmorphophobia, etc.)
   B. Psychopathy (pathology of temperament and character, a partial
   anomaly of the development of the central nervous system)
      1. Delayed or inhibited development (infantilism)
         a. Unstable or excited personalities
         b. Hysteroid personalities
         c. Pathological lying and fantasy formation
      2. Disproportional development
         a. Cyclothymic personalities (hyperthymic, depressive)
         b. Schizoid personalities
         c. Epileptoid personalities
         d. Psychasthenic personalities
      3. Damaged development (organic brain damage in the early years
      of life)
   C. Neuropathy (functional vegetative, vascular, and gastrointestinal
   disturbances with psychic syndrome of irritability, impressionability, excitability, and fatigability)

III. Oligophrenia
   A. Endogenous forms
      1. Enzymopathy
      2. Chromosomal aberrations
      3. Other genetic factors
   B. Pathology of intrauterine development
   C. Perinatal factors (birth trauma, asphyxia)
   D. Postnatal damage in the first two or three years of life

Source: G. E. Sukhareva, personal correspondence, September 1969.

the other hand, rheumatic fever (*revmatizm*) has moved from a separate category in Appendix III to a kind of chronic systemic infection in
Table 4. This change may reflect the diminishing frequency of rheumatic
fever with or without psychic symptoms.

Minor psychiatric disturbances appear in Table 4 as "borderline
forms." Here, the term "borderline" is used in the Soviet sense of minor
disturbances, exclusive of forms of retardation. Although Appendix
III allows for a "reactive psychosis," I never in actual Soviet practice
saw a case described in this way. Both versions have three major sub-

groups: reactive states, psychopathy, and neuropathy. The expanded meanings of these terms are discussed later. In correspondence, Sukhareva mentioned that the problem of grouping borderline disturbances was complicated by the fact that the reaction to the same psychic trauma may differ, depending on the personality of the patient and the social environment in which he lives. Also, the attempt to make a purely etiological schema fails because, she said, there is a series of psychogenic reactions which are more characteristic of a particular phase of development than of a particular etiological factor. The major difference between Table 4 and Appendix III with respect to reactive disturbances stem from this fact. In her later version, Sukhareva has introduced a category of age-specific psychogenic reactions formerly absorbed into the list of subacute psychogenic reactions. The other significant difference is the disappearance of the category paranoid personality disorder or psychopathy in the later version. This may reflect the feeling that a paranoid personality is not manifest in children and only begins to appear in adolescence. In both versions, Sukhareva remains firmly committed to the idea of a congenital neuropathy, distinct from the kinds of organic central nervous system dysfunction which produce psychopathy.

Of the third major division, Sukhareva wrote in her letter of September, 1969: "We regard oligophrenia as a group of pathological states, varying in their etiology and pathogenesis, united by one general sign: They all present clinical phenomena of general psychic lack of development (associated with dysontogenesis of the brain). We assign to oligophrenia only those forms of general lack of psychic development which are characterized by two signs:
  1. The existence of an intellectual defect, in various levels of its expression.
  2. The absence of progressiveness."
This latter factor Sukhareva feels is one of the distinctive features of her classification. She excludes all forms of degenerative disease or progressive deterioration, leading to dementia, and defines oligophrenia as a fixed state. I found it puzzling that having separated the dementias, Sukhareva did not list them as a separate category of gross childhood psychic disturbances.

In the grouping of oligophrenia, as in the grouping of reactive states, a purely etiological classification is not possible. The other factor is the time of influence of the pathogenic agent: genetic, intrauterine, perinatal, or postnatal. This approach, Sukhareva feels, distinguishes her grouping from others with which she is familiar. In the later version, chromosomal anomalies of a nongenetic nature are added, she said, because of the recent advances in cytogenetic research.

The Concept of Residual
Organic Brain Damage

A variety of disturbances are attributed to residual damage after brain trauma or infection during the intrauterine period, at birth, or during infancy and early childhood. Tracing the relationship of these etiological factors to the clinical manifestations of disease is a major focus of the research studies of S. S. Mnukhin and his co-workers, whom I met in Leningrad. In one study, Mnukhin reported a review of the anamnestic data on 900 children, divided into four groups (10):

1. Psychic disturbances (including psychopathy and oligophrenia), 280 cases.
2. Seizure disorders, 340 cases.
3. Motor disorders (paresis and hemiparesis), 62 cases.
4. Mixed group: more than one type of disorder, 218 cases.

Mnukhin examined the histories of these patients for clear-cut pathology in the parents or in the child. He did not describe the criteria by which he made a causal connection between these factors and the disturbance which brought the child into the research group. He reported that in 14 percent of the total series, the etiology of the child's illness remained unclear. This was most frequent in the seizure group, suggesting to him the operation of an unidentified factor contributing to the etiology of seizures. Pathological inheritance was found in 13.5 percent but as a single factor in only 6 percent of the whole group and most frequently in the seizure patients. Clear-cut pathology during the mother's pregnancy with the patient which Mnukhin interpreted as evidence for the existence of intrauterine damage was found in 15 percent—an indication, he said, of the importance of paying more attention to the toxemias of pregnancy. Prematurity, which was not defined, was found in 8 percent of the patients, as compared with 5 percent of one group of normal children. Evidence of birth trauma was found in 25.5 percent, a figure Mnukhin claimed was considerably more frequent than in normal children, though he cited no comparative figure. In 22 percent, he found infectious agents which he took to be responsible for "residual encephalitis." There was evidence of postnatal trauma in 13 percent and toxic-dystrophic states were found in 20 percent. This term was not defined.

In discussing his results, Mnukhin noted that it was not possible to establish correlations between the type of pathogenic agent and the clinical picture. Nor could correlations be made between the time of the influence of the pathogenic agent and the clinical state. He said the older the child at the time of damage, the milder the impairment of global functions. He also thought the clinical picture would depend on the localization and the massiveness of the damage. On the other hand, he added, compensatory capacities in the child are greater than in the adult and even EEG changes at times disappear.

Major syndromes which result from residual organic brain damage were outlined by Professor V. V. Kovalev in a lecture to trainees I was privileged to attend:

1. Cerebrasthenia
2. Neurotic-like syndromes
3. Psychopathic-like syndromes
4. Cerebroendocrine deficiency
5. Delayed or inhibited psychic development
6. Mild and latent hydrocephalic syndromes
7. Syndromes of partial lack of development (speech, gnosis, spatial orientation)
8. Cerebral palsy
9. Organic dementia
10. Oligophrenia
11. Epileptiform syndromes

It was interesting to me to observe how frequently compensated hydrocephalus was diagnosed and considered a contributing factor in behavior disorders. Also noteworthy is the Soviet concept, explained by K. S. Lebedinskaya, of neuroendocrine disturbances. She had studied cases of precocious puberty, delayed puberty, and the adiposo-hypogenital syndrome and attributed the endocrine disturbances to residuals of damage to the diencephalon, mostly due to encephalitis. Her training activities and research interests are described in chapters VI and VII below.

I. V. Dimitrieva reported on toxic psychoses appearing in three children with grippe during epidemics in 1953 and 1955 (2). The clinical picture included sleep disturbances (both somnolence and wakefulness), fears, and mood changes, all accompanying grippe. Later, a delirium developed with visual and auditory hallucinations. Dimitrieva attributed the mental symptomatology in the children to a general toxic state, though in adults she reported a more serious psychosis with amentia, coma, and sometimes death, due to a real encephalitis.

The case of Boris, an eight-year-old boy whose symptomatic psychosis developed at the beginning of the grippe epidemic of 1968–1969 in Moscow, was presented to a group of students to illustrate the concepts discussed above. Boris was admitted to the neuropsychiatric hospital in a state of fearful excitement with sleep disturbances. His history revealed toxemia during the mother's pregnancy and dysentery at four months. Tonsils and adenoids were removed at three years; the operation was followed by pneumonia. Early development and premorbid personality were normal. At five, Boris entered kindergarten but was allowed to stop going because he missed his grandmother too much to adjust comfortably. When he was eight, he was seen by a psychiatrist because of irritability, poor sleep, enuresis, passivity, and easy fatigability. He improved on librium. When he became physically ill with grippe and fever, there was an acute exacerbation of fear, restlessness, and excitement with a fluctuating course. The symptoms recurred in spite of medication with librium and chlorpromazine. Physical and neurological examination on admission was not remarkable except for gynecomastia. His mood was described as hypomanic. He had frightening visual hallucinations of people and dogs, as well as tactile hallucinations. His fears increased at night. He knew he was ill and asked to be taken to the hospital. At the time of presentation, he was free of psychotic symptoms. In the discussion of the diagnosis, the acute symptoms were attributed to a symptomatic psychosis. The gynecomastia was considered suggestive of a diencephalic syndrome arising at the time of the dysentery in the first year of life. Neurotic traits were noted, especially the enuresis, and infantilism (his persistent attachment to his grandmother). The treatment included dehydrating agents (magnesium sulfate and hypertonic glucose) and sedation with levomepromazine.

V. P. Kudryatseva studied the psychic sequelae of prolonged dysentery in infancy (7). During the acute illness, some children are comatose. After the acute phase they are able to play and to answer questions but they are drowsy, sluggish, fatigued, and show various degrees of "cortical inhibition." When the dysentery takes a more chronic course, development of walking and talking is slow. There are disturbances in play activity, with slow movements and a tendency to fall asleep at play. The children cry with little reason, fatigue easily, and show instability of mood. The intellect usually is not grossly impaired and definite neurological signs are lacking, though general physical development is retarded, and the children are not only undersized but retain infantile proportions. They frequently start school late and do poorly, showing short attention span, unwillingness to prepare assignments, and a wish to play all the time. Their work capability is subject to sharp fluctuations. Their thought processes are concrete and they show poor appreciation of the rights of others and lack respect for other children's property. The intellectual difficulties are attributed by Kudryatseva to a failure of adequate interconnections between the first and second signal systems, with evidence derived from conditioning studies of higher nervous activity. There is sluggishness of the nervous processes and "formation of a weak type of nervous system." Endocrine disturbances, appearing in periods of transitional growth crises, are attributed to a direct involvement of the diencephalon and its connections with the hypophysis. These claims are difficult to establish, since no autopsy studies are available. There is no consideration of the possible effects of prolonged hospitalization in the first year of life on emotional and intellectual development, or of the effects of prolonged separation from the mother.

The case of Sasha, a nine-and-one-half-year-old boy, presented at consultation to Professor Sukhareva, is given in Appendix IV. The child presented a problem in differential diagnosis between psychosis with organic brain damage and schizophrenia. The discussion of the case illustrated the importance Russians attribute to the distinction between a process and a state. There were signs of organicity with evidence of progression. This presented a dilemma, because the diagnostic schema did not allow for an organically based progressive psychosis distinct from schizophrenia.

The Concept of Rheumatic Involvement
of the Central Nervous System

A second concept in Soviet psychiatry differing from American psychiatry is that of rheumatic process involving the brain: chiefly the vascular system and perivascular infiltration around smaller vessels. *Revmatizm* should be translated "rheumatic fever" or "rheumatic process" rather than "rheumatism." A rheumatic inflammatory process affecting the central nervous system is a concern of child psychiatry, for it is this age group that is chiefly affected by any form of rheumatic disease.

What kind of evidence do Soviet doctors present to justify this concept? T. V. Kovaleva screened 9,700 adult patients admitted to Lvov Psychiatric Hospital during 1948–1952 (6). Two hundred patients were found who had "various rheumatoid psychoses." One hundred of these were carefully studied. Only patients who had unmistakable signs of rheumatic fever were included: 95 had EKG disturbances, such as A-V conduction block, changes consistent with myocardial disease, extrasystoles, signs of coronary insufficiency. The psychic manifestations were broken down into seven groups: 43 patients had symptoms resembling schizophrenia (catatonic, depressive, paranoid, and hypochondriacal syndromes). Kovaleva found it hard to differentiate rheumatic manifestations from schizophrenia. Sixteen patients had a delirious form of amentia which began with unmotivated fear followed by hallucinations and disturbances of consciousness and ended in a state of apathy and asthenia. Twelve patients had a choreiform psychosis with a stormy course. Smaller groups included rheumatic epilepsy in 9, neurotic-like syndromes in 8, gross vascular disturbances (thromboangiitis, embolism, hemorrhage) in 6, and psychosensory symptoms (illusions, hallucinations, body image disturbances) in 5.

V. Ya. Deyanov reported a series of 200 children with rheumatic disturbances who had been in a psychoneurological hospital (1). One hundred three cases had the asthenic syndrome. Thirty-four patients had neurotic symptoms pertaining to the vascular system (fainting, fear of impending death, heart pains) or epileptic symptoms (grand mal, loss of consciousness without seizure, hysteric-like spells). Twenty had "rheumatic psychoses" and 19 had characterological changes or psychopathic-like behavior. Deyanov also observed 50 patients in an acutely rheumatic state; 75 percent showed the asthenic syndrome. Another 50 patients with a history of active rheumatic inflammation, were studied in a quiescent period; 50 percent showed the asthenic syndrome.

A follow-up study two to four years after discharge from a psychoneurological hospital was done on 117 patients. Fifty percent were symptom free, either in school or working. Of the others, those able to go to school or work showed diminished work capacity. Of 17 patients with a history of rheumatic psychosis, 10 were recovered and the rest "in a state of serious asthenia." An acute psychosis had a better prognosis than a chronic one. In the group with vascular or epileptic symptoms, 50 percent had continuing symptoms. Two could neither attend school nor work. In the group with the asthenic syndrome, all could work, though usually with lowered capability, except for 2 patients who also had chorea. There was a group with characterological changes which persisted after the active rheumatic process. The author considered the nonchoreic form of rheumatic fever with psychic manifestations to be a specific rheumatic involvement of the central nervous system. Deyanov also noted 12 patients in whom the psychic disturbances and the somatic disturbances did not appear together: either could come first. The asymptomatic interval is therefore considered a time of continuing, imperceptible rheumatic activity. The author concluded by emphasizing the importance in preventive work of the recognition of the psychic disturbances accompanying rheumatic fever.

In short, the evidence presented for rheumatic involvement of the central nervous system is not conclusive. It points to the coexistence, in some children and adults, of psychiatric disturbances and episodes of rheumatic fever with cardiac involvement. In Sukhareva's grouping, six kinds of rheumatic involvement of the central nervous system appear: cerebrasthenia, epileptic seizures, cerebropathia with dementia, psychoses, neurotic-like syndromes, and rheumatic chorea (see Appendix III).

Rheumatic cerebrasthenia is described in Deyanov's study of 103 children 8–16 years of age as a triad of symptom complexes: motor, emotional, and sensory disturbances. The usual boy-girl ratio for neurotic disturbances is reversed: 15 boys, 88 girls. Fifty had a form of rheumatic fever with involvement of the heart or joints, and 53 had chorea. In the motor sphere, hypermotility was noted in 12 children. Some had tics, some general restlessness. Twenty-eight children had diminished activity, slowing down of the tempo of speech and movements. Their faces seemed "grey" and expressionless, their voices monotonous. The children were irritable, depressed, cried easily, without adequate reason, sometimes for hours on end. They experienced sudden, unmotivated fears, general anxiety, concern for the health and safety of those close to them. The mood disturbances were worst in the morning and tended to improve toward evening. Disturbances in the visual sphere included double vision, spots before the eyes, things surrounded with "grey fog," and the feeling that things were not anchored solidly in space. There was also intolerance of noises. Some children had taste disturbances. Vestibular disturbances included vertigo and the sensation of falling, especially at night in the state between sleep and waking. Some patients manifested body image disturbances, for example, the hands felt enormous or very long and thin. Along with these specific symptoms the patients showed generally increased fatigability, disturbances of attention, and hence diminished work capacity. They frequently complained of headaches.

Vera, a 16-year-old girl, was brought for consultation to a clinic for diagnostic problems because of fears, nightmares, difficulty falling asleep, easy fatigability, depression, and slipping marks in school.

Vera was slender, short in stature, quiet, reserved, and looked as if she were about to cry. She was expressive and talked readily about her condition, but said she did not know the reason for her fears. She was aware of fear of elevators and fear of the dark. She denied difficulty studying, but knew she was having less to do with other girls than formerly. She felt exhausted much of the time, but could not sleep. She thought she was getting worse. The girl said her symptoms began about five months ago when a neighbor died. She spent ten days in a hospital on the neurological service, where she was treated with chlorpromazine and librium and improved. Then her fears returned. On the one hand, she didn't want to live, and on the other, she feared serious illness and death. She cried frequently and was further frightened by bad dreams.

A brief physical examination revealed the patient was undersized for her age, rather poorly nourished, and had a heart murmur. The differential diagnosis included cerebrasthenia on the basis of a rheumatic infection, a neurotic-like state, and early schizophrenia. Hospitalization in a psychoneurological hospital was recommended. Further study was to include investigation of the cardiac status.

Soviet psychiatrists say rheumatic fever is becoming much less frequent in all its forms, a trend noted also in the United States. I saw no documented examples of rheumatic psychoses in my visits to the various psychoneurological hospitals, although the condition was considered in the differential diagnosis in some cases. Nevertheless, Soviet psychiatrists have described in detail such states, which in American psychiatry are not recognized at all.

Schizophrenia

Soviet and American descriptions of childhood and adolescent schizophrenia appear very similar. There seems no reason to believe schizophrenia in its juvenile form is any different in the Soviet Union from the illness in the United States. After considering Soviet descriptions, certain differences between Russian and American diagnostic approach to the problem of schizophrenia are discussed.

The following discussion of childhood schizophrenia is based on the works of the three Soviet psychiatrists (13, 14, lecture 23). Affective disturbances include emotional emptiness, coldness, flatness, mood fluctuations. Developmental disturbances include delayed speech, persistence of infantile habits like thumb sucking and masturbation. While intellectual development may be precocious at the beginning, the children adapt poorly to the demands of school. Thought disturbances, poverty of thought processes, or excessive fantasy formation bordering on the delusional and obsessive states are reported. Motor disturbances include underactivity, excited states, rituals, and perseverative play. The profound alteration in relationships with others is well described. An important diagnostic sign is diffuse fears without adequate reason. Hallucinations and delusions are rarer in childhood than in adolescent schizophrenia. An insidious onset and course with progressive impairment are more characteristic of the childhood form. Though the prognosis for the group with preschool onset is the worst, there can be at times a favorable outcome. Intellectual development in these children may be severely impaired.

Kanner's syndrome of infantile autism is, particularly in Leningrad, considered a manifestation of early brain damage. In Moscow, autism is seen as schizophrenic. The controversy involves whether the gross developmental and interpersonal disturbances should be regarded as a process or a state, in either case appearing so early that development at very basic levels cannot occur. However, in Leningrad, in the preschool department of the Bekhterev Psychoneurological Institute, they showed me such a child and considered him schizophrenic. Dr. L. P. Saldina, who had worked in Moscow before coming to Leningrad, felt the difference between these two main centers was not significant.

Victor, a ten-year-old boy, illustrates the Soviet idea of mild childhood schizophrenia. Many Americans might disagree. The complaints on admission were general irritability, stubbornness, and uncooperativeness in school. Study of the family revealed that the paternal grandfather was probably a schizoid character. Paternal uncle had been diagnosed schizophrenic and had a schizophrenic daughter. Father also had a history of a psychiatric illness and was still irritable. Mother had neurotic traits.

The developmental history revealed toxicosis during the pregnancy. Birth history and early developmental milestones were unremarkable. In the second year, Victor cried a lot and did not play with toys. When he went to kindergarten at three years, he did not play well with other children. He was soon removed because of his unwillingness to attend. At home, his parents noted apathy and poor sleep patterns. He was stubborn, demanding, and moody.

When he entered school at seven years, he showed intolerance for noise, rapid fatigability when he was with other children, and a preference for playing alone. At first he learned adequately, but in the second class, Victor's inattentiveness and gloomy attitude were interfering with his learning. After a conditional promotion to the third class, his difficulties remained severe enough so that he spent three months in a sanatorium for neurotic children. He returned to regular school, still irritable and stubborn, and was held back in the third class. That fall, he refused to study or answer questions in class.

In the hospital, Victor first was tearful and sullen and would hardly answer questions. He was moody and suffered from diffuse, inarticulated fears, particularly at night. He slept fitfully and complained of headaches. He adapted poorly to the ward routine and made no friends. Victor was just as reluctant to attend school at the hospital as he had been at home. His class work revealed a poor foundation in first- and second-year work. The teacher said he was irritable and frequently in conflict with other children. Physical and neurological examinations were not remarkable. During hospitalization, he improved on librium and levomepromazine.

Victor was a plump, reserved boy whose behavior in the interview was not so negative as had been reported in the history.

Sometimes he would smile, but frequently looked troubled and fearful. He said at present his mood was good and he hoped to be going back to school and to be able to study well. At first he denied difficulty studying or thinking, but blamed the teacher for not explaining enough. However, Victor would not ask when he did not understand. He was vague about what school work gave him trouble. In Russian grammar, he admitted mistakes and could not answer simple questions. He answered simple arithmetic problems correctly but became confused if there was more than one step. He said his fears, most vivid at night, concern school and things he has read or seen on television. He expressed a vague fear that someone would come and kill him. In the morning he would awaken tired, heavy-eyed. Although he felt fearful and had unpleasant moods, he could not give a clear picture of his inner experiences. There were no definite hallucinations or delusions.

The differential diagnosis was between schizophrenia and a "neurotic state with psychopathic-like behavior on an organic basis." The consensus was schizophrenia. Although schizoid personality as a variety of psychopathy appears in Sukhareva's classification, it is not frequently used. Soviet psychiatrists see mild childhood schizophrenia as frequently manifested by symptoms of neurosis or "psychopathic-like behavioral disturbances."

Sukhareva described the pubertal form of schizophrenia (14, lecture 24). Among prodromal symptoms, she included appetite disturbances, estrangement from other people, altered relationships with close ones, diminished scholastic achievement, and strange behavior. At this stage, she said, it is difficult to tell the disease from a reactive state. The beginning of the psychosis is characterized by fear, anxiety, a sensation of change, altered perception, depersonalization, hallucinations. The height of the psychosis may include a catatonic excitement with impulsiveness, aggressiveness, overproductivity of speech, stereotyped movements, posing, mannerisms. Thought disturbances are present, including delusions and disconnected thought processes. Affective disturbances range from emotional lability to manic or depressive states. Negativism is frequent. In acute disturbances, there may be disorientation in the conventional spheres, withholding of urine or feces. Frequently, patients refuse to eat.

Schizophrenia of puberty has a more acute onset and a more intermittent course than childhood schizophrenia. The illness in puberty resembles adult schizophrenia. The first episode in girls is often associated with the menarche. The physiological implications are more stressed than the psychological significance. Sukhareva commented that the differential diagnosis of schizophrenia, the infectious psychoses, and the reactive psychoses is often difficult. The Russian psychiatrist never describes a "reactive form of schizophrenia." A case considered wholly a reactive state would not be called schizophrenia. In the Soviet view, reactive psychogenic factors could cause an exacerbation of latent schizophrenic process.

The case of Ivan, given in Appendix IV, illustrates many points in Russian diagnostic thinking about adolescent schizophrenia. Ivan's intellectual development had surpassed his motor development. Lifelong obsessional fears and poor peer relationships are features described in Soviet studies of insidious schizophrenia, the prodromal phase merging imperceptibly with the manifest illness (see O. P. Yureva's work, described in Chapter VII below). The case of Ivan shows a type of course considered in Soviet psychiatry to be common in adolescent schizophrenia: intermittent with slow progression and failure to recover completely. None of these aspects of the case differ from an American case. However, the poor response to medication was linked with a history in childhood of chronic pneumonia as possibly indicating "diencephalic insufficiency." This concept is unfamiliar in American thinking.

Other cases of adolescent schizophrenia seen at the same mental hospital included a 14-year-old girl with an acute onset of depression, with vague, paranoid ideas of reference, and feelings that her thoughts were known to people around her. Another was a 15-year-old girl with emotional apathy, coldness, and auditory hallucinations. This girl thought that young boys were talking about her and asking her to meet them in order to make love to her or marry her. She believed the hallucinations and disagreed with everybody who thought she was ill. The interviews included careful clarification of the affective state and estimation of its appropriateness. When patients expressed fear, effort was made to find out the content. The patients' own attitude toward delusions and hallucinations and ability to criticize them were evaluated. The "dynamics" were emphasized. Since schizophrenia is seen as a chronic illness, there is interest in longitudinal study of its natural history.

In general, Russian psychiatrists diagnose schizophrenia in childhood and adolescence more frequently than Americans, particularly in cases where the symptoms were depressive and diffuse anxiety or vaguely structured fears. Some of these children did not appear schizophrenic to me, because their affective state and ability to relate to people were intact. In others, the anxiety seemed to me more motivated by identifiable unconscious conflicts and therefore not the diffuse anxiety of incipient schizophrenia. Further, among the cases Soviet psychiatrists were diagnosing schizophrenia were many which an American would call borderline, a term with a completely different meaning in the Russian sense. In Sukhareva's classification, borderline refers to all reactive states and personality disorders. It does not mean a state close to psychosis. This observation was confirmed by Professor V. V. Kovalev, who has talked with many Western psychiatrists.

Where there was a question of an infectious base for the psychosis or a history of rheumatic involvement, Russian psychiatrists diagnosed schizophrenia less readily than I would. One 12-year-old girl's illness began with fears seemingly unrelated to external events, visual hallucinations of crosses and bugs, bizarre mannerisms, and inappropriate laughter. She was terrified and complained, cowering, of feeling sick. She looked out the window and said she could see crosses, then complained of being frightened because she felt dirty, insisting she would never get well until she could be cleansed. She also had pains in her heart and legs. To me, this was schizophrenia, but the child's doctors felt that they would have to study the course of her illness further before they could make a firm diagnosis.

In summary, the differences in diagnostic approach lay in three main areas: First, the Russian interest in the course of the illness frequently leads them to diagnose schizophrenia when the leading symptoms are depression and fear, since these symptoms often mark the beginning of a schizophrenic process. Second, because internal conflict and unconscious motivation are not investigated, states of depression and fear seem to them more "unmotivated." Third, there is a difference of conceptualization, because infections and their sequelae (grippe, dysentery, etc.) and rheumatic involvement of the central nervous system are seen at times to cause psychotic disturbances with schizophrenic symptomatology. While there was widespread recognition of the syndrome of infantile autism, there was some disagreement as to whether to regard it as a form of schizophrenia. Nobody spoke of symbiotic psychoses. The quality of the mother-child relationship was never considered a major etiological factor in the development of schizophrenia.

In discussing the influence of the midnineteenth-century German medical model on Russian psychiatry, we saw how the diagnostic ideal is to develop a classification in which each illness is an independent entity, both in its etiology and pathogenesis. While Russian child psychiatrists are sophisticated about childhood and adolescent schizophrenia, they talk as if they would like to regard it as a single entity, a process which can be slow or rapid, mild or severe, intermittent or steadily progressive. Soviet psychiatrists reject the position taken by some Americans that schizophrenia is a loose, poorly defined collection of varying etiology.

Other
Psychoses

True states of mania and depression before adolescence are probably as rare in the Soviet Union as in the United States. During several weeks in Moscow, no cases were observed. In Leningrad, one adolescent girl was seen who was said to have emerged from a manic state. A. S. Lomachenkov reported on 54 cases admitted over a ten-year period to a small Leningrad mental hospital with either manic or depressive episodes (8). He described typical depressive episodes alternating with manic excitement usually not beginning until after puberty. Depressive episodes were commoner than manic. In girls, the illness began two or three years younger than it did in boys and was frequently associated with the menarche.

Sukhareva included in her classification a group of periodic psychoses whose nosological status is still not established (see Appendix III). There are affective disturbances resembling the manic depressive psychosis, motor disturbances resembling the excited or inhibited stages of catatonic schizophrenia but without negativism, and also a group of sensory disturbances and disorders of consciousness. Psychotic disturbances falling in this category she thought to be caused by birth trauma or infections early in life, sometimes accompanied by endocrine insufficiency. Sukhareva believes a psychosis can become manifest five to ten years after a brain insult. It is not clear how she distinguishes these states from schizophrenia where the same kinds of external etiological factors are mentioned. It is of interest that residual organic brain damage is thought to have late sequelae and can cause disturbances characterized by periodicity.

Neurotic
Reactions

What role does psychogenesis play in the thinking of leading Russian child psychiatrists? Sukhareva maintained psychic trauma can cause a reactive neurosis or act as the precipitating factor in a vulnerable personality with somatic predisposition. Unless the relationship between a definite external event and the appearance of symptoms is very clear, a "reactive state" is not diagnosed. Table 5 shows how neurotic children in special schools were actually classified. One school was in Kiev; the other was in Pavlovsk, a suburb of Leningrad. Severe psychopathy and psychoses were excluded. Only 7 percent of the children admitted to the Kiev sanatorium were considered to have wholly psychogenic disturbances. The Pavlovsk children were classified by the diagnosis with which they were admitted to the school, following terminology of Mnukhin. The three major categories are: neuropathy, 60 percent; asthenia and cerebrasthenia, 23 percent; and inhibitions of psychic development, 17 percent. The neuropathies and asthenias are considered organically based. Cerebrasthenia is subdivided into disturbances of embryonic development and brain damage at birth. Even among inhibitions of psychic development, psychogenic factors are not explicitly mentioned. Mnukhin's view of learning problems is further discussed in Chapter VII.

Aside from acute and subacute neurotic reactions caused by obvious psychic trauma, Sukhareva's grouping allows for neuroses which develop over a period of time in response to chronic stresses in family life (Appendix III). Myasishchev's neurosis of development is a similar concept, resembling the category of distorted character formation due to unfavorable conditions of upbringing (9). At the time of my visit, there was interest in the problem of character and its relationship to organically based psychopathy and to social factors. The work of V. V. Kovalev on this subject is presented in Chapter VII. As in the United States, most children with neurotic character distortions are handled in psychiatric and pediatric outpatient facilities. Many of the children in sanatoria for neurotics were recommended for admission because of unfavorable family situations, but this factor was underemphasized in formal diagnostic evaluation.

An example of a neurotic child is 11-year-old Sonya, whom I saw in outpatient consultation with Professor Sukhareva because of refusal to go to school, moodiness, and headaches. The child had

Neurotic
Reactions

Table 5. Etiology and Types of Neuroses

Etiology

Multiple factors	44.0%
Infections of the brain and meninges	7.0%
Intrauterine disturbances	7.5%
Birth trauma	9.0%
Postnatal trauma	4.5%
General infectious illnesses (measles, etc.)	9.0%
Somatic weakness	2.5%
Psychogenesis	7.0%
Intoxication	1.5%
Genetic	1.0%
Unknown	7.0%

Types

Neuropathy	31%	
Neuropathic disturbance of childhood	22%	Neuropathy 60%
Neuropathic character traits	7%	
Asthenia	11%	
Asthenia from physical illness	7%	Asthenia + Cerebrasthenia 23%
Cerebrasthenia	5%	
Disturbance of embryonic development	2.5%	
Brain damage at birth	2.5%	
Inhibitions of psychic development with neurotic syndrome	9%	
Inhibitions of psychic development with difficulties forming basic habits: reading, writing, arithmetic	1%	
Inhibitions of psychic development on a somatic base	4%	Inhibitions of psychic development 17%
Psychophysical infantilism with difficulties forming basic habits: reading, writing, arithmetic	2%	
Psychophysical infantilism with neurotic tendencies	1%	

Source: Data on etiology obtained from Children's Psychoneurological Sanatorium, Kiev, 68 children. Data on types obtained from Sanatorium-Forest School for Nervous Children, Pavlovsk, 147 children.

always been withdrawn and had difficulties adjusting, beginning with kindergarten. In the first class, she was frightened and unable to stay in school. Her best years were the third and fourth class. When confronted with a new teacher in the fifth class, Sonya ran out of the classroom and wrote a letter, saying she had headaches and did not want to return to school. She refused to go after that and became moody and irritable, especially in her relationship with her grandmother.

Sonya was a neatly dressed preadolescent girl in long pigtails. She was shy and smiled in an embarrassed way. She said she had remained in contact with her girl friends by telephone. She refused to write for the doctor. She said she was afraid of school and of getting bad marks. Professor Sukhareva spoke affectionately with her, holding her, patting her. The suggestion was given that some medicine would help her feel able to go to school. The possibility of hospitalization was mentioned lightly if the child found herself unable to return to school.

Sonya was accompanied by her mother, who was a teacher, and by her doctor-father, who volunteered to give the history. The impression was of intellectual, overly anxious parents focusing all of their attention on an only child who had learned to manipulate adults but also had occasionally provoked a beating from her mother over the issue of attending school. The mother was so guilty over this that she cried as Professor Sukhareva told her the child was ill and needed medicine rather than punishment.

This case was diagnosed as a neurosis due to unfavorable conditions of upbringing and resembled cases of school phobia seen in the United States. While no psychotherapy was recommended, the consultation itself, conducted in a warm, supportive way with a strong element of suggestion and some opportunity for the expression of guilty feelings on the part of the mother, appeared to be a form of brief psychotherapy.

Other children diagnosed neurotic had tics, fears, and the whole gamut of symptomatology familiar to psychiatrists in the United States. Hysteria was not a very common disturbance, but was recognized as one cause of seizure-like episodes. A 12-year-old girl with a history of dizziness, headaches, and spells of altered consciousness with pronounced fear of death was presented at a conference to Professor Mnukhin at the Leningrad Psychoneurological Hospital for Children. There were changes in the pneumoencephalogram suggestive of arachnoiditis and EEG changes consistent with a temporal lobe focus. Suddenly, the child was carried into the conference, in the middle of a spell. She held herself somewhat stiffly, her head rotated to the right. She kept her eyes tightly shut and whimpered, crying for her mother. She stuck her tongue out on request and obeyed all other commands. The neurological examination was within normal limits. She was still in the same state when she was carried out of the room. In the discussion of the case, the doctors present were impressed with the signs of organicity. When I was asked for my opinion, I said I thought this was a case of hysteria (by this time I was accustomed to being a minority of one when psychogenic factors were considered). To my surprise, Professor Mnukhin conceded that the behavior we had witnessed was "hysterical" and that, intuitively, one would have to consider neurosis, in spite of the changes in the EEG and the pneumoencephalogram. This incident reaffirmed my observation of the sensitivity and clinical judgment Soviet doctors demonstrate in their dealings with patients, in spite of their (to me) excessive concern with organicity.

One psychogenic reaction in Sukhareva's grouping is of particular interest: the reaction of protest (see Appendix III). At all ages, symptoms may appear as the child's way of protesting against the conditions of his life. The specific symptomatology depends partly on the period of life. This reactive state represents a conflict between the child and his environment. In its passive form, the child may protest in covert ways such as selective mutism or vegetative somatic disturbances, the latter commonly seen in pediatric practice at the preschool age. Another passive protest is suicidal attempts commonly encountered in adolescence. In the active form, the child may protest by temper tantrums, aggressive or rebellious acts. If the reaction continues over a period of time, it may gradually turn into a more permanent distortion of character formation. The reaction of protest seemed to me a useful way of describing an external conflict between the child and the environment with no direct counterpart in American classifications. What is lacking in the Soviet schema is an adequate conceptualization of a *psychogenic process* whereby conflict becomes internalized and then perhaps latent, to reappear later in life in altered form with new symptom formation.

We have seen how the condition called asthenia, neurasthenia, or cerebrasthenia is considered organically based. It is also listed in Sukhareva's grouping among the psychogenic reactions, both in Table 4 and Appendix III. Symptomatically, cerebrasthenia is indistinguishable from the category of neuropathy or nervous predisposition. Neuropathy can exist from birth in a congenital form, or it may be acquired as the result of cerebral trauma or infection early in life. Sukhareva wrote me as follows regarding her thinking on neuropathy, differentiating it both from reactive psychogenic states and from psychopathy: "From the group of psychopathy we considered it necessary to separate those clinical forms of borderline states which bear the name, 'neuropathy.' A cardinal feature in the pathogenetic basis of neuropathy is a disturbance of function of the vegetative nervous system and associated with this a lowering of the threshold of excitability in relation to various stimuli. In the clinical picture of neuropathy, functional vegetative vascular disturbances occupy a prominent place as well as disturbances of the gastrointestinal tract. In the psychic state of these children, the syndrome of excitable weakness predominates with increased impressionability, easy excitability, and rapid fatigability. On this base, neurotic phenomena easily appear in children and adolescents under the influence of insignificant factors. But in these children, pathology of temperament and character characteristic for psychopathy is lacking."

Professor Kovalev described cerebrasthenia in a lecture to trainees as a state of "psychic weakness" with lowered work capability, emotional lability, fatigability, and no gross disturbance of intellectual functioning. Psychosensory phenomena include altered body feelings, vestibular and vegetative disturbances. The neurasthenic state after grippe is characterized by depression, moodiness, unmotivated fear, and startle reactions. There is frequently heightened sensitivity to sound and under- or overactivity. Kovalev considers the differential diagnosis from similar symptomatology on a psychogenic basis very important, because psychotherapy does no good for the organically based syndrome.

Professor Kovalev saw in consultation Karla, a 12-year-old girl whom he diagnosed as posttraumatic encephalopathy with cerebrasthenic syndrome. Although the history revealed the father was alcoholic and had killed himself, psychogenic factors were not emphasized. When she was nine, Karla fell under a car and was hospitalized for two months. Following this head trauma, her speech was unclear, she slept poorly, was fearful, and complained of headaches. She was unusually sensitive to noises and seemed sluggish and underactive. Her attention span was poor. She had been hospitalized previously with some improvement and then was readmitted because the symptoms returned. On physical examination, she was found to be a large, well-developed girl, whose speech was dysarthric. Other findings were very slight facial asymmetry, awkward tongue movements with a tendency of the tongue to deviate slightly to the right, and generalized hypotonia. When we saw Karla she expressed a positive attitude about the speech department. She was self-conscious about her speech defect and wanted to improve. In the discussion, the asthenic syndrome was considered most important, but there were some hysterical trends in the personality and there was a "functional insufficiency of the diencephalon with a basal vegetative syndrome." Therapy included medications (librium, pyridoxine, and a dehydrating agent) and speech therapy, which emphasized tongue exercises. A general psychotherapeutic approach was advised to discourage somatic fixations and to encourage positive interests such as dancing.

Anorexia
Nervosa

Anorexia nervosa is a well-recognized syndrome in the Soviet Union. One leading Russian psychiatrist, T. P. Simpson, described a state of anorexia caused by an urge to grow thin, characteristically beginning at puberty with the appearance of the secondary sex characteristics (12, pp. 38–45). The adolescent is ashamed of her developing full figure and strives to eat less and less frequently. Somatic characteristics of these patients are an asthenic body build with infantilism and hypogenitalism. The patients are frequently negativistic and restless. Additional symptoms are depression, sleep disturbances, and emotional excitability. In the initial stages the patients struggle against hunger, but later on they lose their appetites. Some throw away food or try to deceive the personnel into thinking they have eaten. Simpson believed the functions of the diencephalon and the endocrine system are disturbed. She noted the amenorrhea, but did not present other evidence of endocrine disorder. She acknowledged that anorexia nervosa must be differentiated from Symond's disease.

Sukhareva, too, described the syndrome of anorexia nervosa in puberty (15, lecture 12). She thought the crucial factors are pubertal sexual development and unpleasant experiences occurring at that time. She recognized the importance of the changes which occur in the "sensation of the self." Interoceptive and proprioceptive sensations are also connected with disturbances in the harmony of the internal secretory apparatus, chiefly the hypophyseal-thalamic system. In Sukhareva's clinic, K. A. Novlyanskaya observed 11 cases in adolescence, 14–16 years of age. Observation for two or three years was needed to establish the diagnosis of anorexia nervosa as a form of pathological reaction of puberty or as a form of schizophrenia.

In one study of 60 schizophrenic patients, 2 girls and 1 boy were described as having the syndrome of refusal to eat because of altered body perception and fear of growing fat (13, pp. 27–30). In each case, there was a family history of psychosis and a past medical history of frequent infectious illnesses. The boy had a severe sore throat and difficulty swallowing, which precipitated the refusal to eat. The symptom developed gradually and was accompanied by personality changes: irritability, withdrawal, awareness of illness or some impending catastrophe (though without insight), ambivalent attitudes, ideas of reference. As the weight loss continued, the patients became emaciated, with pallor and dry skin. The authors considered the syndrome characteristic of puberty and more frequent in girls, though sometimes present in boys.

N. S. Rotiniyan, an associate of Sukhareva in Moscow, kindly permitted me to read her unpublished paper on anorexia (11). She reviewed the literature on anorexia nervosa, citing the first Russian description by A. A. Kisel in 1911. She then presented the findings in a series of 66 cases, falling into two groups: the first, 34 girls, showed a pathological reaction of puberty; in the second group were 23 girls and 9 boys with a form of schizophrenia. The premorbid personalities of the children in both groups were characterized by activity, conscientiousness, self-consciousness, and rigidity. The males were all in the schizophrenic group. The syndrome in both groups was highly uniform. The onset in both groups could be considered to be psychogenetically determined, with disturbed, anxiety-laden attitudes toward the body (a form of "dysmorphophobia"). Both groups also had ideas of reference, affective disturbances, feelings of people noticing their fatness and laughing at them. Some patients were depressed, agitated, reluctant to be with contemporaries, or refused to go to school. The differences between the two groups lay in the quality of their thought processes and affective experience. The first group showed fixation on sensations of the gastrointestinal tract, while the more disturbed group showed depersonalization and disintegration of thought processes. Affective changes, more pronounced and rapid in their onset in the second group, included sullenness, exasperation with parents urging them to eat, coldness, reserve, and apathy. In some activity was diminished. There was preoccupation with questions of life and death. Rotiniyan reported the follow-up of 25 cases over a ten-year period. Uniformly, the syndrome disappeared after puberty. In the reaction of puberty group, the syndrome lasted three or four years while in the schizophrenic group, symptoms lasted a few months to ten years.

Rotiniyan also described a patient observed for 23 years, first hospitalized at 14 because of refusal to eat and exhaustion (11). The illness began at 13 with an increase in irritability, moodiness, and a tendency to withdraw from friends. The girl did less well at school and began to limit her food intake. She became secretive, because she thought people noticed she was fat. The youngster would hide herself, only venturing out at night. Sometimes she would overeat and induce vomiting. The relationship with her mother deteriorated. On insulin therapy, there was some improvement, although the patient still limited her food intake. Twenty-three years after the onset of the illness she was experiencing tension, headaches, and lack of interest in life. Sometimes the thoughts about being fat recurred, but she was no longer limiting her food intake. Her disturbed relationships with other people were still prominent, and she feared that the neighbors were talking about her and therefore she did not want to work. The long follow-up made it possible to see the anorectic syndrome as part of a more diffuse insidious schizophrenic process with an intermittent course.

It was of great interest to me to see two cases of anorexia nervosa with Dr. Rotiniyan (Ira and Olga, Appendix IV) and to compare their histories and clinical picture with those we have seen and reported in the United States (19). In our discussion, Dr. Rotiniyan said she regards the fear of fatness as the central feature of the syndrome. I described a concept of anorexia nervosa as a disturbance of the body image, which explains many facets of the disorder (18). The children frequently have a conviction that there is something physically wrong and are often so frightened that they avoid seeking medical help. The illness is often experienced as a sensation of fullness and heaviness in the abdomen, indeed just the sensations described by Olga. The fear of fatness, I said, was secondary to this fundamental disturbance in the body image. Dr. Rotiniyan appeared to understand this formulation, but she was puzzled how in America we could treat anorexia nervosa without specific drug therapy. I told her about patients I had treated who were so afraid of losing control of their eating and their situation in general that I felt drug therapy would arouse more anxiety than it would alleviate. Why then, she wondered, do we hospitalize patients against their will? I described two basic indications for hospitalization:

first, a dangerous physical state, and second, an emotional crisis in the family of intolerable proportions, arising as the parents witness their child slowly starving.

Dr. Rotiniyan considered neither of the two patients we saw together suitable for psychotherapy. I was inclined to agree, since it would have been difficult to form a therapeutic alliance with either one. Both were given subcoma insulin and tranquilizing drugs. However, Sukhareva, in her discussion of the syndrome, indicated the need for psychotherapy and the importance of attempting to change the patient's attitude (15, lecture 12).

Age Peculiarities and Transitional Growth Periods

The last category in Sukhareva's grouping of psychogenic reactions is reactions characteristic of transitional growth phases (see Table 4). This is not unlike the American Psychiatric Association (APA) categories, adjustment reaction of childhood and adolescence. In Soviet thinking, symptoms and syndromes can arise in a transitory, self-limited way as a reaction to the developmental stages through which all children must pass. But in the absence of psychoanalytic theory, what developmental stages are recognized and how is the psychopathology of neuroses and psychoses related to the stages?

Descriptions of child development are physiologically based, theoretically tied to the teachings of Pavlov. Simpson outlined development, starting with sensorimotor processes in the first year of life, at the same time recognizing the importance of the child's growing ability to distinguish himself from the world around him, first through sensations in the mouth and respiratory apparatus (12, pp. 7–16). Subsequent development includes discovery and recognition of the arms and legs as part of the self plus the process of learning to differentiate both image and voice from those of the mother and others in the environment. Simpson based this part of her discussion on the work of I. M. Sechenov, with some recognition of the contributions of Piaget.

She described three growth crises as nodal points in a child's development (12, pp. 17–20). They are usually decisive and rapid in the sense of establishing new levels of integration. The first of these, two to four years, is the period of stubbornness. The child has learned how to walk and to run and has the rudiments of speech; in short, he has many avenues through which he can explore the world around him. He begins to want to do everything for himself and to ask incessant questions. Physically, the body form and proportions change from those of infancy to those of childhood. Possibilities for tension and conflict stem from a failure on the part of the parents to recognize the new requirements of the new stage, in contradistinction to the old requirements in the period of babyhood. The successful completion of this stage provides the foundation for the child's individuality and character.

The second growth crisis appears at seven or eight years and is less stormy than the first. The somatic basis is the cessation of the activity of the thymus gland which up until this time has exerted an inhibitory influence on the functioning of the sexual glands. Motor development now permits the child to acquire fine, skilled movements. Childhood spontaneity disappears and is replaced by fact and the capacity for inhibition and self-control. Simultaneously, the demands of school make it necessary for the child to acquire the basic skills of reading and writing, to conform to society's norms of behavior, and to expand peer relationships. Possibilities for conflict stem from the sudden increase of external demands on the child.

The third or pubertal crisis is usually most intense at 14–16 years and is caused by the endocrine changes leading to physical growth and development of secondary sex characteristics. A dissociation of cortical-subcortical relationships, Simpson claimed, causes motor disturbances, such as awkwardness, grimacing, poor control over timbre and pitch of the voice. The adolescent senses the metamorphosis. His emotional life is much richer, but also more unstable, because of the imbalance caused by the unequal development of the internal organs and their functions. The focus of attention on the self leads to egocentricity. The possibility for conflict with parents is heightened if they fail to recognize the adolescent no longer requires the care and protection of childhood.

Soviet child psychiatrists stress the influence of age characteristics and developmental crises on the form and course of psychopathology, both the neuroses and psychoses. While self-limited pathological reactions can appear in the three major crisis periods, age factors alone are not usually sufficient to cause neurosis or mental illness (15, lecture 12). In fact, it is emphasized that these periods can be negotiated peacefully, free of conflict and friction, if the parental approach to the child is correct. This is in sharp distinction to the psychoanalytic theorists who see within the developmental stages the potentiality for internal conflict just by the inherent nature of the developmental processes. From these differences in points of view might arise differences in the diagnostic assessment of an unusually peaceful, uneventful adolescence. An American psychiatrist might see in adolescent turbulence the opportunity for undoing pathological defenses, a second chance at the resolution of old infantile conflicts, and an opportunity to reorganize the personality along healthier lines. A Soviet psychiatrist might view with less concern the conforming kind of teenager who seems to have skipped adolescent turbulence altogether.

In discussing age factors and neuroses, Simpson emphasized psychogenic somatic disturbances of infancy and early childhood (particularly gastrointestinal disturbances and respiratory difficulties) and the ease with which the child loses recently acquired habits of speech and cleanliness (12, pp. 20–23). The school-age child, in the second growth crisis, is prone to such disorders as stuttering and tics. Sukhareva vividly described frequently encountered syndromes of adolescence (15, lecture 12). These include pathological intellectualism, sometimes picturesquely described as philosophical intoxication, hypochondriacal fixation on bodily sensations, dysmorphophobia (excessive fears of physical inadequacy), psychogenic anorexia with fear of fatness, and, finally, psychopathic-like forms of behavior. These include delinquency and various forms of sexual deviant behavior.

Age factors are also recognized as influencing the form of symptomatology and type of course in schizophrenia. In Sukhareva's view, the childhood form was described with one type of symptomatology and the adolescent form with another type. The insidious course was considered most characteristic of the childhood form and the intermittent course with progression most characteristic of the adolescent form. M. S. Vrono confirmed Sukhareva's findings in a study of 200 children. He described how the catatonic symptoms of childhood rarely if ever reach the extremes of stupor and excitement observed in adolescents and adults (17). The slow, insidious course of schizophrenia was more characteristic of the childhood form; a periodic form, with or without a slowly progressive defect, was more characteristic of adolescence. Vrono concluded that age is not the only factor influencing the degree of destructiveness of the schizophrenic process and the extent of the residual defect.

It is of interest that even organically based conditions, such as epileptic seizures or psychopathic-like behavior, based on residual organic brain damage, are considered more likely to appear at transitional growth periods. The relationship between age and the appearance of the manic depressive psychosis has already been discussed.

Lydia can serve as an example of a neurotic problem in which the reaction to adolescence itself was considered the major factor. Lydia was a 12-year-old girl seen in consultation by Professor Kovalev after she had been admitted to a psychoneurological hospital because of refusal to go to school. The facts of this child's family history were noncontributory except that the mother was considered to be rigid. Lydia's infancy, early development, and school history were uneventful. She was large for her age and the menstrual periods began at 11 years. Around this time, her parents noted she was interested in sexual questions.

Lydia's refusal to go to school began in the fifth class when she was 11. She simply lay in bed with her eyes closed. She became moody and irritable in her relationships with her mother and her grandmother. Her summer was spent uneventfully at a summer cottage with her mother. In the fall, Lydia began the sixth class, but stopped after the holidays. At first she kept up with her lessons, but after the New Year's holiday she did not even try to do that much. She was becoming increasingly disagreeable with her grandmother. When Lydia's first symptoms developed, she was taken to a psychoneurologist who advised medication, which she refused. A school report revealed that she was an able student. She had been enrolled in a special foreign-language school.

When Lydia was admitted to the hospital, the physical examination was not remarkable except that she was extremely large and well-developed for her age. She was in contact with reality, but quite indifferent to her problem. She could give no real reason for her refusal to go to school. However, she expressed interest in becoming a writer for a magazine. She acknowledged some fear of the dark and denied that she had been particularly cruel to her grandmother. In the hospital, she attended school classes willingly and it was noted that her behavior was best when she was occupied with school work.

When Lydia appeared for the interview, she was a well-developed, large adolescent girl who related well and expressed interest in becoming a journalist. She said that she liked to read Dickens, Gorky, and Turgenev. Her reason for refusing to go to school was not clear.

She did admit poor relationships with other girls and some depression, although formerly she had felt generally cheerful. Lydia's discomfort about going to school had prevented her eating breakfast in the morning. Her mood did not seem depressed and her attitude and bearing were appropriate for an adolescent of 14 or 15. She indicated the medicine which she had previously received had not done any good.

In the differential diagnosis, early schizophrenia and circular psychosis were ruled out. It was considered that Lydia was reacting to an unusually early puberty, although the age factor did not completely account for her refusal to go to school. However, Professor Kovalev was opposed to psychotherapy, which I suggested. He was afraid it might fixate Lydia's attention on her sexual thoughts. In his opinion, the sexual preoccupation should be suppressed with chlorpromazine and the energy rechanneled into other interests such as sports. Lydia seemed to me to illustrate in a striking way *belle indifference,* one classical sign of hysteria, although this aspect of the case was not discussed. This type of patient at home would be less likely to be hospitalized. The doctors who were present agreed with me that an important aspect of managing the case would be active encouragement to return to school.

Personality Disorders

The Russian term *psikhopatiya* is probably more accurately translated "personality disorder" than "psychopathy." In discussing the etiology of these disorders, which would include psychopathic personality, Sukhareva mentioned inheritance and factors acting during the intrauterine period or early childhood (15): systemic or brain infection, brain trauma, and factors of "intoxication and autointoxication" (alcohol, syphilis, harmful radiations, and extremes of temperature). Sukhareva also recognized the role of an unfavorable social environment, particularly conditions of upbringing. For the diagnosis of psychopathy, it is necessary to establish severe forms of abnormal personality development. Some general characteristics are increased emotional excitability and lability, pugnaciousness, unstable behavior patterns, lowered work and study capability, and the predominance of primitive instincts and impulses.

While Sukhareva considered it very important to distinguish between psychopathy and changes in character associated with unfavorable conditions of upbringing, she conceded that frequently at the beginning the distinction is impossible and observation must be continued for a period of time to establish the diagnosis. Factors favoring the diagnosis of character changes due to unfavorable upbringing include the absence of symptomatology showing central nervous system involvement, the decrease of excitability under favorable external conditions, greater work and study capability, and the presence of normal interests and intact psychic thought processes such as attention and memory.

P. B. Gannushkin, in his book *The Clinical Picture of Psychopathy,* published in 1933, is credited with the most complete description of the personality disorders. Sukhareva's grouping was most influenced by this work. She distinguished three main varieties of psychopathy (Appendix III). The first is infantilism or inhibition of development, the mildest form, since gross signs of organic brain damage are lacking. This category includes emotionally unstable and excitable personalities, hysterical personalities, and *pseudologia fantastica*. The hysterical personality, Sukhareva said, is found predominantly in the female sex, with increased suggestibility and a tendency toward fantasy formation, along with egocentrism, moodiness, and general emotional instability.

Sukhareva's second main variety is disproportional development, or an unevenness and lack of harmony in the development of the personality. She considered this form of psychopathy the most likely to be genetically determined. Included here are cyclothymic personalities and schizoid personalities. The psychasthenic personality is classified by some Russian authors as a neurosis but by Gannushkin and Sukhareva as a form of psychopathy. It is characterized by a general impressionability, fearfulness in the presence of anything new, hypochondriasis, and tendency toward the formation of phobic fears. In Pavlovian terms, the second signal system is considered strong but the first signal system is weak, and so the interrelationship between the two is disturbed. The paranoid personality Sukhareva claimed is not seen until puberty. Its main features are aggressiveness and egocentricity as well as ideas of reference. The epileptoid personality is characterized by high irritability, defects of moral judgment, and mood disturbances. This term does not imply the presence of seizures. The patients are likely to be aggressive and hostile. This, too, Sukhareva considered not a common disturbance during childhood.

The third variety of psychopathy is damaged development, the form most frequently seen in children's clinics. The evidence of central nervous system involvement is much plainer than in the other varieties. Behavior disturbances are also present. If the picture is predominantly failure of inhibitory controls, the child demonstrates instability, in-

creased motor activity and excitability, profound distractability, with
quick transitions from one interest to another and an inability to inhibit
inappropriate responses. The form characterized by excitability presents
the picture of an impulse-ridden child who expresses primitive instincts
and emotions and in general resembles the picture of the epileptoid
personality.

The case of an adolescent boy, Peter, given in Appendix IV, illustrates one form of psychopathy. It is interesting because of the open
sexual tendencies expressed by the patient and the way in which they
were handled. It also shows how Soviet psychiatrists attribute a global
personality disturbance to organic factors operating early in life, while
Americans would be more likely to search for social and intrafamilial
factors.

Sukhareva's concept of personality disorders was shared by other
leading Russian psychiatrists I met. It is rare for Soviet psychiatrists to
diagnose psychopathy during childhood. Since observations over a
period of time are considered necessary to establish the diagnosis, it is
more usual to speak of a psychopathic-like syndrome which may eventually be established as some form of psychopathic personality or perhaps part of a schizophrenic process. Specific categories differing from
the American classification include the epileptoid personality and the
psychasthenic personality.

The Contribution
of Psychology

The role of the medical psychologist in the Soviet Union is to assist in
diagnosis, to conduct research, and to teach. M. P. Kononova wrote
about the work of the psychologist in a clinical setting (5). She said
psychology is too much isolated from medical practice, although
Pavlov, Korsakov, V. Kh. Kandinski, and I. M. Sechenov had long ago
shown the need for the psychiatrist to know about age characteristics
and normal development. Kononova attributed the isolation of psychology to the pedagogical decree in 1936, but reiterated Soviet criticism of testing from that era; she objected particularly to the use of
quantitative methods and the cultural bias of the Binet, which she
claimed penalized the child of working-class parents. She outlined the
aims of psychological research in a psychiatric clinic:

1. To gather psychological observations to be used in differential diagnosis.
2. Analysis of the structure of intellectual and personality defects.
3. Forensic psychiatry: determinations of the intellectual level of the patient, questions of responsibility, malingering.
4. School problems, special class for the retarded, etc.

The isolation of the clinical psychologist is indeed a fact. While patients in a psychoneurological hospital are frequently referred for psychological study, I never saw a psychologist attend the type of consultations described in previous sections, though the report of the psychologist would be included and frequently referred to in the discussion, particularly in difficult differential diagnostic problems. Further, while there was much talk about the need for an interdisciplinary approach to such problems as oligophrenia, epilepsy, and functional retardation of psychic development, the psychologist was usually omitted from the interdisciplinary list. In visits to several homes and schools for retarded children I was told about interdisciplinary commissions responsible for selecting patients for special educational programs (see, e.g., Chap. II above). In no case was it suggested that a psychologist sit on such a commission.

In her description of the work of the psychologist, Kononova emphasized the qualitative factors in examining a patient, particularly his behavior, his approach to a problem, his response to the intervention of the experimenter, and his attitude. She included sections on age characteristics, methodology (tests of perception, attention, memory, thought, understanding, imagination), investigation of schizophrenia, epilepsy, brain trauma, retardation, psychological disturbances of intellectual development, intellectual characteristics of physically weak children. Under inhibited psychological development is a description of "psychic infantilism," the Russian concept which most closely corresponds to the American idea of "learning inhibition." Kononova described these children as retaining the intellectual and emotional characteristics of younger children. They want always to play and never to work, are unable to sit and apply themselves to school assignments. They are frequently held back a grade or more and may be mistaken for retarded. On psychological investigation, their thought processes tend to be concrete, but they are able to grasp complex situations.

The psychologists in the Medical Psychology Department of the Psychoneurological Hospital for Children and Adolescents in Moscow demonstrated for me their method of examining a patient and evaluating the results. Many of the individual experiments, as they were called, resembled parts of standard tests familiar in the United States. Others were methods worked out by Soviet psychologists.

Vanya, a ten-year-old boy, was referred for aid in differential diagnosis between intermittent schizophrenia and cerebrasthenia secondary to posttraumatic encephalopathy. The clinical history revealed the child had entered the hospital with fatigue and behavior problems. The family history, pregnancy, birth, and early development were not remarkable. At four months, the patient fell from a bed, though there is no mention of head trauma at this time. At eleven months, he had dyspepsia. At seven years, he went to school and was able to study well, but his conduct was poor and he was restless. In the second and third class, his behavior was even worse and there were three episodes of loss of consciousness with no memory for the attacks. When he was nine, Vanya sustained a head injury, with an open head wound but no loss of consciousness. More recently, the child developed mannerisms and began demanding that people call him by his formal name, as if he were an adult. He had many fantasies which he would not share. In the hospital, he was placed on chlorpromazine, trifluoperazine, and magnesium sulfate. His clinical state improved.

When Vanya came in, he said he was ten years old, in the fourth class, that he had been in the hospital for two months because of bad behavior. He was unaware of any particular difficulty with studying. He did not present a surface picture of a psychotic disturbance.

The first experiments concerned memory and logical connections between words. First, immediate recall was tested with 10 words and the answer timed. Vanya correctly repeated 8 out of 10. Then, the following 15 words were given, slowly and distinctly: day, appointment, fire, rain, fight, troop, theater, mistake, strength, meeting, answer, grief, holiday, neighbor, difficulty. The patient was also given 28 cards with pictures and asked to choose the card which most closely described each word. At the end of the session, about 40 minutes later, Vanya was asked to name as many of the cards as he could. At first, he remembered 4; on successive trials, he remembered 7, 7, and 8. The qualitative analysis of this test included the child's reasons for associating a given picture to a card.

The second series of experiments had to do with abstract thinking. The first part was a list of paired words for which the patient was to give both similarities and differences and his reasons. Sometimes the words bore no relationship to each other, and the patient was expected to say so. Examples follow: birch–thicket, river–bird, bus–streetcar, cat–smoke, elephant–fly, glass–rooster. The second part was card sorting, or arranging pictures according to categories. Pictures were included of fruits, people, furnishings, tableware, plants (including flowers and vegetables), animals, birds, clothing. The experimenter asked the reason for the grouping quite early in the procedure. When Vanya was about three-quarters of the way through the task, he began to show fatigue and anxiety. At the end, he was asked what mark he would give himself.

The third series concerned attention. The experimenter presented the patient with a pack of 49 cards with 7 shapes and 7 colors. Each task was timed with a stopwatch: simple counting; counting and simultaneously arranging according to color; counting and arranging according to form; simultaneous counting and arranging cards on a chart, according to both color and form. Vanya showed anxiety very soon in this task and began fiddling with the stopwatch. Later, he showed more concern about how well he was doing.

In evaluating the results of these experiments, the psychologists stressed qualitative factors. For example, while testing memory in the first series, the kinds of associations the patient made between the words and the available pictures were carefully noted. Bizarre associations they mentioned were rooster–fire, because the rooster has a red comb on its head; answer–clock, because a clock ticks and therefore is answering; neighbor–factory, because the factory had two smokestacks which were neighbors.

The quality of the similarities for Vanya was quite variable. Some responses were considered adequate, some were not. Where there was no similarity, he found inappropriate ones.

The card-sorting test is considered good for demonstrating peculiarities of schizophrenic thought, since such patients will often choose inappropriate reasons for grouping. The number and quality of mistakes are noted and also the child's reaction to correction. This patient was thought to be able but not always willing to use the most usual, acceptable classifications. His distractability, especially playing with the stopwatch, was considered like the behavior of a five-year-old.

On the attention test, a normal child should be able to do the most complex task of counting and sorting for both color and form in the same time as the sum of the time for counting and sorting. Vanya took much too long for the more complex task because of his fatigue and impulsiveness, though these factors alone were not considered enough to explain his behavior.

In summarizing this evaluation, the psychologists agreed the child's responses were more characteristic of a schizophrenic thought disorder than of cerebrasthenia. However, the final diagnosis would be up to the doctors.

A second example of psychological investigation was the work of psychologists at Moscow Internat No. 31 (described in Chapter II) for boys and girls with neurological disease. The psychologists here analyzed educational problems and gave recommendations to the teaching staff. They demonstrated their method on one little girl with a complex problem of neurological disease with a strong emotional overlay.

The patient was Lisa, an eight-year-old girl who arrived at this school three weeks before on the recommendation of a special commission because she had been unable to function in regular school, where she had been for one semester in the first class. The history revealed the mother had tried to abort the pregnancy and the child was born at six and one-half months gestation, weighing one kg. She was for a long time in an incubator. Details of her development were not presented. Her situation was further complicated by difficult, unspecified home conditions.

Lisa was quite small for her age, giving the impression of a five-year-old. She was attractive, with short wavy auburn hair. When she entered the room where a group of doctors and psychologists had gathered, she was very shy and cowered in the corner. She was allowed to leave for a while and then return. This time, she smiled shyly and murmured a greeting but had to be gently encouraged to move into the room and sit down. All through the examination, she seemed troubled and unable to try, though not really restless. It was rather that she expected always to fail and in fact did fail frequently. She was very forlorn, but said she liked being at the school and wanted to stay, so she could learn better.

Some of the tasks given her are as follows:

1. Resembles digit symbol on the Wechsler-Bellevue. A symbol was placed inside each of five abstract shapes. There followed

a page of the shapes into which the patient was supposed to draw the correct symbol. The task was timed.

2. Difference. A series of four pictures was presented and the child was asked which one did not belong. Examples are three pictures of clothing with one of a tool; three flowers with one butterfly.

3. Simple arithmetic with plastic forms. The forms were placed in a row in front of the child. She was asked to close her eyes. Some of the forms were removed. The child was asked how many were gone.

4. Attention and immediate recall. A list of ten things were given and Lisa was asked to repeat as many as she could. The list is given several times, until the child recalls all of the words or it is clear no more will be recalled.

5. Card sorting. Here, the test was only used to test Lisa's form perception, since she had done very poorly on the digit-symbol type of experiment.

6. Resembles picture arrangement on the Wechsler-Bellevue. A series of three cards was presented for the child to arrange in correct sequence. Then the child was asked to tell the story shown by the pictures.

7. Tests of right-left understanding, including the ability to determine the right and left of the examiner, who faces the patient.

This patient failed abysmally in everything. She was extremely hesitant to try and gave up easily. No one would say the child was retarded, and everyone agreed she was very disturbed. It was abundantly clear she could never in her present state function in regular school where classes usually have 40 children. In the United States, every effort would be made to offer the child and her family individual psychotherapy, as well as to find a suitable educational program, but the help would probably be given on an outpatient basis if possible. In this instance, one would anticipate considerable improvement in Lisa in her special school setting because of the warmth and understanding shown by the staff.

The procedures described are capable of giving a comprehensive picture of intellectual functioning. There is considerable flexibility about which experiments to apply in a particular case. The refusal of Soviet psychologists to use quantitative, statistically standardized procedures makes their job difficult. In discussing American psychology, they were not only critical of the intelligence quotient but also seemed insufficiently aware that the American clinical psychologist, too, is concerned with qualitative analysis and the more experienced the psychologist, the more he emphasizes the patient's attitude and behavior and the points at which anxiety and fatigue disrupt performance.

Some psychologists expressed interest in personality testing, although the investigation of the personality was not routine. One Soviet worker, V. E. Kagan, reported the use of the TAT (Thematic Apperception Test) on a small group of patients 8–20 years old: eight patients with oligophrenia, three with psychopathic-like behavior, four with reactive states, and four with anxiety and depression (3). He considered the test useful, particularly for exposing special emotional experiences or family circumstances which may be connected with the development of the illness as well as the personality, and which the patient may not reveal to the doctor in the history.

In general, the clinical psychologist was confined in his role to study of intellectual functioning in patients who presented diagnostic problems. A notable exception was the Medical Psychology Department of the Psychoneurological Institute named for Bekhterev in Leningrad. Here, under psychiatric supervision, psychology students from Leningrad University were being taught medical psychology. I was told they would gradually begin to do some psychotherapy.

Summary and Conclusions

Soviet child psychiatrists emphasize diagnosis and classification more than we do in the United States. Russian case material presented to illustrate the major diagnostic categories seemed very similar to our own clinical problems at home. Two major exceptions in the adolescent age group are identity crises and drug problems, seen regularly in the United States and not in the Soviet Union. In the concluding chapter of this study, we return to the problem of character distortion and its relationship to culture. Problems in character development and identity formation do not so frequently reach the attention of Russian psychiatrists because they are considered part of normal development and are frequently brought to the attention of educators. Open manifestations of sexuality in adolescents are not well tolerated. Case material is presented which shows they are suppressed with drug therapy.

Of the influences on child psychiatry described in Chapter I, the German medical model was the most obvious one on the diagnostic thinking which I actually observed. One example of the tendency to equate psychiatric disease with brain disease is the importance attributed to residual organic brain damage in Soviet psychiatry. It is evoked as an explanation for neuroses and personality disorders as well as for organic brain syndromes recognized in American psychiatry. Russians refer frequently to psychic disturbances following infections such as grippe, chronic tonsillitis, or infantile dysentery. Rheumatic involvement of the central nervous system is believed to cause several different categories of psychic disturbances which have been described.

One key Soviet diagnostic point is the distinction between a process and a state, a distinction which seemed to me quite valid and useful. Psychogenetic factors are recognized but are far less emphasized than in American psychiatry. They are conceived in Soviet psychiatry as causing reactive *states* and distortions of character development. They are also recognized as precipitating factors in predisposed people for the formation of neurotic symptoms or for the manifest psychotic phase of a schizophrenic process. Psychodynamic formulations are lacking. There is no concept of a *psychogenic process* beyond the recognition that some states, originating in early conflict between the child and his environment, crystallize as character distortions in later development. The reaction of protest with its active and passive forms and vegetative manifestations is to me the most interesting of the Soviet psychogenetic concepts.

Soviet psychiatrists diagnose schizophrenia more readily than their American counterparts, because they emphasize the course of the illness over a period of time and recognize neurotic-like and psychopathic-like syndromes as frequently indicative of an insidious schizophrenic process. Some conditions American psychiatrists would call borderline states would be called slow, insidious schizophrenia in the Soviet Union. Some psychoses an American would not hesitate to call schizophrenia are thought to be periodic psychoses on a rheumatic or infectious base in Soviet practice.

The process of working up a patient and presenting the completed case to a senior consultant is not so different in the large teaching centers of the Soviet Union and the United States. Except for the absence of detailed descriptions of family interaction and parent-child relations, the case studies were careful and thorough. The practice of having the consultant interview the patient and sometimes the family as well seemed to me a valuable addition to the conference procedure. Neither the doctors nor the patients minded the lack of privacy. The Russian emphasis on clarity and precision in the summary statement of symptoms and syndromes gives a solid foundation for the diagnostic formulation. While there is not the conceptual framework of ego and superego functioning to assess which aspects of the personality are impaired by the disease and which are left intact, the close attention to the course of the illness over a period of time permits an evaluation of the breadth and depth of impairment and of the remaining strengths.

Finally, psychologists are more isolated in the clinical setting than their American counterparts. They contribute mostly to the diagnostic study of intellectual disturbances, emphasizing the qualitative aspects of a patient's performance. In my opinion, their contribution could be broadened, including more attention to affective factors and other aspects of personality. Also they could be more fully integrated into the diagnostic and therapeutic team.

IV

General
Treatment
Methods

The general aim of the treatment methods Soviet psychiatrists apply is to create a state of peace, calm, and relaxation. This stands in contrast to many American methods, especially those derived from the psycho-analytic model. In addition to classical psychoanalysis, for example, individual psychotherapy, family therapy, and group therapy all encourage exposure and mastery of disquieting conflicts, catharsis of strong feelings, and tolerance of anxiety. Sometimes, we say, things have to become more turbulent before they can get better. I found no such expectation in Soviet treatment.

In Soviet medicine, the term psychotherapy is used in two different senses: general psychotherapy and special psychotherapy, the latter described in Chapter V. In its general sense, psychotherapy should be practiced by everybody who surrounds the patient, whether he be physically ill or suffering from psychiatric disturbance. No special psychiatric team is considered necessary to apply the principles of general psychotherapy. In the third year of their undergraduate training, medical students learn the general principles of psychology and are taught some basic facts about the doctor-patient relationship, to be applied in all branches of medicine. In a psychiatric setting, general psychotherapy is the business of every member of the team. In the Soviet Union, the professionals involved are the psychiatrist, the *pedagog* or special educator, the nurse, and the upbringer or nurse's assistant. There is no professional social worker. Soviet doctors were unaware of the role of a psychiatric social worker in the United States. Soviet psychiatrists and pedagogs fulfill some social work functions. They provide an atmosphere of warmth and emotional support for the patient and include the family and sometimes the school in therapy aimed at helping those close to the patient to modify their attitudes and expectations.

A second broad aim of psychiatric treatment in the Soviet Union is to strengthen and reconstruct the child's relationship to the collective, especially the school and the peer group. The power of the collective is also used in the healing process by the pedagog in his daily work with patients in groups. It is curious that the Soviet educators I met showed no interest in the study of the dynamics of group formation or group process as it is known in American psychiatry and education.

Medication

Table 6 lists some common drugs used in Soviet and American child psychiatry where Soviet nomenclature differs from American terminology (7, 9). This discussion, where drugs are arranged according to their Soviet names, is limited to reporting those drugs I actually saw used in the hospitals and clinics. Where a medication was used on one of the patients described in the illustrative case material, a cross-reference is provided to furnish concrete examples of the application of several common agents.

Aminazine (generic name, chlorpromazine; synonyms, plegmazine, thorazine). This basic phenothiazine is widely used by Soviet psychiatrists in the treatment of schizophrenia. A. N. Korganova described, among the indications for the drug in schizophrenia, catatonic phenomena, excitement, affective tension, and fear accompanying hallucinations and sometimes delusional states (4). Chlorpromazine was also recommended in the treatment of symptomatic psychoses due to infectious illness or a general state of fear and excitement where hallucinatory experiences dominate the clinical picture. Sukhareva recommended use of chlorpromazine for "borderline states," including phobias, neuroses, fear, and obsessional states (5). In personality disorders, chlorpromazine is considered particularly good for overactivity and excitement or impulse disorders of either a sexual or aggressive kind. Sukhareva said the drug was introduced in her clinic in 1956.

The use of chlorpromazine to control sexual manifestations deserves

Table 6. Comparative Nomenclature: Common Drugs Used in Soviet and American Psychiatry

Soviet name	Generic name	Common synonyms
Aminazine	Chlorpromazine	Plegmazine, thorazine
Amizil	Benactyzine	Diazil
Doxine	Diazepam	Valium
Elenium	Chlordiazepoxide	Librium
Endoksin	Meprobamate	Meprotan, andoksin, equanil
Ethaperazine	Perphenazine	Trilafon
Haloperidol	Haloperidol	Haldol, halol, haloperazin, sereans
Imizin	Imipramine	Trofanil, melipramin
Iprazid	Ipraniazid	Marsilid
Luminal	Phenobarbital	
Mazheptil	Thioproperazine	Thioperazine
Mellaril	Thioridazine	Melleril
Meridel	Methylphenidate	Ritalin
Neuleptil	Propericiazine	
Pavlov's mixture	Caffeine benzoate and sodium bromide	
Phenamine	Amphetamine	Benzedrine
Tizertzine	Levomepromazine	Methotrimeprazine
Triftazine	Trifluoperazine	Stelazine
Triptizol	Amitriptyline	Elavil

special comment. Chlorpromazine was prescribed to control masturbation in sanatoria and schools for neurotic children and in psychoneurological hospitals. In the case of Peter (App. IV), chlorpromazine was used to control the urge to masturbate and to control his sexual excitement in the presence of women. In the case of Lydia (Chap. III), chlorpromazine therapy was used to diminish her sexual preoccupation, which had been the reason for her admission to the sanatorium.

The use of chlorpromazine for fear and excitement is illustrated in several of our cases. Sasha (App. IV), was a child with psychotic symptoms, excitement, and obsessive preoccupations where it seemed that a schizophrenic process might be superimposed on an organic deficit. Chlorpromazine was also used in two cases with a probable diagnosis of cerebrasthenia: Vera (discussed in Chap. III to illustrate rheumatic cerebrasthenia) and Vanya (see Chap. III, discussion of psychological testing).

The dosage recommended for preschool children by V. P. Kudryat-seva (personal conversation) was 25 mg once or twice a day. Sukhareva suggested 1–2 mg per kg of body weight in a course of treatment lasting two or three months. In children 7 to 10, the dosage range is usually 50–75 mg. In prepubertal and adolescent patients age 10–14, the dosage is usually 50–75 mg and in older adolescents 14–17, 100–200 mg (5). These doses are somewhat lower than those recommended by various American workers who stress that children can tolerate higher doses per unit of body weight with fewer extrapyramidal effects. Barbara Fish, for example, advocated 1 mg per pound per 24 hours as an average dose with a range of 0.5–4.0 mg per pound (6, p. 4).

Soviet doctors frequently used chlorpromazine with other drugs, especially trifluoperazine, in the treatment of schizophrenia. Sometimes dehydrating agents, typically magnesium, were used if the cerebrasthenic syndrome was present and thought to be based on the sequelae of brain trauma. Chlorpromazine was also combined with other calming agents, for example, phenobarbital and calcium gluconate, a practice with which I am unfamiliar in the United States.

Bromides. Bromides were prescribed in the form of Pavlov's mixture, which contains caffeine benzoate, 0.5 gms, and sodium bromide, 1.0 gms, in 200 gms of distilled water (9). Pavlov's mixture is prescribed in children with neurotic disturbances such as restlessness, difficulties in sleeping, and fearfulness. In the sanatorium for neurotic children at Pavlovsk, near Leningrad, Pavlov's mixture was used for nearly all the children for the first two or three weeks of their stay. It was also occasionally used with luminal in epilepsy. Sometimes Pavlov's mixture was combined with other medications such as librium or calcium gluconate.

Calcium gluconate. Calcium gluconate was combined with librium, phenobarbital, or chlorpromazine in a variety of neurotic states and personality disorders.

Elenium (generic name, chlordiazepoxide; synonym, librium). Librium was used with other medications in a variety of neurotic states, including enuresis, and particularly frequently in tics. It was also used in schizophrenia where apprehension and fearfulness were prominent symptoms. Librium was prescribed for Sasha (App. IV) along with chlorpromazine to control his excitability and apprehension. Librium combined with chlorpromazine was also prescribed for Boris (Chap. III), who was showing symptoms of psychosis secondary to grippe with fear, restlessness, and excitement. Librium and chlorpromazine were a favorite combination for fear and restlessness. Finally, librium was given with levomepromazine to Victor, whose moodiness, irritability, and diffuse fearfulness were felt to be symptoms of pseudoneurotic schizophrenia (Chap. III). In one case of anorexia nervosa, Ira, librium was prescribed in combination with insulin (App. IV).

Haloperidol (generic name, haloperidol; synonyms, haldol, halol, haloperazin, and sereans). Haloperidol is a diphenyl methane derivative of butyrophenone. Soviet doctors used Hungarian and French preparations in schizophrenia where paranoid ideas and auditory hallucinations are prominent. In contrast to American practice, in which the drug was still not approved for use in children in 1970 (except for Gilles de la Tourette syndrome), Soviet doctors were using haloperidol for younger children in excited states and for retarded children with behavior disorders. In this group, the recommended dosage according to Kudryatseva (personal conversation) was 50–60 mg a day. Haloperidol was also frequently used in combined therapy with trifluoperazine in schizophrenia of adolescence with either paranoid ideas or auditory hallucinations. It was combined with levomepromazine when agitation and fear were prominent.

Insulin. Insulin coma treatment was still used in the Soviet Union in 1969 for the beginning stages of schizophrenia in childhood and adolescence, particularly paranoid and pseudoneurotic forms. Children were observed undergoing insulin coma therapy in one adolescent department of the Moscow Psychoneurological Hospital for Children and Adolescents and also in the Psychoneurological Hospital named for Pavlov in Kiev. Insulin coma may also be tried in cases that do not respond to chlorpromazine. In the case of anorexia nervosa reported by Rotiniyan (Chap. III) insulin therapy was used, as this illness was considered part of a schizophrenic process. In the cases of anorexia nervosa I personally observed, subcoma insulin was administered in combination with other agents (App. IV).

Luminal (generic name, phenobarbital). Soviet doctors use phenobarbital as we do in the treatment of epilepsy and to some degree for behavior problems and neurotic manifestations such as enuresis and fears. Sometimes it was prescribed in combination with dehydrating agents, with calcium gluconate, or with chlorpromazine.

Magnesium sulfate. Magnesium is the commonest dehydrating agent, used in a variety of clinical states when it is felt that hydrocephalus even in a mild compensated form is present. It is combined with numerous other agents depending on the primary symptoms. The frequent use of dehydrating agents in psychiatric syndromes in the Soviet Union differs from American practice. This reflects the Soviet conviction that many clinical psychiatric states are due to the residuals of organic brain damage (Chap. III).

Mazheptil (generic name, thioproperazine, synonyms, thioperazine, thioproemazine). Mazheptil was mainly used in little children with early schizophrenia, old forms of schizophrenia with a deep disturbance and residual defect, and adolescent catatonic states. The dose suggested for little children (personal conversation with Kudryatseva) was 5 mg daily.

> Anna, an adolescent girl, was observed in a Leningrad hospital. She had experienced the sudden onset of acute fears while she was with her mother on a summer vacation in the south. Although her mother had been previously seriously ill, she was recovering when the child began to develop fear for her mother's health. Anna was hospitalized that fall when she began to hear voices and was unable to stay in school. Since evidence was found of a rheumatic carditis, the differential diagnosis lay between a rheumatic psychosis and schizophrenia. The psychotic symptoms disappeared, only to return in the middle of the winter following a visit from her mother. Anna became fearful, hallucinated, and developed catatonic symptoms, including waxy flexibility. When we saw her, she was lying in bed, glassy-eyed. When her arm was lifted, it would remain motionless in midair wherever you left it. She fixated her gaze on me as if aware of a stranger but would not respond. She was receiving 20 mg a day of thioproperizine. She was interesting from a diagnostic point of view, since I would not have hesitated to call her schizophrenic, but her doctor said that her diagnosis was not established (cf. Chap. III).

Mellaril (generic name, thioridazine). Mellaril is a phenothiazine derivative with a dosage similar to chlorpromazine. It was used by Soviet doctors to control sexual expression in older children and hyperkinetic disturbances in younger children. In states of excitement, mellaril might be combined with chlorpromazine or used instead of chlorpromazine if the latter were poorly tolerated. Mellaril is known to have fewer extrapyramidal affects than chlorpromazine.

Meprobamate (generic name, meprobamate; synonyms, meprotan, endoksin, andoksin, equanil). As in the United States, meprobamate is prescribed in a variety of neurotic states and in some symptomatic psychoses, the major indication being a presence of anxiety or specific fears.

Neuleptil (generic name, unknown; synonym, propericiazine). Soviet psychiatrists described propericiazine as a French preparation which they prescribed for severe behavior disorders of a preschizophrenic or psychopathic-like type. One example was a child with an encephalopathy on a posttraumatic or postinfectious basis. The major symptoms were headaches, dizziness, poor schoolwork, sensitivity to noise, and difficult behavior which included stealing. It was also used in another child with a more severe behavior disturbance who had many fantasies which bordered on the delusional. On the adolescent ward of the Moscow Psychoneurological Hospital for Children and Adolescents, propericiazine was prescribed in combination with levomepromazine or with chlorpromazine.

Triftazine (generic name, trifluoperazine; synonym, stelazine). This phenothiazine derivative was frequently prescribed, as in the United States, for schizophrenia with hallucinations or pseudoneurotic symptoms. In the cases I observed, trifluoperazine was always prescribed with other drugs: haloperidol in paranoid states with or without hallucinations; chlorpromazine in an adolescent with pseudoneurotic schizophrenia. The combination of trifluoperazine and chlorpromazine was given to Sasha (App. IV), whose clinical picture was one of a psychotic process superimposed on an organic base. The combination was also used for Vanya (Chap. III), in whom there was a problem in differential diagnosis between cerebrasthenia and schizophrenia. Trifluoperazine was sometimes combined with librium as in the case of Ivan, the adolescent schizophrenic presented in Appendix IV, and in many other patients with pseudoneurotic schizophrenia. Occasionally trifluoperazine would be combined with levomepromazine if anxiety and apprehension were particularly prominent. Cases where trifluoperazine was used in nonpsychotic states included Olga, the adolescent girl with anorexia nervosa, who was also receiving subcoma insulin. (App. IV).

Triptizol (generic name, amitriptyline; synonym, elavil). This tricyclic antidepressant was occasionally used in states of fear and depression. One boy receiving amitriptyline had headaches and night fears with a paranoid tinge and little evidence of depression. Ivan was receiving 100 mg daily of amitriptyline in combination with levomepromazine at one point in the therapy for his ongoing schizophrenic process (App. IV). This combination of drugs was chosen because Ivan was experiencing states of depression—feeling that he would never recover—accompanied by considerable anxiety.

Tizertzine (generic name, levomepromazine; synonyms, methotrimeprazine, nozinan, noridol). This phenothiazine derivative is described in American literature as having strong analgesic properties as well as a tranquillizing effect. While levomepromazine is used more in the United States for its analgesic effect, in the Soviet Union it is prescribed for psychotic states and is widely used in emergency psychiatric aid because of its strong and rapid sedative action (1, p. 20). It is also said by Soviet doctors to regulate the mood without a depressive effect. It was being used in various neurotic states in a Moscow sanatorium and was recommended by K. S. Lebedinskaya in a lecture to trainees on delirium and twilight states and hallucinations in the symptomatic psychoses. Levomepromazine was used in schizophrenia where there was a strong component of anxiety and moodiness or depression as in the case of Ivan (App. IV). Victor, the boy with pseudoneurotic schizophrenia in Chapter III, also received levomepromazine with librium. He had diffuse anxiety states, fear without obvious cause, mood fluctuations. Some patients experiencing fearful hallucinations are given levomepromazine in combination with haloperidol.

Much emphasis was placed on medication in the treatment I observed in the Soviet Union. This was particularly true of the handling of neurotic states and personality disorders, both under sanatorium conditions and in the outpatient clinics. There was more use of major tranquilizers in such conditions than I am accustomed to. Medications not widely used in the United States included Pavlov's mixture, calcium gluconate, dehydrating agents, haloperidol, thioproperizine, and levomepromazine. Dosage levels of antipsychotic drugs, chlorpromazine in particular, tended to be lower than those many workers use in the United States. Combinations of drugs were used frequently. I heard no discussions of the use of stimulant drugs, except for the caffeine in Pavlov's mixture to achieve better cortical control and integration. Neither was there any interest in the use of lithium for manic attacks in adults or emotional lability in adolescents. At Kashenko, an adult psychoneurological hospital, lithium is not approved.

Physical
Therapy

Baths. Russian medical folklore includes a belief in the healing powers of naturally occurring waters. At Sochi, a health resort on the Black Sea, elaborate therapeutic regimes are built around the healing powers of "Matsesta water." Sanatoria exist at resorts for both adults and children. Financial assistance is given to patients recommended by their physicians for sanatorium treatment. I wondered whether such a system, linking rest and vacation with problems of health and illness, might foster secondary gain in neurotic states with somatic symptoms. Some Russian psychiatrists said they did not believe in sending children to the warm southern climates, since they found them worse after they returned home.

Bath therapy is used in the sea resorts, in sanatoria for neurotic children in the major cities, and in the mental hospitals. Sukhareva, in discussing the treatment of borderline states, recommended tepid water for stimulation and hot water for a calming effect (5). The tepid baths are prescribed in children who show sluggishness, apathy, and diminished appetite. The overreactive, restless children are given warm baths. Sea baths with warmed water are recommended in preparation for seabathing. At one sanatorium in Pavlovsk near Leningrad, each child received bath therapy fifteen minutes a day.

Specific cases in which bath therapy was used in the neurology department of a general pediatric hospital in Kiev included one patient with restlessness, tics, and a history of rheumatic infection. This child was also receiving medications. Another preschool child on this ward with restlessness, enuresis, and behavior problems was receiving a combination of bath therapy and electrophoresis.

Electrophoresis. A galvanic current is used in the process of iontophoresis to introduce ions of medicinal value into the organism (5). The ions chiefly used are calcium, bromide, novocaine for relief of pain, and sometimes phosphorus or iodine. Electrophoresis is used for its sedative effect in restless children in hospitals and sanatoria. One example was "a galvanic collar" with bromides, vitamins, and glucose for an 11-year-old girl hospitalized because of restlessness and behavior problems. Electrophoresis is also used in cases of enuresis accompanied by other signs of anxiety. In Forest School Sanatorium No. 9 in Moscow, it was claimed that the treatment for enuresis was over 90 percent effective where outpatient treatment had failed: a combination of electrogalvanic stimulation and medication, particularly strychnine. At a sanatorium in Kiev, N. I. Krasnogorski's regime for enuresis was recommended: no liquids after 3:00 p.m.; record time but do not awaken child if he wets at night; electrophoresis with novocaine and medication including strychnine.

Electroson. A distinctive Soviet treatment was electrical sleep or *electroson.* Indications included psychopathic-like behavior in children, neurotic states, rheumatic involvement of the central nervous system, sleep disturbances, and motor restlessness. Usually electroson was combined with medication and a regular regime. The method I observed in several places was to induce a state of quiet and relaxation in four or five patients lying down in bed with subdued light and quiet surroundings. A weak, alternating electrical current was passed through the brain between electrodes placed on the frontal and occipital regions. The electrical stimulation, which continued for thirty minutes, was experienced by the patient as pleasant and relaxing. The patients appeared drowsy but did not lose consciousness. They were encouraged to sleep an hour or so following the treatment, which was given five days a week, for a month at a time.

Physiotherapy. Departments of physiotherapy offered courses of massage and exercise. This was an important part of therapy in one special school for children who had primarily neurological disorders. The atmosphere surrounding the administration of physical forms of therapy was warm and supportive. Children were handled in small groups with plenty of personnel. The general psychotherapeutic effect of such care, aside from the effect of the specific physical treatment, should not be underestimated. The gratification of passive and dependent longings was evident, though never discussed. Sometimes I wondered what could possibly motivate the patients to get well and return to usual conditions of Soviet life!

Regime

A balanced schedule of daily activities including rest, schoolwork, physical exercise, and recreation in a milieu where order and quiet prevail is considered extremely important in Soviet psychiatric treatment. The regime is used in sanatoria, special schools, and mental hospitals. The general characteristics of a representative sanatorium regime were outlined by V. A. Gamza, director of Children's Psychoneurological Sanatorium No. 44 in Moscow (2). He advocated a daily schedule with a balance of activity and rest to enable the formation of new, healthier connections in the central nervous system. The children are under the constant observation of the personnel, who preserve a quiet, stable atmosphere. School lessons are reduced from the usual 45 minutes in regular school to 35 minutes with a recreation period after each two lessons. Educational measures are applied as much as possible on an individualized basis. Children enter this sanatorium for a limited three-month stay. They are divided into classes of 17 to 25 children in the first three days after the doctor, the educator, and speech worker have become acquainted with each child and his parents.

Sanatorium No. 44 was opened in 1930 at Sokolniki, a section in the northern part of Moscow near a wooded park. In 1965, the sanatorium moved to different quarters. As urban Moscow grows, these sanatoria and special schools tend to move farther from the center of the city, to maintain contact with nature. Sanatorium No. 44 in the winter of 1969 was a 350-bed complex of three large green buildings on the edge of the city with a forest behind the school. Nearby was an urban development of new apartment buildings, at the end of the streetcar line. Inside, the buildings seemed cold and drab though extremely clean, with large empty spaces. There were boys and girls in classes 1–8. The children slept in wards with no personal privacy. The atmosphere was subdued. During recreation periods, the children had free access to the forest, a recreation area for residents of the region.

Indications for admission to the sanatorium were outlined by Dr. Gamza (2):

1. Neuroses, asthenic states after infection or illness (rheumatic fever, tuberculosis).
2. Neurotic-like or asthenic states and cases of inhibited development following intrauterine damage, birth trauma, postnatal head trauma, residuals after central nervous system illnesses (encephalitis meningitis).
3. Neuroses, reactive states, pathological character development due to unfavorable upbringing, psychic trauma of an acute nature or of a more protracted nature.
4. Children with innate nervousness (neuropathy). Children with complex characterological structure requiring individual training and education.
5. Mild forms of neurotic-like mental illness, including pseudo-neurotic schizophrenia.
6. Mild psychopathic-like states, epileptiform syndromes of varying etiology.
7. Speech disturbances (stuttering, dysgraphia, dyslalia, and others) accompanying more established illnesses. In Soviet terminology, reading and writing disorders are included.

Contraindications to admission include the following:

1. Manifest mental illness with gross conduct disturbance.
2. All degrees of intellectual retardation.
3. Manifest psychopathy and psychopathic-like states.
4. Severe central nervous system damage.
5. Frequent epileptic and epileptiform seizures.
6. Serious physical illness requiring special treatment.
7. General contraindications for all children's sanatoria.

Dr. Gamza enumerated frequent psychic symptoms encountered in children admitted to Sanatorium No. 44: sleep disturbances, variations of appetite, behavior problems (including both lowered or excessive motor activity, excitability, proneness to conflict), disturbances in the emotional and volitional spheres (lability of mood, fears, a tendency to be easily offended, obtrusiveness in personal relationships, withdrawal, impressionability, lack of self-confidence, etc.) (2). Intellectual disturbances included inability to function academically at an age-appropriate level, poor memory, shortened attention span, speech disturbances, inability to help oneself. Additional specific symptoms frequently encountered were headaches, dizziness, tics, compulsive moments, enuresis, stuttering, masturbation, nail biting, seizures, and twilight states.

The team at Sanatorium No. 44 consisted of the director, a special educator, a speech therapist, nurses, and assistants. Work with parents was one function of the team (2). On admission, when the doctor and educator interviewed the parents and the child, the educator focused on how the child had behaved at home and at school, difficulties the child had experienced in family living, and difficulties in school. If school problems were important, the educator might seek direct contact with the teachers at the child's school. The doctor focused on the general medical background and previous treatment. The parents continued to participate, both through individual conversations with the doctor and the educator and on parental visiting days in group meetings in which general recommendations about upbringing and helping children to learn were discussed. The active participation of parents was further encouraged by the fact that the sanatorium stay is limited to three months and the parents are expected to resume the care of their child. At discharge, recommendations may be given to the parents and the school for further management.

At Sanatorium No. 44, consultation for the staff was available with senior people. Professor Kovalev was kind enough to include me in a consultation with Martia, a rebellious adolescent who like her sisters in

America was leading her parents a merry chase (App. IV). The case was delightful, because the youngster seemed so familiar and because through Martia we get a glimpse of what Soviet youth think of American culture. Martia shows a problem diagnosed psychogenic and judged amenable to treatment through the sanatorium regime. Although interviewing technique is underemphasized in the Soviet Union, many of the professors were very skilled at it, and this interview with Martia is a good example.

Another type of setting in which children with "borderline states" are treated is Sanatorium Forest School No. 9 in Moscow, an institution similar to the one described by Skolnick in the American literature (10). This forest school was built in 1956 in the country; by 1969, it was surrounded with apartment buildings, and no wooded areas remained. There were 325 boys and girls in classes two to eight. In contrast to the sanatorium, the children spent Saturday and Sunday at home. Each class had 25 children, the building was cold and barren, although the sleeping wards were smaller than in the sanatorium; 8–10 children instead of 30.

The school was saturated with communist propaganda to a degree that I had not seen in other settings. There was a special Lenin room, like a chapel. Children prepared wall displays on various aspects of the life of Lenin and his contribution to the building of the Soviet state. There was one huge display in which macabre hooded figures were labeled members of the Ku Klux Klan from the United States to illustrate the evils of Christianity. I told Vasili Akimovich, the director, that the Ku Klux Klan was not a very important aspect of life in the United States, since it distressed me to see the children exposed to this aspect of American society and no other. There was no opportunity to discuss this further. The general atmosphere seemed warm and accepting of the children, who were subdued and orderly in their behavior and obviously not permitted much freedom of expression.

Forest schools such as No. 9 were institutions administered through the Ministry of Education where children with "borderline states" were admitted for an academic year. They usually returned to regular school after one year, exceptions being children admitted to the seventh class. Since it would be difficult to complete the eighth class in regular school, some remained for two years. The emphasis was on education rather than on treatment. The Moscow forest school system included three for neurotic children and nine others for physical illnesses such as tuberculosis and rheumatic disease, although these were decreasing in the Soviet Union. In contrast, the sanatorium described above was a medical institution under the Ministry of Health with the focus on treatment and the secondary emphasis on education. Children remained in the sanatorium for only three months. The two types of institutions were similar in utilizing the therapeutic power of the regime.

Indications for admission to the forest school were like those for the sanatorium:

1. Reactive states, neuroses, asthenic and cerebrasthenic states of various etiology.
2. Compensated mental illness, chiefly schizophrenia.
3. Neurotic-like states on an organic basis.

Contraindications include:

1. Psychopathic-like behavior and psychopathy.
2. All degrees of oligophrenia.
3. Physical disabilities requiring special care.

Children were selected for forest schools and sanatoria by a special commission of the Central City Psychoneurological Dispensary for Children and Adolescents: psychiatrists from the dispensary, directors of the forest schools or sanatoria, and special educators attached to the school and trained to work with emotionally disturbed children. Children were referred to this commission from the various regions of Moscow by schools or psychoneurologists in the polyclinics. Psychiatric reports and school reports were available. Important decisions about children are made, in accordance with the collective emphasis in Soviet society, by groups rather than by individuals.

The director of Forest School No. 9, Vasili Akimovich, was enthusiastic about the results with the children under his care. On one of the upper floors was an exhibit showing each forest school in Moscow and pedagogical methods used. These exhibits emphasized correct political indoctrination along with an individual approach to the problems of each child. Medications were used to some degree, and there was a department of physiotherapy. The forest school was closer to a regular school in its program and general demands on the students than the sanatorium. The two following cases indicate the kinds of problems handled in a forest school setting.

Valodia was an eight-year-old boy admitted because of fatigue, irritability, inattentiveness, enuresis, headaches, fears, and poor appetite. He was an only child. The pregnancy, delivery, and neo-natal period were normal. Before he was a year old, he had pneumonia twice. At around five years, he had an adenoidectomy. At kindergarten, Valodia experienced day wetting and played with children younger than himself. In school, he experienced easy fatigability and the gradual onset of the other symptoms.

Physical examination was not remarkable. Although the skull x-ray revealed some asymmetry, there was no definite pathology. Mental status revealed a quiet, inhibited boy whose contact with reality was not impaired. In the forest school, his behavior was good but he did not relate well to the other children. He was home-sick, particularly missing his grandmother. He began to masturbate after admission to the school and chlorpromazine was started.

Treatment of the neuresis claimed to be 95 percent effective, involved physiotherapy, electrophoresis, and various medications, one including strychnine. The doctors said they encouraged Valodia to discuss his fears although they did not elaborate. He was selected for admission because the doctor at his polyclinic was familiar with the school and its effectiveness. He had been treated as an outpatient for his enuresis without any effect. His fatigue and inattentiveness had made it difficult for him to work well in school.

The second case illustrates how the forest school regime is used for schizophrenic children in a mild phase of their illness.

Lena was a 16-year-old girl admitted for periodic headaches, social withdrawal, and general apathy. She was an only child. Her mother experienced toxicosis during the pregnancy and there was evidence of asphyxia at birth. During the first year, Lena had severe measles and mumps with elevated temperature. Then she developed normally until the fourth class, when she had grippe, followed by easy fatigability, general slowness, and apathy. Because of these symptoms, she entered a mental hospital when she was eight, and a diagnosis was made of a postinfectious psychosis.

Following discharge, Lena made a satisfactory adjustment until puberty at 14, when she began to feel poorly and became irritable with her parents. She fell ill with pneumonia. She was under close observation in her polyclinic and was presented to Professor Suk-hareva, who confirmed the diagnosis of insidious schizophrenia. When Lena began to refuse to go to school, she was recommended for admission to the forest school. Medication included trifluoperizine, 6 mg daily, and 50 mg of chlorpromazine, continued after she came to the forest school where she showed signs of improvement. She attended classes willingly and showed evidence of a good intellect.

Lena was one of 15 schizophrenics out of 325 children who attended this forest school. Schizophrenics must be in a compensated state to be eligible for admission. Soviet psychiatrists, consider the protected environment of the forest school preventive of more serious decompensation.

The doctors here spoke of handling one severe behavior problem by fostering a close relationship between the child and the staff which was subsequently extended to include the relationship of the child with the collective. This boy had a schizophrenic mother and was himself particularly vulnerable. He remained at the forest school for two and one-half years, then managed to enroll in a music school. In addition to warmth and affection, the staff encouraged his interests in drawing and music.

I asked about how the complaint of headache was handled, since many aspects of Soviet therapy seemed to me to encourage somatization. The doctor said that first they would try to find the reason for the headaches. They would use dehydrating agents if hydrocephalus was found. Usually headaches diminish because of the regime, which they felt was the most effective agent.

I sensed a cooperative spirit among the staff. Doctors spoke of observing in classes, talking to teachers about a child's performance and capability. The upbringers, too, had access to the medical staff.

Two other similar institutions were visited. One was a small sanatorium for 75 children in the first three classes, housed in an old mansion on a wooded hill in the center of Kiev, the capital of the Ukrainian Republic. Here, the emphasis was on treatment; each child received bath therapy everyday and many received medication. Lessons did not start until the afternoon, and school demands were held to a minimum. The other institution was Sanatorium Forest School No. 2 in Pavlovsk, a suburb of Leningrad. This school received 150 children with neuroses and personality disorders from the city of Leningrad and its environs.

Table 7 summarizes the comparative features of the four institutions: two sanatoria and two forest schools. All accepted children with neurotic states, characterological problems, and compensated psychotic states. They refused the more severe forms of behavior disorder associated with psychopathy or overt psychoses. They varied in size: 75–450 beds. They took both boys and girls and emphasized a balanced, regular schedule of schoolwork, rest, and physical activity. While the details of the regimes vary, the regime itself is valued. According to Sukhareva, "Exact rhythmical repetition of one and the same processes organizes the conditioned reflex activity of the nervous system, enables the establishment of a specific dynamic stereotype, which in its turn is important for the harmonization and calming of the overly excitable psychic activity of the child" (5, p. 389). The regimes all leave little unstructured time. Sukhareva claimed children with inadequate social and work habits do not have the capability for independent organization of their free time.

In each institution, the children were given four meals a day. In some cases, regular school lessons were supplemented by medical work with a speech therapist. Physical culture, with calisthenics and gymnastics, was an important part of the recreational activity programs. The two forest schools, scheduling five classes a day (except for four classes a day in one of them for younger children) emphasized schoolwork more than the two sanatoria did. The specialized educational approach to the children was considered as important as the regularity of the regime.

Role of the
Educator

In the Soviet system, the *pedagog* or educator is largely responsible for carrying out the therapeutic regime in mental hospitals and sanatoria, in close cooperation with the doctor. The educators I saw working with disturbed children were on the whole dedicated, gifted young women with personal warmth, assertiveness, and an intuitive responsiveness to children. Their special training begins after ten years of regular school and is offered in teacher training institutes. The one in Moscow is staffed by the Institute of Defectology. Courses include education, child development, and special techniques for handling exceptional children. Some educators become specialists in retardation, deafness, blindness, as well as psychiatric illness.

Sukhareva, describing the general principles of pedagogical work, cited common symptoms in various types of psychopathy which require special educational measures: psychomotor restlessness, overexcitability, egocentricity, poorly formed habits necessary for life in the collective, diminished work capability, and sometimes a negative atti-

Table 7. Regimes at Sanatoria and Forest Schools

	Children's Psychoneurological Sanatorium, Kiev	Sanatorium Forest School No. 2, Pavlovsk	Sanatorium No. 44, Moscow	Sanatorium Forest School No. 9, Moscow	
				Lower School	Middle School
7:30 AM					Get up
8:00	Get up	Get up Exercises	Get up Breakfast	Get up Breakfast (8:10)	
8:30	Breakfast	Breakfast (8:40)	Lesson 1 (35 min)		Breakfast (8:30)
9:00		Lesson 1 (40 min)	Rest (10 min) Lesson 2 (35 min)	Lesson 1 (40 min)	Lesson 1 (40 min)
9:30	Outdoor recreation	Rest (10 min) Lesson 2 (40 min)	Speech and language work, recreation (9:50)	Rest (10 min) Lesson 2 (40 min)	Rest (10 min) Lesson 2 (40 min)
10:00					
10:30	Physiotherapy, hydro-therapy, music	Rest (10 min) Lesson 3 (40 min)		Recreation (60 min)	Rest (10 min) Lesson 3 (40 min)
11:00					
11:30		Rest (10 min) Lesson 4 (40 min)		Lesson 3 (40 min)	Recreation (60 min)
12:00					
12:30 PM		Rest (10 min) Lesson 5 (40 min)	Dinner (12:45)	Rest (10 min) Lesson 4 (40 min)	Lesson 4 (40 min)

Time					
1:00	Dinner	Recreation		Dinner	Rest (10 min)
1:30	Nap (1:40)		Nap	Nap	Lesson 5 (40 min)
2:00		Dinner			Dinner
2:30		Nap			Nap
3:00			Snack (3:15)		
3:30	Lesson 1 (35 min)		Recreation (3:45)		
4:00	Snack			Snack	Snack
4:30	Lesson 2 (35 min)	Snack		Homework and Pioneer work	Homework and Pioneer work
5:00	Outdoor recreation	Homework	Lesson 3 (5:10, 35 min)		
5:30			Homework (5:45)		
6:00	Lesson 3 (35 min)				
6:30	Recreation	Recreation	Supper		
7:00	Free time		Preparation of speech assignment		
7:30	Supper	Supper	Quiet hour	Supper	
8:00		Free time		Games and library	Supper
8:30					Games and library
9:00	Bed	Bed	Prepare for bed	Prepare for bed	Prepare for bed
9:30			Sleep	Sleep	Sleep
10:00					

tude towards work and study (5, p. 388). Although Sukhareva said a theoretical rationale for pedagogical work with disturbed children has not yet been worked out, she related it to the regime. A correct balance between rest and work she regarded as specific therapy for restlessness and overexcitement, along with physiotherapy and pharmacotherapy.

At Sanatorium No. 44 in Moscow, Dr. Gamza and his staff worked out detailed instructions for the educators to follow in their daily work with the children. The following discussion is based on his unpublished paper (2). My personal reaction is expressed only in the concluding paragraph.

The educators begin their duties in the morning, when the children get up, receiving reports on night behavior from the nurses. Bed wetters are handled tactfully, but are made to feel that they must cooperate actively with the therapy. A child might be told that he himself is partly to blame, for he ran around too much yesterday evening at the outdoor period and became overtired. The children are helped to acquire neat personal habits, within their capabilities, and are encouraged to help each other. Children on medication are observed carefully and any symptoms or behavioral changes are reported to the doctor. After inspection for cleanliness, the children file in for breakfast. They must be absolutely quiet before they are allowed to sit down. They are expected to finish one course before starting another. Sometimes children with eating problems may be left in charge of the nurse. After breakfast, the educator helps the children receive any necessary treatment from the doctor. After class work with the teachers, the children go with the educator for outdoor recreation. The children walk quietly in pairs to the play area. The educator organizes games and activities, always controlling the level of excitement and activity. Conflicts between children are prevented wherever possible or are resolved by the educator. At rest hour, an effort is made to prevent the children from masturbating by requiring them to lie on their right sides. With the exception of formal class time, an educator is with the children during all of their waking hours.

In the classroom, the atmosphere is orderly. The children sit in the same place every day. They must answer the teacher standing. Some children with special needs may have individual instructions. In warm weather, classes may be held in the fresh air. The program includes physical culture and sports.

The individualized approach to each patient, within the framework of the collective, requires thorough knowledge of each child and an understanding of the collective. To assist the teacher in developing an individualized approach, there are frequent consultations with the doctor and conferences within the department. Special consultations may be held with experts from the teacher training institute. Teachers are encouraged to increase their qualifications by attending seminars, reading current literature, and, above all, by the study of the individual patient. Children are stimulated to perform well by a daily marking system. The teacher gives the academic marks while the marks for conduct are given by a class monitor, appointed daily. The marks are displayed publicly on a chart: red for good, blue for satisfactory, and black for unsatisfactory. Emphasis is placed on the need for agreement between the educator and other personnel, since lack of agreement is recognized to have a disorganizing effect on the children. Much undesirable behavior is avoided through control of leisure time and arousing the child's interest in studies, workshop activities, and "social work."

With each new group of children, the educator must work to create the collective. This is difficult because of the nature of the symptoms, especially excitability and egocentricity. At the beginning, the educator makes it clear this is not a camp but a sanatorium where children come to study and to receive treatment. The children are taught to ignore symptoms in each other such as stuttering, tics, and bed wetting, to avoid teasing, and to help each other. While at first the children are told they are here because of illness, later, sickness is deemphasized and normal behavior is expected. The standards of conduct encouraged are those adhered to in normal school and Pioneer groups, where communist values are stressed: a conscientious attitude toward learning, "cultured conduct," and habit training.

In the Pioneer organization of the sanatorium, the children are organized into small groups. The monitor, appointed each day, wears a special armband, leading the class whenever they are walking. At the end of the week, there is a "line-up" at which the daily marks are totaled for each group, competing for the award of the red pennant, inscribed with the words, "fifty years of Soviet power." The educator manipulates the collective to achieve a better adjustment for each individual child.

Individual approaches are recommended for specific behavioral patterns. A restless, argumentative child may be given a job with the condition that there be no arguing. When conflicts appear, they are taken up quickly with the child, who is taught to analyze his behavior and to believe in his ability to control himself. These techniques lend a psychotherapeutic dimension to the work of the educator, who can take up disturbed behavior right on the spot. A withdrawn, timid child may at first be given tasks which require a minimum of interaction with others. For example, in outdoor play, a shy child might first be encouraged to gather leaves and flowers. Later, when the child is ready, he is drawn into the group. The educator may hold a discussion with the group about violations of conduct on the part of an individual child, always guiding the children toward correct social opinions and conclusions. Sometimes, the educator may appeal to the group to help a particular child.

Further, the educator manipulates the identifications of the children through the use of literature, movies, T.V., and other cultural material chosen as positive and negative models of conduct. National heroes of the October Revolution and holidays are also used. Children are encouraged to do special projects. Wall displays on Lenin's childhood are common. (One Soviet educator I met who had traveled extensively in the United States was surprised, when she visited an American school on Lincoln's birthday, to find the teacher making no use of this opportunity. She was critical of the American deemphasis on national pride, national holidays, and patriotic symbols.) The educator solicits the active participation of children in planning games and other activities of the collective, consulting with the doctor, who advises about the child's activity, fatigability, and capacity for concentration.

The principles of reward and punishment are applied concretely. For good behavior, the child may receive praise from the educator, a good report on the wall chart which helps his group win the pennant, or perhaps a small gift. Special achievements may merit a letter to the parents. For misconduct, the child receives personal attention from the educator who may also bring the matter up for discussion in the class room or in the Pioneer Council. A poor conduct mark on the wall chart pulls the average of the group down. For unusual circumstances, a letter to the parents may be written, or the child may be excluded from a favorite activity. Group pressure is brought to bear on children who misbehave, since their individual performance lowers the average mark for the group. For "malicious hooliganism" or destruction of sanatorium property, a child may be expelled.

In applying principles of reward and punishment, educators are reminded that children have frequently been punished and criticized for laziness before admission to the sanatorium. The resulting reaction of protest and symptom formation leads in turn to more punishment, more rebellion, and a vicious circle. So parents and children are told from the beginning that restlessness and excitability are symptoms, not willful "hooliganism." They are phenomena of a weakened nervous system and the focus of the sanatorium program. Everyone on the staff is there to help the child become relaxed, healthy, strong, and able to study. The child's active cooperation is stressed. The aim of the work is to achieve "active inhibition." Praise is used lavishly, even for little achievements, such as not arguing. Some behavior is ignored. *Social censure in the collective is used sparingly, only after consultation with the doctor.* If a child must be excluded from the group, the educator should advise the nurse on how to handle the situation. Sometimes, a neutral staff member may be asked to step in if a child has come in direct conflict with one educator. A child who has misbehaved is told his nervous system is still weak, but with training he will be able to control himself. When punishment is necessary, the educator must be certain the child really experiences punishment. It does no good to exclude a child from a movie, only to permit some other pleasant activity, or to deprive the finicky eater of sweets.

For each child, the educator is expected to prepare a report (see Table 8) (2). After describing the major symptoms, the educator must report on the child's social habits, work skills, attitudes toward work and other activities, relationship to the collective. She also describes the child's basic mood and ability to control himself. The report is concluded by recommendations when the patient is discharged from the sanatorium.

Under sanatorium conditions, regime therapy and the educational approach described are applied mainly to children with neuroses or neurotic character disorders without extreme behavior problems. In my opinion, children with neuroses do not need a therapy directed towards strengthening repression and other inhibitory controls. Children with severe character disorders and psychopathic personalities in the American sense might benefit greatly from the sanatorium program, especially if parents could become involved and help the child to maintain some disciplined regularity after discharge. I told Dr. Gamza I thought his program might be good for children with psychopathy. He said he excluded such children because he would need more personnel to handle them. I wonder whether some adaptation of the sanatorium regime could be used in American residential treatment centers, including the limited residential period, which stimulates maximum motivation for parental involvement. Not only can parents witness concrete results, but they must prepare themselves to support and perpetuate the results. The use of social pressure, especially public censure, may be so distasteful to Americans that the value of the total program

Table 8. Outline for Educational Report

    I. Basic complaints

   II. General level of development in comparison with group.

  III. Level of habits

      A. Possesses cultural-hygienic habits

         1. Cleanliness

         2. Tidiness

      B. Possesses work habits

  IV. Possesses technical skill commensurate with group and age

   V. Relationship to work

      A. Attitude toward various kinds of work

         I. Works enthusiastically

         2. Works willingly

         3. Does not like to work

         4. Refuses to work

      B. Favorite kinds of work? What?

      C. Sloppy work? What?

  VI. Relationship to other forms of activity

      A. Favorite activities? Games?

      B. Basic content of play? Games?

 VII. Relationship to collective

      A. Attitude toward collective

         1. Loner, does not relate to children

         2. Relates to children only when they engage him

         3. Not very friendly but himself enters relationships with children

         4. Relates to majority of children in collective

         5. Organizer of collective

      B. Influence on collective?

         1. Yes/no

         2. What kind of influence? How is it expressed?

         3. Positive/negative

         4. Presence of conflicts

           a. Rarely

           b. Frequently

           c. Never

           d. Source of conflicts; describe

VIII. Self control

      A. Adheres to regime and discipline

         1. Yes

         2. No

         3. Not always

      B. Carries to completion work which interests him; describe work

         1. Yes

        2. No

        3. Not always

    C. Carries to completion work which does not interest him; describe work

        1. Yes

        2. No

        3. Not always

    D. Adheres to demands of educator; how does he react to demands?

    E. Does he relate the same way to all educators?

IX. Basic mood

    A. What mood predominates?

    B. Is it stable or does it change?

    C. What situations evoke undesirable behavior? Give examples

    D. Are undesirable habits evident? Describe specifically

        1. Masturbation

        2. Nail-biting

        3. Others

    E. What measures influence and quiet the child?

    F. What reasons does the educator see for the child's difficulties?

X. Summary and recommendations

    A. Dynamics of training and development

    B. Recommendations of educator and speech worker for continued training

        1. Speech school

        2. Regular school

        3. Special school for mildly retarded

        4. Other

Source: V. A. Gamza, "Instruktivno-metodicheskoe picmo dlya pedagogov detskogo psikhoneurologicheskogo sanatoriya No. 44" (Instructive Methodological Letter for Educators at Children's Psychoneurological Sanatorium No. 44), Moscow, 1968.

is overlooked. I think we need to stand off from our cultural biases to make a useful evaluation.

A Special Therapeutic Program
for Speech Disorders

In the Soviet Union, speech disorders are the concern of psychiatrists as well as educators. An elaborate network of services exists in the Moscow area, as shown in Table 9. Children with simple speech diffi-

Table 9. Organization of Services for Speech Disorders in Moscow

	Logopedics Department of Children's Polyclinic	
Prekindergarten speech child-care centers	Visits to child centers Visits to kindergartens Exam before entering school Cooperative work with pediatricians Consultation	Logopedics department regular schools
Speech groups in kindergartens	Office of Logopedics and Speech of the Moscow City Psychoneurological Dispensary for Children and Adolescents	Logopedics department special schools for retarded
Dzerjinski hospital for kindergarten-age children		
Hospitals in Moscow, Kiev, Leningrad for children to 14 years	*Logopedics Department in District Psychoneurological Dispensary Services for Adolescents*	Speech schools 3 boarding schools in Moscow
Preschool and school-age children to 14 years		
Hospital for adolescent stutterers from 16 years, Botkina-Moscow	Cooperative work with psychiatrists and other specialists Work therapy Consultations, referrals	Logopedics day care center for stutterers of kindergarten age connected with Psychoneurological Dispensary, one region—

culties may be handled at the polyclinic. Special nursery and kindergarten groups exist for stutterers. Speech workers attached to regular
schools provide additional services. More complex cases with psychiatric symptoms may be referred from the polyclinic to the Moscow
City Psychoneurological Dispensary for admission to the hospital program. Special boarding schools also exist for children with speech disorders without serious psychopathology.

The speech workers and doctors I talked with about the etiology of
stuttering considered organic brain defect more important than neurotic
disturbances. No specific brain lesion is responsible, they said, but there
may be a functional imbalance between cortical and subcortical processes. A pure speech neurosis and neurotic overlay on an organic base
are considered less important in childhood than in adolescence, when
the patients become more self-conscious about their disability.

At Department XI of the Psychoneurological Hospital for Children,
attached to the City Dispensary in Moscow, there was a 50-bed speech
unit for boys and girls in classes one through four. They were admitted
for a four-month program of intensive speech therapy. During the
summer session, somewhat older children come—classes five through
eight. Indications for admission were stuttering, alalia, dysarthria,
dysgraphia, dyslexia, and inhibited speech development in children who
also had disturbances of intellectual development or of behavior. The
children accepted were primarily held back in their development and
capacity to use regular school by the speech problem. Some children
were accepted from far-off regions of the country where extensive
speech services were not available.

The atmosphere was warm and cheerful. The children did not seem
nearly as subdued as the sanatorium children. Increased spontaneity
was one of the explicit therapeutic aims in the speech program. The
children were helped to lose their self-consciousness by speech therapists who met with them in small groups and encouraged them to speak
loudly in unison, even to shout. The children spent their mornings with
speech therapy and physical culture, followed by outdoor recreation.
Afternoons were devoted to school subjects. Each class had about 20
students and periods were reduced to 30–35 minutes. Children with
intellectual retardation or gross language disturbances received individual instruction.

A team approach characterized the work of the department. The key
personnel were the psychiatrist, the speech worker, and the educator,
supplemented by teachers, upbringers, nurses, work therapy and physical culture instructors, and music teachers. Consultations were oc-

casionally held with professors of psychiatry. One speech worker, who had worked in a polyclinic before she came to the hospital unit, said the hospital program achieved far better results.

The initial diagnostic workup included physical, neurological, and psychiatric examinations and an evaluation of language skills by the speech therapist. One therapist demonstrated the investigation of three areas constituting the "fundamental basis of speech." She said, first, the child's ability to see and to name simple objects is ascertained. If the visual apparatus is intact, visual memory and spatial relations, with particular reference to right-left discrimination and sequence, are tested. In the auditory sphere, the child's ability to hear simple sounds, to discriminate and reproduce rhythms is investigated. Motor coordination is observed, and the child's capacity to make the voluntary movements necessary for writing is noted. In addition, the speech therapist is interested in general intelligence, assessed by some tests of abstract thinking such as differences and picture arrangement. Since the Soviet speech worker deals with not only spoken speech but all aspects of language, she also tests reading ability, spelling, and writing.

> The speech therapist who explained the diagnostic evaluation demonstrated her examination on a nine-and-one-half-year-old boy, Igor, who was not progressing in the first class, because of his inability to master the fundamentals of reading and writing. During the year before admission, head shaking and enuresis had appeared. There was disagreement between the psychologist, who felt the child was retarded, and the psychiatrist, who thought he was not retarded but had suffered organic brain damage and showed signs of psychic infantilism.
>
> The mother had a history of a heart ailment. The delivery was breech with asphyxia. Early feeding was satisfactory. Developmental history showed some slowness: Igor walked and said his first words at two years, did not use sentences until three and one-half years. Until he was four and one-half, Igor's speech was so poor that only his mother could understand it. At ten months, he was hospitalized with dysentery. He had pneumonia on two occasions during the first year of life, followed by asthma, which stopped when he was five. He also had head trauma at six months and at one year, on the latter occasion with loss of consciousness and vomiting but no convulsions.
>
> When we saw Igor, he was a plump, reserved boy who seemed small for his age. He spoke indistinctly but without stuttering. The

visual examination showed he could recognize and name simple objects and could identify two images, one superimposed on the other. He was unable to distinguish right and left completely and also had difficulty with the concept of behind and in front. He worked with his left hand, somewhat awkwardly. He reversed serial numbers and counted from right to left. Simple designs with plastic sticks were reproduced as mirror images. Auditory perception was grossly intact but rhythms were not accurately reproduced when they became complex. Sequences of thoughts were not accurately remembered, though the patient understood what was said and substituted other words for the ones he forgot. In the motor sphere, fine movements and sequential movements were somewhat disturbed.

The boy's performance on the various aspects of the language examination suggested a global disturbance of which the speech disorder was only a small part. The practical question as to whether Igor should be treated as a retarded child had not been resolved. The procedures for assessing language skills used by the speech therapist included psychological and educational methods.

Following diagnostic study, the children were assigned for speech therapy in small groups. Four boys and one girl in the fourth class were observed and recorded on audiotape while they had a speech lesson. They had entered the hospital three months before, all with severe stuttering. During the half hour while they were working with the speech therapist, there was *absolutely no stuttering.* The exercises were varied, with much emphasis on rhythmicity in individual and group participation. The children appeared confident and willing.

First, each child told how the day went: "My day went well, I had no complaints. I prepared my lessons. At the table, I ate everything," and so forth. They did breathing exercises in unison, reciting the basic vowels, then adding a consonant in front of the vowel, then adding more syllables. This exercise ended with a verse in unison and individual recital of verses. Next, with mirrors, the children did tongue exercises, individually and together. Then again they recited verses individually and in unison. Further rhythmical speech was elicited to the beat of a hammer. Then each child recited an incident he had learned about everyday life. One child spoke about going out, playing ball, buying ice cream. The therapist asked a few questions about the stories, which the children answered. A ball game was played in which the child to whom the ball was thrown had to give quickly a word with a particular vowel sound or be eliminated from the game. The children read a story aloud about an Eskimo dog and a bear in Siberia. They answered questions in turn about the story. Then they marched around and stopped, started on command, marked time, and marched, reciting left, right, left, right. They also rehearsed a scene of a play they were putting on for their parents, in celebration of the New Year holiday and the end of their course of therapy. The lesson ended with warm encouragement from the speech therapist for their success, and her hope they would continue to do exercises and to speak at home as they had in the hospital.

The doctor and speech therapist met with the parents to emphasize the need to continue training and practice at home. One parent was in tears after hearing her boy, formerly a severe stutterer, speak clearly without a trace of hesitation. The New Year's play permitted most of the 50 children to show their progress in public.

I was impressed with the fact that speech free of stuttering could be induced with use of rhythm and group speaking and then transferred to more spontaneous speech, at least in the context of the lesson and a public performance. I wondered whether in the United States we might consider developing special therapeutic programs with an initial, limited hospitalization or residential period, followed by outpatient follow-up. The principle might apply not only to speech disorders but to a wide variety of other common problems with a psychiatric component. Perhaps such an approach could make available the advantages of residential treatment, with its total control of the therapeutic environment, to a larger number of needy children and at the same time enlist the positive participation of the parents in maintaining the good results of the therapeutic program.

Work
Therapy

The positive value attached to work in Soviet thinking reflects the Marxist view of man's economic relationships as the basis for the development of social relationships and personality. Myasishchev has constructed a theory of work therapy which establishes the basis for a scientifically rational prescription of work, with its correct dosage, in a given patient (8). He saw work therapy as a specifically human activity, with the patient both the acting subject and the acted upon object. Since the patient's work activity changes the external world, work therapy is distinguished from psychotherapy, where the patient is also both object and consciously experiencing subject. He also pointed out the diagnostic value of studying a patient under conditions of work activity, since to study an organism only at rest is artificial and misleading.

How does this all apply to the field of child psychiatry? In actual practice, work therapy was less emphasized than I had anticipated in the therapeutic programs I saw. Young children of preschool age and in the early school years were given supervised periods of hand work in hospitals and sanatoria. There were no adolescent workshops in the inpatient institutions visited in 1968–69. One psychoneurological dispensary in Leningrad had an ambulatory workshop for some children, selected for the placement by a special commission: imbeciles, schizophrenics, and a few with severe organic brain syndromes. They lived at home and commuted to the workshop, under the supervision of their families, five days a week. Under the guidance of work instructors, they worked part of the day at folding cardboard forms into boxes. They also had instruction under a specially trained educator who met with them in small groups. The children had one meal at the workshop and returned home around 3:30 P.M.

Residential schools for the mildly retarded and homes for imbeciles in Moscow and Kiev had a variety of workshops, including sewing for girls and bookbinding and woodworking for boys. One director claimed nearly all his graduates, children with mild retardation, were able to get jobs in industry. Since I was not allowed to visit hospitals and colonies for children with chronic severe psychoses, I do not know to what degree work therapy is used in such programs.

Soviet society values work as a positive force in the construction of the social order and the development of an individual with a collective, social conscience. There is a tendency in the west to regard work as a necessary evil. Freud's well-known criterion for mental health and maturity is the ability to work and love. One loves in order to meet instinctual needs and works to meet reality demands, without expectation of much pleasure or need-gratification from work.

In the context of Soviet thought, it is not surprising that psychiatry has become known for utilizing the therapeutic potential of work. The historical development of work therapy for psychiatric patients in the Soviet Union is the subject of a book by M. Ya. Grebliovski, who describes some of the aims in utilizing work processes (3). There is disagreement among Russians about the boundary lines between work therapy, rehabilitation for employment, and utilization of a patient's residual intact capacities for production. As a therapeutic tool, work is used to dissolve or diminish symptoms of mental illness, to alter the pathophysiological process itself, to regulate and stabilize behavior, to prevent further deterioration of the personality, and to utilize the patient's residual capacities. Partly the disagreement about how to describe work processes reflects which point of view prevails: work as therapy for an individual or work as production of goods and services to meet the needs of society. But even so, dividing lines can become quite artificial.

The Soviet attitude toward work in society and in therapy appeared to me quite constructive. Soviet hospitals and sanatoria for adolescent psychotic and neurotic patients in particular could utilize more workshops, as Soviet psychiatrists were quick to admit themselves. American psychiatrists, planning programs for adolescents with psychopathy and severe character disorders, as well as for the grossly disabled, might benefit by adopting a similar attitude toward the therapeutic potential of work and its value in preventing deterioration of very handicapped people to a vegetative level.

Conclusions

The psychiatric treatment methods I saw in the Soviet Union were influenced by the Pavlovian concepts outlined in Chapter I above. The aim was to achieve stability of nervous processes, with an optimal balance between excitation and inhibition. The use of Pavlovian concepts was much more evident in treatment practices than it was in diagnostic thinking. The treatments observed were all applied with the aim of promoting a state of quiet, with no attempt to expose psychopathology for the purpose of "working it through." The use of major tranquilizers, individually or in combination, to achieve impulse control (especially sexual impulses) and in the treatment of neuroses and personality disorders was more prevalent in Soviet than in American practice.

The educational aspects of Soviet psychiatric treatment showed an emphasis on training for communist morality. It was in this area and in the readjustment of the child to life in the collective that the ideas of Makarenko were most influential. The manipulation of the collective, when skillfully done in the sanatorium setting, served the therapeutic needs of individual patients as well as the aim of the communist society.

There were aspects of the Soviet approach to the parents of children in treatment which made me reexamine some of my own procedures. In particular, the concrete level at which the parents were included in the therapeutic program may be more helpful in some instances than traditional American psychiatric casework. The Soviet parents visiting in the mental hospitals and sanatoria were encouraged actually to see what produced results with their children and to continue the techniques at home.

V

Special
Psychotherapy

As we saw in Chapter IV, psychotherapy in its general sense has been recognized as important in all branches of Soviet medicine. The relationship between doctor and patient is considered a decisive therapeutic factor. Psychotherapy in its special sense refers to special psychotherapeutic techniques. These fall into two major categories: suggestive psychotherapy and rational psychotherapy. Both have become increasingly important in Soviet medicine with the widespread recognition since the early fifties of the importance of functional complaints.

Suggestive techniques in the Soviet Union are based on the method of autogenic training developed in Germany by J. H. Schultz. In 1969, V. E. Rozhnov was one of the leading professors of the Moscow school of psychotherapy. He was using autogenic training and hypnosis with adults. His pupil, B. Z. Drapkin, was extending these techniques to a program for adolescents. The other major school, derived from the work of Myasischev in Leningrad, was applying the techniques of pathogenetic psychotherapy to adolescents. Considered in historical perspective, Soviet psychotherapy and American psychotherapy shared influences from the nineteenth-century interest in France in hypnosis. Soviet psychotherapy retained more interest in suggestive techniques, while American psychotherapy, following the development of the psychoanalytic movement, tended to reject techniques based on hypnosis.

Suggestive
Psychotherapy

SCHULTZ'S METHOD OF AUTOGENIC TRAINING

At the turn of the century, J. H. Schultz found that hypnotized subjects spontaneously experienced heaviness in the limbs, indicating muscular relaxation. The subjects also reported warmth in the extremities, which Schultz attributed to vasodilation. Suggestions could reproduce these spontaneous psychophysiological effects. From these observations, Schultz evolved a technique which he called autogenic training. His basic textbook was published in German in 1932. After World War II, there was increasing interest on the European continent in autogenic training, and in 1959 Schultz and W. Luthe introduced the technique to an English-speaking audience (5). Without exception, Soviet doctors who discussed psychotherapy with me referred to Schultz. His work is less known in the United States.

Schultz's subjects either lie or sit in a relaxed position in a quiet environment. Lighting is reduced and eyes are closed. The subjects are instructed to avoid pressure points on the extremities or muscular tension and to adopt an attitude of "passive concentration," with a casual attitude toward the outcome of suggestions to be given by the therapist. The subject first is asked to think about his right arm and to be able to feel it. Then suggestions are given repetitively; each suggestion is kept simple with stress on calm and peace. Only mental or physical effects which would naturally be expected are suggested. During the initial part of the training, the suggestions are given for brief periods, 30–60 seconds each, three times at each sitting. The subject is encouraged to repeat these three times a day at home. Autosuggestion is ended by having the subject flex his arms and legs, breathe deeply, and open his eyes. A sharp line is preserved between the waking state and the autosuggestive state.

Schultz described a series of standard exercises for all subjects. The first set has to do with the sensation of heaviness in a limb when relaxation is complete. For right-handed people, the exercise is begun in the right arm and continued until a definite effect is noted. The heaviness is extended until it includes all extremities. This may take three to four weeks. The second standard exercise suggests that warmth will be experienced in the right arm; then, generalization of the sensation is established to all four extremities. This may take another three or four weeks. The third exercise is the suggestion that the heartbeat is calm and regular. The fourth exercise induces a subjective experience that breathing is automatically controlled. The specific formula Schultz recommended was the expression, "It breathes me," to suggest automatic control. The fifth standard exercise is the sensation of abdominal warmth in the region of the solar plexis. Finally, the sixth exercise is the suggestion that the forehead feels cool.

A series of special exercises may then be introduced to subjects who have been successful in the standard series. Examples of these are, first, the achievement of the standard series with the presence of interfering environmental stimuli. For psychosomatic disturbances, special exercises involve specific organic formuli, for example, for the bedwetter. Or special exercises may be elaborated around specific neurotic symptoms. These are called "intention formuli."

Schultz and Luthe indicated that the autosuggestive state is similar to but not identical with the states of hypnosis, sleep, and certain drug-induced conditions. Attention is focused not on the environment but on the mental process of passive concentration. They hypothesized that there is reinforcement of "trophotropic" changes and a diminution of "ergotropic" mechanisms. The functions of the parasympathetic nervous system and self-regulation are enhanced, and voluntary activity is diminished. They believed that there is a normalization of diencephalic functions, achieved through a modification of cortico-diencephalic connections which restores self-regulatory mechanisms. They noted improved general functioning of the subjects, which was not directly suggested during the training. The subjects experience an overall increase in their adaptability; their physical health becomes better and their resistance to stress is greater. For Western readers this is an important point, because a common criticism of suggestive techniques is that they simply remove symptoms and are not directed toward the general emotional and physical health of the patient.

V. E. ROZHNOV AND THE MOSCOW SCHOOL

It was my privilege to talk with Professor Rozhnov who held the chair or *kafedra* of psychotherapy at the Central Institute for the Increased Qualifications of Physicians in Moscow, established in 1967. Professor Rozhnov impressed me as a firm, assertive man who has had relatively little contact with the West, although he told me that one of his papers on the psychophysiology of the hypnotic state had been presented at an international congress in Paris. He said the other major chair of psychotherapy was in Kharkov, in the Ukraine, under Professor I. Z. Velvovski. I asked to visit there, but was not granted permission.

The third chair of psychotherapy was being organized in Leningrad, distinct from the Department of Medical Psychology at the Institute named for Bekhterev where Myasischev was working.

Professor Rozhnov distinguished between general psychotherapy and special psychotherapy, a series of techniques taught to his trainees. Only physicians should be doing psychotherapy, he claimed, since this is a form of treatment of sick people. Psychotherapy is used for neurosis and other disorders, such as asthma, dermatitis, and gynecological problems. In Rozhnov's view, there is no such thing as a universal psychotherapist, such as he understood us to have in the United States. Various medical specialists are trained to use psychotherapy as one method in combination with others .

Professor Rozhnov's training program was of particular interest. Doctors come to the Central Institute for Increased Qualification of Physicians in Moscow for two- to three-month cycles. In 1969, there was a cycle of specialization lasting three months for doctors who wished to become psychotherapists and who had no previous training in this area. There were two-month "cycles of increased qualifications" for psychotherapists who wished to learn more. The methods taught emphasized hypnosis and the autogenic training of Schultz, although some rational psychotherapy was taught as well. The trainee's day was occupied by two hours of lecture material and three hours of clinical practice.

The research activity of Rozhnov and his co-workers centered on the physiology of the hypnotic state: relating EEG changes in various states of cortical inhibition and excitation to stages of hypnosis, the role of the reticular formation in the hypnotic state, comparison of the autogenic method of Schultz and the hypnotic state. Rozhnov also was training doctors at a more academic level, supervising dissertations for the degree of Candidate of Medical Science.

B. Z. DRAPKIN'S PSYCHOTHERAPEUTIC PROGRAM FOR ADOLESCENTS

Dr. Drapkin was one of Professor Rozhnov's students. He prepared his dissertation for the Candidate of Medical Science degree in child psychiatry. He had formed a new hospital department of psychotherapy in the Moscow Psychoneurological Hospital for Children and Adolescents. Dr. Drapkin and his associates, Dr. N. E. Polyakova, held a unique position as the only child psychiatrists administering a full-time hospital program devoted to psychotherapy. I visited them for several days in the Fourteenth Department of this hospital. A new unit was being formed where they expected to have 50 beds for adolescent boys and girls 12–16 years of age and also facilities to receive ambulatory patients. This new department was another indication of the importance Soviet medicine attributed to psychotherapy at the time.

Dr. Polyakova invited me to sit in on consultations to select patients for psychotherapy in their department. The indications for their treatment (hypnosis and autogenic training) are as follows. The patient should have clear evidence of motivation and should be of at least normal intellectual capacity, as estimated by the doctor. The patients were generally not under 12 or over 16. Other indications for suggestive therapy were favorable attitudes toward hypnosis and a successful trial of suggestibility. Contraindications included mental retardation and schizophrenia. However, Dr. Drapkin and Dr. Polyakova hoped to extend services to some schizophrenic patients with pseudoneurotic symptomatology. The sources of referral were other hospital departments of the mental hospital, the Central Psychoneurological Dispensary, and polyclinics around Moscow.

We interviewed Kolya, a 14-year-old boy in the dispensary, to see if he would be suitable for the hospital therapeutic program. He was referred because of stuttering.

The mother was uncertain about the exact onset of the stuttering. She was sure that Kolya could speak clearly in early childhood. When he was between 3 and 4, he went to his grandmother in the country where he developed fears. This time may also have marked the onset of the speech disturbance. He began school at the usual age without difficulty. When he was 8, he was hit by a car and suffered unconsciousness. After this accident, the stuttering became worse. Kolya experienced spells of unconsciousness when he was 9 and 10, without convulsions. When he was 11, his father left home. Mother cried as she spoke of the separation, adding that the boy was very upset about his father. Kolya's speech had become worse during the past two years, and he had begun to fear speaking, especially in school. His mother considered him an outgoing boy, not particularly anxious in other aspects of life. At times he would take a long time falling asleep. Three families were occupying one apartment and this family with two children had one room. However, it was said that there were no conflicts with those neighboring families.

Kolya was able to relate well and to talk some about his difficulties. He complained that it was hard for him to answer in school, and he said his grandmother thought his stuttering began when he was about five years old. He commented that he could read better than he could talk in general conversation. It appeared to me that he stuttered most when asked about the summer. A brief physical examination revealed a slight right facial weakness and increased tendon reflexes in the right arm. There was slight incoordination in the right arm, as indicated by some unsteadiness on the finger-to-nose test. Kolya had a slight residual neurological defect from his accident, but his stuttering problem was part of a chronic, long-standing neurosis.

In discussing this case with Dr. Polyakova, I commented about the boy's disturbance over his father. We learned from the mother that the boy was so disturbed about his father's leaving the family that he does not want to see him and throws his gifts away. Dr. Polyakova agreed this was important, but the boy was too upset about it for her to question him in this initial interview. She felt it would have to be brought out gradually later on after he was admitted to the hospital. The boy had also lost a friend last summer, which further upset him. Kolya was apprehensive when Dr. Polyakova recommended hospital treatment, so he was invited to come the following day for a visit before admission so that he could feel more comfortable.

In discussing cases with Dr. Polyakova, I noticed that she intuitively touched on many of the same issues which I consider important. We saw an 18-year-old boy with a variety of somatic complaints: headaches, general weakness, palpitations, pain in his heart, and anxieties about his cardiac function, including fear of death. He had gone to technicum for two courses and then was hospitalized at a special psycho-neurological hospital which offers hypnosis and autogenic training. After discharge, his periodic fears of death continued, and he was neither working nor going to school. I commented that the boy's passivity would be a major issue, since he conveyed an unspoken demand that something should be done for him and become impatient when questions were devoted to his family situation. It was clear that he wanted only to have specific treatment for his heart symptoms. Dr. Polyakova told this boy that his treatment would demand a lot of work from him and that it was a serious matter. She recommended that he join an ambulatory group for autogenic training and placed the responsibility on the patient for coming in two weeks to start with a new group if he wanted to. She was quite firm in telling him that he was emotionally sick and that he must work.

The hospital part of this program for intensive therapy, lasting three months, was being conducted in an old brick building, not unlike many of our less modern state hospital facilities. The rooms were decorated in a festive way for the traditional Russian New Year. The atmosphere was friendly and supportive. Doctors, nurses, and educational personnel all seemed devoted to helping the patients establish friendly relationships in the collective and restore their damaged feelings of self-confidence. Some received medication. There was a strong therapeutic recreation program. I accompanied the teenage patients and their attending personnel to the Pushkin Museum in Moscow to see a special exhibit of French art from the Louvre. There was a casual atmosphere as the young patients wandered, frequently arm in arm, and mingled with the crowd. I also attended a ward party which included a program of public speaking, guitar playing, singing, and dancing. These parties were planned to help overcome social anxiety and fear of speaking. The patients were warmly praised when they performed well. One girl sang in English, about discrimination against Negroes in the United States.

During their hospital stay, the patients kept notebooks in which they wrote their own personal answers to such questions as, "What's the matter with me?," "What is good about me?", "How do I think a person should be?" The patients were encouraged to express their concepts of their illnesses and their personal ideals. Later, in their hospital stay, they were asked to write on such subjects as, "Do you like it here?," "What do you find good here?," "What do you not like about being here?," "What would you like to see changed here?"

I noticed one young girl who appeared to be about 14 years old. She had teased hair and seemed quite conscious of her appearance, although she was not extreme in her dress style; I saw very few Soviet teenagers with either extremely short skirts or, in the case of males, extremely long hair. This youngster had sung particularly well at the party; but when she returned to the group, I noted a sullen expression on her face and a tendency to withdraw and remain aloof from the other youngsters. With help, I read her clinical history and the answers she had put in her notebook. She was actually 17, admitted about three weeks previously because of stuttering, unwillingness to study in school, and a feeling of exhaustion. Her family situation was said to be unfavorable, though the details were not available except that her father had a drinking problem. She had entered voluntarily, enjoyed the hospital, and did not want to go home. She fulfilled all the requirements of treatment very willingly but did not like to do school work. About herself, she wrote that she was moody and easily angered, but had "high aims in life." She followed this comment with a verse, saying she carried a "pain in her heart." She felt that there were two kinds of people, the first phony, and the second, apparently her own choice, impulsive or emotional. It seemed to me she recognized her moodiness as a symptom of illness; on the other hand she cherished it as a character trait of positive value. The staff felt that since her admission she was relating more positively and had begun to show an open interest in boys. I observed this youngster again during autogenic training. When the suggestion had been given that the right arm would become warm, I was sure the left hand was warmer! I wondered whether this was a symptom of her negativism but her doctors did not so interpret it.

An additional important aspect of the general therapeutic program is the work with parents, conducted both by doctors and educators. Work with parents has never achieved the formal character that it has in our own clinics; I never heard any discussion about technique. One day when I arrived at the hospital, Dr. Polyakova was talking with the mother of a 13-year-old boy who had recently been admitted with fears, predominantly of other youngsters his own age. The talk with the mother was lengthy, the third since the boy's admission. Dr. Polyakova was advising the mother on how to handle the boy. Everybody had treated the youngster as sick and incapable. She advised the mother that demands should be made within his capabilities. She pointed out that the mother worked at a job, the sister studied and helped around the house, and this patient should have tasks assigned to him at home.

However, this boy was good at creating a feeling that he was fragile. When he was in a group of five patients undergoing hypnosis, Dr. Polyakova noticed that he was not in a hypnotic trance. She did not confront him and later told me that in rational psychotherapy he would first be encouraged to tell how he was sick and what his fears were, and the therapeutic task would be to show him how he could be strong and self-confident. However, there was a question in her mind of underlying schizophrenia, and if this were so, the boy should not be having hypnosis, since she considered such patients too suggestible; therapy should be directed toward strengthening their will, rather than weakening it. So this boy had managed to create a feeling in his therapist, as well as in his mother, that he could not meet usual expectations. At home he had no duties; in hospital he was not required to enter a hypnotic state. In my own work, I try especially to notice my own emotional reaction and to compare it to the response patients elicit in those close to them. This conscious use of the doctor's own feelings, of which countertransference is one aspect, was not a feature of Soviet work I observed.

One part of the program was the autogenic training method of Schultz. Dr. Drapkin demonstrated this method with a group of 18 or 20 adolescent boys and girls who met together in a large classroom. They sat in a relaxed position with their eyes closed. In the subdued atmosphere, Dr. Drapkin gave suggestions somewhat as follows: "There is not a thought in my head. My head is light, separate, apart. I will be at peace. I will be relaxed in all the muscles of my body. The muscles of my right hand are relaxed. I am at peace. My right hand is relaxed and is becoming heavy. I am at peace. My right hand feels all heavy. My right hand has become completely, completely heavy. I am at peace. The heaviness is going from my right hand into my left hand. I am at peace. My hands are very heavy. I am at peace. The heaviness is going into my legs. My right leg is relaxed and has become heavy. I am at peace. My legs and hands are becoming weak and are becoming heavier. I am beginning to feel a sense of fullness in my right hand. I am at peace. My right hand feels full and swollen. My right hand feels as if it has been in hot water. I am at peace. My right hand feels full. I am at peace." The effectiveness of the suggestions is tested by demonstrating a noticeable temperature difference between two extremities. Patients are trained to continue self-suggestion after they are discharged from the hospital and to continue their treatment in follow-up groups. The autosuggestive state was ended with the suggestions that the patients would move and awaken feeling refreshed.

After a group of patients has achieved some success in the auto-suggestive program, they meet in groups of six to eight with a speech therapist if their major symptom is stuttering. I saw how the speech therapist used autogenic training on the problem of stuttering in a group of five boys and one girl. First they worked in a waking state on speech exercises such as smiling, showing their teeth, and counting. They also recited some tongue twisters which I have practiced myself and find difficult to repeat! They seemed full of good humor and laughter when they stumbled over the words.

Then the speech therapist began the autogenic training. After inducing relaxation and vasodilation, she added suggestions that had to do with deep breathing, relaxation of the muscles of the chest, neck, and face. She added that the voice and the whole head felt calm and lacking in tension. Then each member of the group was encouraged to say, individually, his full name. Each patient read aloud a short story about a Russian general who had been on a long journey for about six years and who emerged from the forest and was slowly dying of hunger. For the most part, these patients could speak in the auto-suggestive state free of stuttering, although there was one young boy who had considerable difficulty. The speech worker later told me he was considered to have poor motivation. There was no attempt to use the situation to make direct suggestions that stuttering disappear but rather to demonstrate to the patients that they had the capacity to talk without stuttering if they were calm and relaxed.

In this program, the educator had become psychotherapist, in spite of what has been said above about psychotherapy's being reserved for medical practitioners. The team approach and the need for interdisciplinary cooperation was recognized. The educators and the doctors worked closely together. Combined conferences were held fairly frequently to coordinate the work of the two disciplines.

Dr. Drapkin demonstrated hypnosis individually on an adolescent girl with a hysterical personality and the dramatic symptom of swallowing pins. She was so suggestible that she went into a trance very quickly. Dr. Drapkin massaged her right arm, pushing the blood proximally from the superficial veins; then he suggested that she could not feel anything there, and pushed a needle through a fold of skin. The girl did not even wince. Before withdrawing the needle, Dr. Drapkin suggested that the place would not bleed, and it remained bone dry after he removed the needle. He suggested that she taste a lemon and that it would taste sweet to her, which evidently it did. Before wakening her he noticed a wart on her hand and suggested that it would be gone in a week. She awakened as quickly as she had fallen into the trance and the needle wounds immediately began to bleed. In her waking state, this girl was in good contact and said she felt completely well. She liked Dr. Drapkin and felt she had been helped by his therapy.

Hypnosis was also conducted in groups of five or six boys and girls. They came into a large room with couches, got blankets and pillows, and lay down in a relaxed posture. The lighting was cut down and background noise was reduced, as with the autogenic training sessions. The main difference was that after suggesting peace, relaxation, and calm, the doctor went on to suggest a state of sleep, in a soft, repetitive voice. The sessions lasted about 40 minutes and were mainly used for rest and relaxation. There was no effort to get the patients to express fears, fantasies, or conflicts. Occasionally, suggestions directed toward particular symptomatology were whispered to an individual patient. The suggestions given to the group were more general, encouraging relaxation, a good mood, cheerfulness, a feeling of being rested, mentally clear, full of joy, and so forth. The suggestions before awakening were made in a gradually increasing loud voice, telling the patients that they would be fully awake when the count of ten was reached. As he counted slowly, Dr. Drapkin added that the mood would be marvelous, that the patients had had a wonderful rest, the sensation of heaviness was becoming less and less, their heads would be clear, and they would feel alert and full of joy. At the count of ten, the suggestion was given that they open their eyes. They began talking informally with each other and with the doctor.

I asked Dr. Polyakova what signs she used to determine the state of hypnosis, and she mentioned regular slow breathing, diminished eye movements and blinking, complete relaxation of the body; if you pick up a limb and let it drop, it falls limp and supine. Voluntary movements decrease and then stop, and the patients sometimes appear flushed, as if sleeping, and yet they maintain contact with the hypnotist. In general, the patients appeared to have a favorable attitude toward the program and the doctors. I am sure that this positive transference played an important role in the results achieved, although this concept does not enter Soviet thinking. The gratification of longings for care, nurturance, and passivity was another prominent feature of the program difficult to assess for its contribution to therapeutic effect.

Dr. Drapkin asked me about what I did and I tried to explain that through play and conversation, we encourage young patients to express fantasies, fears, feelings, and thoughts that are connected with their symptoms. When the patients can express such fantasies, we try to show them how they are connected with the symptoms. He said that they try to do this kind of thing, too, in their rational psychotherapy, but that what I had described resembled more closely the type of therapy conducted by the Leningrad school. I added that I thought many of the feelings and fantasies of the patients at the beginning were unconscious, which did not seem to surprise Dr. Drapkin. I further tried to convey my opinion that Soviet psychiatrists stress the rational aspect in their conversations with patients perhaps more than we do and that we consider such conversations an emotional process which depends on the relationship of the doctor and the patient and the transference of earlier thoughts and feelings onto the therapist. Dr. Drapkin seemed to understand all of this. He wanted to know the difference between what I do and psychoanalysis which, he said, he did not practice. I answered in terms of the frequency of interviews, the use of the "basic rule" of free association in older patients, and the more ambitious aim of character change for psychoanalytic therapy.

Dr. Drapkin gave me an unpublished paper which he had written on the psychotherapy of stuttering in adolescents (1). He claimed that 1–2 percent of the children in the general population suffer from stuttering. The basic clinical picture of stuttering he said, is often complicated by secondary psychic layers. The fear of speech leads to social withdrawal, emotional changes, and perhaps eventually to characterological deformation. A vicious circle is set up in which the fear of speech and the suffering over the defect lead to an increase in the spasms of the throat, which in turn worsens the stuttering and heightens the sense of conflict and suffering, and so on. Eight percent of Drapkin's stutterers began having the symptom when they were from two to five years of age. The fear of speech appears much later, in Dr. Drapkin's opinion, usually around ten years, and worsens in adolescence, due to the social anxiety accompanying pubertal development and the increase in pressure of the environment to speak. Many patients have had unsuccessful speech therapy during their preschool years and a long history of therapeutic failure. The adolescent patients frequently have inferiority complexes and secondary negative character traits, such as aggressiveness, egocentricity, and bad habits. Table 10 summarizes the classification Drapkin proposed, following Sukhareva and Simpson, with the recommended type of treatment for each of the varieties of stuttering. Drapkin advocated a program including a brief hospital interval, followed by semihospital conditions and finally by ambulatory treatment and prolonged supportive observation in a psychoneurological dispensary. I agree that this would be the ideal model of a therapeutic program, not only for stuttering but for many symptoms.

General psychotherapeutic rules cited in Drapkin's paper were the following:

1. At the first encounter with the patient, the doctor shows him that he underestimates his ability to speak. This encourages the patient to believe that improvement is possible.
2. In the direct speech therapy, demands are initially minimal and

Table 10. Clinical Classification of Speech Disorders

Kind of Stuttering	Basic Method of Treatment	Auxiliary Method of Treatment
Shock—acute psychic trauma. Acute onset, 1 day–1 week. Other symptoms of neurosis	Psychotherapy, speech therapy, medication	Regime, general supportive treatment, physiotherapy
Speech neurosis— gradual onset	Psychotherapy	Medication
Speech neurosis on a base of residual organic damage	Psychotherapy, speech therapy	Physiotherapy, medication
Stuttering on basis of speech pathology	Speech therapy	Psychotherapy, medication
Stuttering syndrome with other pathology: schizophrenia, epilepsy, etc.	Treatment of basic illness	Treatment of stuttering

Source: Drapkin, B. Z., untitled paper on the psychotherapy of stuttering in adolescence, MS, Moscow, 1969, pp. 3, 5–6.

later gradually increase along with the patient's ability to master them.

3. Demands made on a patient and assignments for extra work must always correspond to his ability to succeed.
4. The whole treatment is conducted at a high level of interest and emotional involvement on the part of the patient. It is clear that the Soviet doctor sets much value on establishing a positive relationship and uses novel methods and materials to help sustain interest.
5. Continued stimulation of the patient is necessary, repeatedly showing him that he has hidden abilities which he has not utilized.
6. The patient is praised warmly for his successes and his failures are underplayed.

In describing special characteristics of psychotherapy for adolescent stutterers, Drapkin indicated that while the patients are waiting for treatment, this period can be utilized to assess their readiness to cooperate and their ability to work independently. Sometimes they are assigned tasks in speech work or in training of the will. In the preparatory period, the patients are given general examinations of the mechanisms of stuttering and the means of treating it. As with the programs described in Chapter IV, the importance of the formation of "collectives" is recognized. Conversely, patients sometimes have a negative therapeutic effect on each other. The approach to treatment must be individualized, depending on the clinical picture, even though much of it is given in a group setting. This means that the patient must be studied carefully as an individual and his psychological characteristics taken into consideration. In actual practice I felt this was done successfully and intuitively. The importance of follow-up observation, after the hospital phase of the program, was repeatedly emphasized in the paper.

Drapkin offered the following schema for the course of treatment:

1. Preparatory
   a. establishing contact with the patient
   b. beginning of autogenic training
   c. rational psychotherapy
   d. introducing the patient to successfully treated stutterers
   e. hypnotherapy: diagnostic study and structuring the treatment for the patient
   f. suggestion in a waking state
   g. complete study of the patient from all angles
   h. medication

2. Treatment period
   a. speech work
   b. autogenic training
   c. rational psychotherapy
   d. hypnotherapy: resolution of secondary neurotic and psychic layers
   e. hypnotherapy: resolution of aspects of the speech syndrome in cases of "pure" speech neurosis
   f. speech training in the hypnotic state
   g. medication

3. Terminating period: suggestion in the waking state

4. Supportive observation in the dispensary
   a. autogenic training
   b. sessions of group hypnotherapy

In a further discussion of hypnotherapy, Drapkin indicated his preference for the group method over individual treatment. Hypnosis has diagnostic as well as therapeutic value, since the patient able to speak in the hypnotic state most likely has a functional disturbance. The emphasis in hypnotic theory is always on the resolution of secondary neurotic disturbances and the normalization of vegetative functions. In speech training during the hypnotic state, life situations may be simulated to show the patient that he can deal with speech problems he encounters every day. One must always be careful never to suggest beyond the patient's capacity.

Dr. Drapkin reported results in treating approximately 500 patients, over a period of several years. He claimed improvement in 65 to 70 percent of the cases where there was a history of severe, intractable stuttering and previously unsuccessful therapy. This seems to me to be a very good record. However, the aim of the treatment is kept limited realistically, for, as Dr. Drapkin says, it is to relieve the secondary symptoms (or the neurotic overlay, as we would say), not to remove the stuttering completely.

HYPNOSIS IN THE TREATMENT OF ENURESIS

A. I. Niss wrote on the treatment of enuresis in children by hypnosis (2). He rejected psychodynamic theories and explained the symptom in Pavlovian terms: a watchful or waking point is formed in normal children in the cerebral cortex around two years of age. This point remains active during sleep, capable of transmitting the sensation of the urge to urinate. In enuresis, such a waking point is not established because of unfavorable toilet training practices, fear, psychic or physical trauma, infection, and so forth. The therapy of enuresis must be devoted to constructing such a waking point through hypnotic suggestion, along with medication, physical therapy, diet, and the general doctor-patient relationship.

Niss reported on the hypnotic treatment of eight boys and one girl with enuresis, aged 8 to 12 years. The duration of treatment was 3 to 11 months and the number of hypnotic sessions varied between 11 and 14. In no case were there less than 7 hypnotic sessions after the enuresis stopped. He reported six patients recovered and two improved significantly in the sense that there was less enuresis and the children slept better. There was also improvement in their general mood. One remained unimproved. The depth of the hypnotic state induced in the children was not discussed. The suggestion given the patient was to sleep as if he were sleeping regularly. Then the child was told, at the time he was falling asleep, "I cannot, I will not, I must not wet the bed." The child's own expression for urination was used. Then, during the hypnotic state, the suggestion was given that the urge to urinate would appear during hypnosis. This was followed by the suggestion that the child would awaken when the urge to urinate appeared during hypnosis. Finally, posthypnotic suggestions were given that at home the child would not wet the bed before sleep, and that if the urge to urinate appeared during sleep, he would wake up.

Niss discussed one example, a 12-year-old girl who had wet the bed every night since infancy, and sometimes twice a night in the wintertime. She stopped the enuresis after the first session. After the sixth session she wet again, at a time when her father, who had been away for several months, came back home and the girl had been excited. Niss theorized that the new waking point established in the cerebral cortex had been inhibited in the general excitement. There was no further wetting after this. The duration of treatment was 12 sessions.

This treatment was conducted in small groups of three or four children, each in a boarding school setting. It is another specific example of the way which suggestive therapy is used with children in the Soviet Union.

Rational
Psychotherapy

The Department of Medical Psychology of the Institute named for Bekhterev in Leningrad is the center of Myasishchev's work. Professor I. M. Tonkanogi discussed with me many aspects of psychotherapy as they practice it. Unfortunately, Myasishchev himself was not there at the time of my visit. The research activities of the department are conducted by psychologists, psychiatrists, and neurologists. For the most part, psychotherapy remains a medical discipline. However, there is a more flexible attitude here with regard to the role of psychologists. Professor Tonkanogi said some psychologists from Leningrad University were being trained to begin psychotherapy in the Clinic for Neuroses under medical supervision.

In his discussion Tonkanogi emphasized that the focus of the treatment is on the actual situation of the patient. He related certain types of conflict in Myasishchev's classification (see Chap. I above) to specific kinds of neurotic character development and symptom formation:

the conflict of wish-versus-possibility is central in the hysterical character, formed typically in children who for various reasons are spoiled as they grow up. Frequently, he said, they are the youngest in the family and are excessively babied. They become moody and capricious and presumably form a faulty picture of what is possible because of their overly permissive handling. A second type of conflict is the internalized one of wish-versus-conscience, central in phobic and obsessive character formation. The Soviet terms would be psychasthenia and the neurosis of fear. These obsessive and phobic states are related to an excessively restrictive upbringing by rigid parents under repressive conditions. This formulation is not unlike the Freudian one for the obsessive character and the obsessive neurosis: a deep-seated, strong conflict between instinct and superego. Furthermore, the presence of *internal* conflict is acknowledged, which surprised me, in view of Lenin's reflection theory (described in Chap. I above). There was more recognition here than in Moscow of the importance of the neurosis of development, or a pervasive personality disorder stemming from a lifetime of family relationships with the human environment.

Professor Tonkanogi went on to define the task of psychotherapy as a change in the patient's attitude toward the environment. At the beginning, the patient usually is unaware of the real reason for his state. He used the term "rational psychotherapy," although Myasishchev has referred to the method as "pathogenic psychotherapy." Tonkanogi had held many discussions with Isadore Ziferstein, an American psychiatrist who had spent 13 months studying psychotherapy at the Institute named for Bekhterev. He had observed the complete treatment of 12 patients by five different therapists. Tonkanogi understood Ziferstein to have felt that therapy at Bekhterev is not as deep as psychoanalytically oriented psychotherapy. However, Tonkanogi pointed out their therapy is "deep," in the sense of producing a profound change in life adjustment, and in the sense of dealing with underlying feelings. He emphasized the widely held Soviet view that the actual situation of the patient is the subject of rational psychotherapy, rather than conflict in early childhood or the development of personality.

However, in one published report of Ziferstein's work, the emphasis was not so much on the "depth" of the Soviet therapy as on the doctor-patient relationship (6). In Soviet work, Ziferstein observed that the doctor-patient relationship was kept positive and used intuitively in the therapy, though not much discussed. In psychoanalytically oriented psychotherapy, said Ziferstein, the transference aspects of the doctor-patient relationship are described and articulated in the form of interpretations made to the patient. Ziferstein used a case example from his observations of Soviet treatment to show how negative transference would be handled when it is used in the service of resistance. The Soviet doctor is much more active and directive, relying on warmth, support, and persuasion, while the American doctor is more passive, relying on the patient to make his own changes as a result of effective interpretation of resistance. Ziferstein concluded the most important factor in the differences with respect to activity or directiveness was cultural: the collectivist values and the emphasis on mutual aid in interpersonal relationships in Soviet life. The more passive and more interpretive technique used by psychoanalysis is more consistent with a concept of ideal adult relationships based on individualism and laisser faire.

What about rational psychotherapy as it relates to the disturbances of children and adolescents? Rational psychotherapy is not available to children in polyclinics. Neither was play therapy or family therapy. So the following observations are limited to work with adolescents, as it was beginning to develop in ambulatory practice in the psychoneurological clinics.

At the Leningrad Regional Psychoneurological Dispensary in Moscow, I talked with Dr. A. S. Meisner, a psychotherapist who said rational psychotherapy is directed toward the patient's conflicted neurotic life situation. The treatment consists of an analysis of the patient's illness, since the patient is unaware of the whole reason for his illness. I ventured the opinion that this means there is an unconscious. Dr. Meisner and the other present laughed and he explained the patient cannot understand his situation because he is under emotional tension. Treatment helps him to understand conflict and to clarify connections between symptoms (the patient's subjective complaints) and the conflict as it appears in the life situation. For example, he had treated an adolescent girl who was in considerable conflict with her parents. They were simple and uneducated, but the daughter, with the benefit of superior education, had developed interests in art which her parents could not understand. The girl was rebelling because she found her parents simple and coarse. In her therapy, she was shown that through her conduct, she was just as simple and coarse as she claimed her parents were. I added I thought it important to help the girl to recognize her parents had good qualities as well, with which Dr. Meisner agreed.

We also discussed briefly an adolescent boy who was spending all of his time studying, but who could not measure up to his own high expectations. He had no outside interests. The therapy in his case, said

Dr. Meisner, had not only to change his attitude toward his life situation and toward significant people, but should change his personality. Since I had been growing quite skeptical about the ability of psychotherapy to bring about significant characterological changes, even in young people, I said I thought this would be quite difficult and I would not know how. Dr. Meisner explained he meant to help the boy to broaden his range of interests and to help him to rechannel some of the energy he was putting into studying. So there was no attempt to modify the perfectionism stemming from rigid superego.

At the Institute named for Bekhterev, it was curious to find relatively little interest in the child department in the problems of personality development, distortions of character formation, and psychotherapy which are so important in the work of Myasishchev. However, I met there a young woman, L. P. Saldina, who had a strong interest in psychotherapy. She had spent several years with Professor Sukhareva in Moscow and had written a dissertation on the families of schizophrenics. She impressed me as warm, intuitive, with a light, humorous approach to patients which should make her an excellent child psychotherapist. She had been conducting psychotherapy on suitable cases, although the main focus of the department's interest, under the leadership of G. B. Abramovich, was on the problem of epilepsy.

We saw Valya, a 13-year-old girl with a history of a longstanding character problem and difficult behavior.

Until she was three, Valya had been in an orphanage. Then she was adopted by the present parents, who failed to tell her she was adopted. There were no serious difficulties in early childhood, but Valya was a very active child who from the very beginning preferred boy's games, like football. She had a tendency to wander away from home. She was always getting her clothes dirty, which exasperated her mother.

Two years ago, some boys in the street told Valya her father was not her real father. Soon after this, she was picked up by the police trying to leave Leningrad by train to go to Moscow. She was admitted to the Institute named for Bekhterev, where she improved with chlorpromazine and psychotherapy. During the past year the difficulties recurred, especially during vacation. She began to smoke and went off several times without her mother's permission. She was readmitted to Bekhterev where Dr. Saldina treated her primarily with psychotherapy.

When Valya came in, she was a gangly, unkempt child who did

not yet appear pubertal in her physical development, dress, or behavior. She was scowling and manipulating a great wad of candy in her mouth. She was as close to rude in her answers as I saw any Soviet child. This didn't bother Dr. Saldina a bit. She remarked later it was hard to be serious when talking to this child. I asked Valya why she was in the hospital. She scowled a bit harder and replied abruptly because of her bad behavior. In response to my questions, she said she felt they had helped her there, but she didn't quite know how. It was obvious Dr. Saldina was important to her, but it seemed equally important for her not to show overt pleasure in the relationship.

Dr. Saldina diagnosed this case as psychopathy, infantile personality. Although we did not dwell on specific technique of psychotherapy in our discussion, I felt the focus was on forming a warm, trustworthy, accepting relationship which the patient would experience as quite different from the disapproval she felt from her mother. It was of interest that the subject of her adoption was forbidden territory, because the child was not supposed to know her mother was not her own. Later, I realized what a muddle Valya could be in if she thought her father was not her real father but her mother was her real mother. Dr. Saldina found no fault with the parents' policy of concealing the fact of the adoption, since the family were afraid of a repetition of the reaction of two years ago. Work with the parents, however, was considered an important and essential part of the treatment. Dr. Saldina said several times, in despair, that the mother simply did not understand the child, although the father was somewhat better.

The application of the techniques of rational psychotherapy to hospitalized adolescents in the Soviet Union is still in its infancy. The more intuitive psychiatrists and educators in fact do psychotherapy without formally designating it as such, as Dr. Polyakova told me. And some may do it well. But there is no formal supervisory program nor any attempt to make the therapist conscious of technique or of the therapeutic use of his countertransference in managing the doctor-patient relationship. I felt the attitude toward discussing the adoption in this case reflected a Soviet attitude and way of dealing with truth, particularly a truth of an anxiety-provoking nature (Chap. I). Truth per se is not highly valued; aspects of the truth are utilized to achieve socially desirable ends.

Some
Comparisons

Ziferstein's comparison of psychotherapy, as he observed it in Leningrad, with psychoanalytically based psychotherapy is interesting and stimulating. Since his observations are based on adults, we must see whether they would be transferable to the field of child and adolescent psychiatry. I think not wholly, because child therapists in the United States as well as those who work with adolescents stand closer to the Soviet position in acknowledging the need for more activity and directiveness, more emphasis on a real doctor-patient relationship of a warm, supportive, positive character. If the activity dimension is not the crucial difference, what is? After a digression, we will return to this question.

A different kind of comparison occurred to me after I became familiar with the method of autogenic training and saw it in operation: the method of Schultz and the sector psychotherapy of Felix Deutsch, based on the associative anamnesis, have both been used in the treatment of neuroses and psychosomatic disorders. Both methods assume that self-regulating mechanisms under autonomic nervous control have been interrupted and disturbed by the intrusion of mental representations of a specific target organ.

In Deutsch's theory of psychophysiological disturbances, faulty associations form between organ function and affect-laden experiences in early childhood (3). For example, asthma may appear in an allergically predisposed young child initially as a symptom of infection. If simultaneously there is a tense emotional climate, psychic trauma or conflict with a key parental figure, wheezing may become associated with a person and an affective state. Later on, the repetition of the original emotional situation may by itself evoke wheezing, since the emotional situation has acquired the power of a conditioned stimulus. The technique of interviewing known as the associative anamnesis exposes these faulty connections. Sector psychotherapy breaks the wrong connections, first by bringing them to full consciousness and exposing their irrationality. Catharsis of long-buried affect and interpretation of these feelings and associations as belonging to the past, not the present, are the effective psychotherapeutic factors. The therapy is active and directive, in the sense of limiting the focus to a certain chosen sector. Transference is used but kept implicit, not interpreted. Ideally, the end result is that the sector is "emptied," the abused target organ is restored to self-regulation. Breathing may now be regulated more by the CO_2 content of the blood and less by the conflicted feelings the child has about his mother.

In the Schultz method, mental representation of the offending organ is consciously established by passive concentration, for example, the chest and breathing of the asthmatic, after the patient has become proficient in the other standard exercises and learned to relax. Under conditions of markedly reduced afferent stimulation and voluntary activity, the patient's mental capacity to regulate the organ's activity is established. In the case of the asthmatic, he learns slow, regular breathing and associates this with peace and tranquillity. Later, perhaps he learns to inhibit faulty mental regulation of the organ's activity, for example, wheezing under stress. The end result, as with Deutsch's method, theoretically is restoration of the abused target to self-regulation.

Both of these methods depend on the establishment of a strong, predominantly positive relationship between doctor and patient, without explicit discussion of the relationship itself. Both methods manipulate consciousness and require of the patient relaxed self-observation. Perhaps Deutsch's method to some degree requires suggestibility, as Schultz's method surely does. Both require a degree of language development. Finally, both aim to free an organ for autonomic regulation.

One major difference is the simultaneous approach to the mind and the body which characterizes the Schultz method, making it consistent with the monistic position. The Deutsch method is more "mental," focusing on the thoughts and feelings evoked by a disturbed body sensation. It might be subject to Soviet criticism on the grounds of the error of idealism.

What if we were to combine the two methods? Schultz himself observed that patients in the autosuggestive state had enhanced ability to free-associate and become more productive in sessions designed to elicit psychodynamic material. I believe Americans have not made more constructive use of suggestive techniques for historical reasons.

The psychodynamic techniques of the West and the suggestive techniques of the Soviet Union had a common origin in the observations of the effects of hypnosis made in Charcot's clinic in the nineteenth century. Freud's rejection of hypnosis in favor of free association seems the decisive factor, still operating to inhibit American research on the application of suggestive techniques, especially to the problems of later childhood and adolescence. The Soviet experience has made this appear an American prejudice, passed on from one professional generation to the next. The trend of development in the West led from hypnosis to free association to psychoanalysis, focused on the working out of the transference neurosis. Then came the modifications of play techniques for young children and character analysis. Psychoanalytically based psychotherapies began to appear. The trend to highlight interpersonal aspects increased in traditional child guidance practice and more recently in family therapy.

The line of development in the USSR also starting from hypnosis led through the rejection of Freud in the thirties (Chap. I above). The effect was the inhibition of the development of a theory and practice of psychotherapy until the reaffirmation of Pavlovian principles in the fifties paved the way for Platonov's Pavlovian interpretation of the hypnotic state and the development of suggestive techniques (4). The Soviet emotional prejudice, then, has had its price.

In this historical context, let us return to the question of essential differences in the psychotherapeutic techniques of the USSR and the US. The outcome for the West is the proliferation of psychotherapeutic techniques which improve the patient's adjustment by *sensitizing* him to his human environment, and his human environment to him. Child guidance, marriage counseling, family therapy are all examples. In contrast, the Soviet trend has fostered a group of suggestive therapies which *desensitize* the patient to his human and physical environment, promoting peace, tranquillity, and relaxation, in spite of environmental stress.

However, on the Soviet side, Myasishchev's school has reintroduced the goal of adapting a patient to his human environment, though the work has not yet sufficiently been applied to the child and adolescent field. But the trend is there, and as matters stand now, the Soviets have more freedom of choice than we do in one sense, for they can choose suggestive techniques far more readily than we. I would not question the validity of observations made in Leningrad that certain conditions, such as psychophysiological disturbances and stuttering, lend themselves better to suggestive techniques. In the child field, enuresis might well fall in this category. Other conditions, notably neurotic character disorders, or the "neurosis of development," are better treated by rational psychotherapy.

In conclusion, we should try to overcome our emotional prejudice and search for new ways of utilizing suggestion, without abandoning our psychodynamic insights. And if our Soviet colleagues give us a chance to export anything, we might try to show them that Freudian and post-Freudian theory has undergone development and change.

VI

Training
Psychiatric
Personnel

The American literature on Soviet psychiatry contains few descriptions of training received either by psychiatrists or by those in the ancillary professions. One brief report was made by the First US Mission on Mental Health to the USSR (1, pp. 63–70). There were some discrepancies between this report and the data I collected. In the Soviet system, there are three grades of medical workers. The higher medical worker is a doctor or *vrach,* a graduate of a medical institute. The middle medical worker or *feldsher* is a graduate of a medical technicum. The lower medical worker, *medsestra* or nurse, is a graduate of a nursing school. There is no profession outside of medicine corresponding to social work, with its special contribution to the field of psychiatry in the United States.

Some differences between the two countries become apparent as we look at the Soviet approach to training. Some of these differences exist in ideology, approaches to diagnostic thinking, and treatment methods, already considered. There is also a multiplicity of levels in the training of Soviet doctors with which we are unfamiliar in the United States, because the Soviet system historically was more closely associated in its development with the European tradition of medical education. This multiplicity has the advantage of flexibility, broadening the opportunity for choice. There is room for a variety of people in the mental health system. The Soviet doctor at the lowest level who cares for psychiatric patients has far less education than the full-fledged American child psychiatrist. So more personnel can qualify for this type of patient care, which in turn is potentially accessible to more people. However, the highest educational level of the Soviet child psychiatrist is above the level of the American child psychiatrist. This acts as a stimulus to academic achievement and research, lacking in our own system.

Another difference between the two systems which I believe might have far-reaching consequences is the separation (with some exceptions) of Soviet psychiatry from university affiliation. This arrangement isolates psychiatry from psychology. Our practice of placing hospitals and medical schools under university affiliation and in turn placing psychologists from the university in clinical settings increases the opportunity for cross-fertilization between the two disciplines.

Finally, the relationship of Soviet child psychiatry to pediatrics and general psychiatry is different from the situation in the United States. The Soviet doctor enters the field of child psychiatry after general pediatric training. At the lower levels, the psychoneurologist working in a polyclinic has a close tie to pediatrics. At the higher levels, advanced study is more under the control of general psychiatry. Dissertations in child psychiatry for advanced degrees are defended in general psychiatric research institutes.

Higher Medical Workers: Levels

Undergraduate medical training is offered at medical institutes after ten years of regular school. The duration of the curriculum is six years. It is possible to elect one of several programs; adult clinical medicine, pediatrics, stomatology, public health (epidemiology), or pharmacology. Dr. A. G. Romanova at the Psychoneurological Hospital named for Kashenko described to me the teaching of psychiatry in the general medical curriculum. During the third year, a course in general psychology is offered: 15–20 hours. Normal development is considered, and the doctor-patient relationship in its general and ethical aspects receives some attention. In the fifth year, psychiatry is introduced as a formal subject with 36 hours of lectures and 50 hours of practical exercises, chiefly demonstration of patients. This does not include child psychiatry. In the sixth year, elective specializations, "subordinatorships," are now possible in the hospitals and clinics attached to the medical institute.

The First US Mission reported somewhat differently: "All medical students, in their sixth and final year, are required to take 96 hours of lectures in psychiatry, followed by a two-week clinical clerkship at the bedside in a mental hospital. Students who elect psychiatry as their prospective specialty receive an additional two months of psychiatric training during this final year at a mental hospital, where they receive instruction by the psychiatry faculty, in seminars of 15 to 30 students" (1, p. 64).

In the pediatric institutes, Professor Kovalev wrote me that psychiatry is taught in the sixth year. Two-thirds of the course is spent on psychiatric disorders of children and adolescents, with practical exercises at children's psychiatric hospitals.

The typical graduate of a medical institute works as a therapist in a hospital or a polyclinic, in general adult or pediatric medicine, often in remote rural areas. There is said to be widespread dislike of these assignments, especially by young people brought up and trained under urban conditions. They are reported to feel they are given too much medical responsibility without easy access to specialized resources. They must live in areas lacking urban and cultural advantages. One child psychiatrist described her experience practicing as a pediatrician in the far east of Russia with a mixed oriental, Eskimo, and Russian population. Her responsibilities were heavy, but she felt she got to know the families of the patients under her care quite intimately and the whole experience was of value to her in her later training as a child psychiatrist. She received high pay by usual standards. Some young doctors are assigned to hospitals in large cities. Placements are made depending on existing demands as determined by the Ministry of Health, USSR, and the ministries of the various republics.

A small minority of students specialize immediately after graduation on special recommendation. These are doctors who have held student appointments and acquired some practical experience in a specialty. If it was necessary, in order to meet the problem of adequate distribution of medical personnel, to assign some doctors to positions without their consent, the problem was not discussed with me.

Concerning training in child psychiatry, V. V. Kovalev, his associate, K. S. Lebedinskaya, and their assistants in Moscow were most helpful in providing information and in permitting me to sit in on lectures, clinical demonstrations, and oral examinations. Supplementary information came from S. S. Mnukhim and G. B. Abramovich in Leningrad and S. N. Zinchkina, assistant to I. A. Polishchuk in Kiev. Training in child psychiatry is offered to pediatricians after some years of practice. Those who wish to specialize may apply to an institute for advanced training of physicians for the "cycle of specialization in psychoneurology," the first step in becoming a child psychiatrist. The prerequisite is graduation from a medical institute in general pediatrics. An intensive four-month program is offered. The graduate works as a "psychoneurologist" in polyclinics, seeing psychiatric and neurological patients. The psychoneurologist works only with children. The first step for a doctor who wishes to become an adult psychiatrist is to take a psychiatric internship at a mental hospital such as Kashenko. These internships have been offered since approximately 1967. Since the subordinatorships have been offered in medical school, I gathered it has been possible for some doctors to specialize in adult psychiatry immediately after graduation from the medical institute. Internships have also become available in child psychiatry in a few cities.

One of the most positive features of Soviet medicine is its stress on continuing education. The graduate medical institutes offer, in addition to initial specialization in psychoneurology, "cycles of increased qualifications." The prerequisite is practice as a psychoneurologist, a neuropathologist, or a general psychiatrist. Some programs also require six months of home preparation, with written reports on four control assignments: the treatment of childhood epilepsy; the clinical picture and classification of oligophrenia; the monosymptomatic neuroses of childhood; the neuroses, including pathogenesis and the theory of Pavlov. Of 35 candidates who prepare these reports at a given time, 25 might be chosen for the three-month program. The curriculum is similar to the one for the initial cycle of specialization, but in more depth.

"Thematic cycles" are also offered to psychoneurologists and neurologists who concentrate on one theme, for example, oligophrenia and residual organic states; neuroses and personality disorders (psychopathy and pathological development of the personality); psychopharmacology. Thematic cycles are chiefly chosen by teachers in training institutes, such as the medical institutes, or teachers of general psychiatry.

The psychoneurologist who wishes to become a child psychiatrist may apply for an "ordinatorship" at a children's mental hospital. Clinical ordinators rotate through the departments of a large mental hospital for two years, with duties similar to the psychiatric resident in the United States. They work up and treat patients. They present their cases at clinical conferences and occasionally prepare reports on selected clinical subjects. I met one young woman who had come to Moscow from her home city of Vladivostok to be an ordinator for two years. She was planning to return to her home after her training to make her specialized skills available in a large city which needs more child psychiatrists. Another young woman who had a special interest in psychotherapy was working in Dr. Drapkin's adolescent department. At the time of my visit, this was the only way a child psychiatrist could acquire training in psychotherapy in a psychiatric training program. Senior ordinators may spend a third year at the mental hospital, working in one department, much as the senior resident does in the United States. The graduate of the ordinator program is a specialist in child psychiatry, qualified to work in a children's mental hospital. His level of training and prestige seems most comparable to the fully trained American child psychiatrist.

Aspirants to the degree of Candidate of Medical Science may enter a three-year program, after completion of two years of ordinatorship. A foreign language is also a prerequisite. Only a small minority of doctors I met could speak conversational English but some, able to read English, showed interest in knowing more about our literature. Aspirants work under supervision, preparing a thesis on a specific clinical subject. They are relieved of most of the responsibility for routine patient care. One doctor prepared a dissertation on the psychic characteristics of school-age children with epilepsy (see Chap. VII below). Another doctor, in the process of collecting data for his dissertation, was doing detailed clinical studies of patients with pathological development of the personality. The supervision and the defense of the dissertations is under the control of one of the psychiatric research institutes. When a dissertation is to be defended, notification is published in the newspaper, and the aspirant reads a summary at a formal meeting at his research institute, attended by senior professors and peers. After invited discussants consider the material, questions are encouraged from the floor. Graduates of the program receive the degree of Candidate of Medical Science. They are qualified to work as "senior scientific workers." In addition to conducting research, they may also teach and are eligible for the academic rank of "docent."

The highest level in the Soviet system is the degree of Doctor of Medical Science, attained only by a very few. Prerequisite is the Candidate of Medical Science degree. A program of independent study and investigation leads to the preparation and defense of a thesis at a higher level than the candidate thesis. Graduates may receive the rank of full professor and be appointed to a chair or *kafedra* of psychiatry. While I was visiting, K. S. Lebedinskaya was working on a doctoral dissertation on the psychic characteristics of children with endocrine dysfunction. Some of her preliminary work is reviewed below in Chapter VII.

Training Centers for Child Psychiatry

Considering the size and population of the country, there are relatively few training centers for child psychiatrists in the Soviet Union. Those in existence in 1969 were located in Moscow, Leningrad, Kiev, and Sverdlovsk (a city in the Urals). Centers at that time were in the planning stage for Riga and Tashkent. Recognizing the need to extend training to republics outside of Russia, Professor Kovalev and his staff were offering one-month courses in psychoneurology to qualified doctors in Riga and Tashkent. The psychiatric situation in Tashkent was described by a doctor from there who was visiting the Children's Psychoneurological Hospital in Moscow. She was interested in establishing a training program for child psychiatrists. She said there was a psychoneurological dispensary and polyclinics with psychoneurological offices for children in Tashkent. However, there was no hospital for children with psychiatric disorders. In the republic of Uzbekistan, of which Tashkent is the capital, there were 3,000,000 children and 41 child psychiatrists in 1969. Professor Kovalev's program was offered through the existing institute, so far organized to train only adult psychiatrists. It would have been of great interest to observe this pilot program, but I was denied permission to visit Tashkent while it was going on. Since there is difficulty in meeting the standard of one child psychiatrist for each 20,000 children in Uzbekistan, according to the visiting doctor, a new training program could be extremely important.

For each of the established centers, the general structure was similar. A kafedra of child psychiatry was the teaching nucleus, associated with an "institute for the increased qualification of physicians." In Moscow, there were associations with two psychiatric research institutes. In Leningrad, one kafedra of child psychiatry was connected with the Pediatric Institute. The programs described sounded very similar at the various levels already outlined.

Each kafedra had special research interests. Kovalev's group was working on psychopathy, pathological development of the personality, and the neurosis of fear. The group in Moscow associated with Professor Sukhareva was interested in epilepsy. Another group in Moscow under the child psychiatrist, M. S. Vrono, was working on the genetic aspects of schizophrenia. This work was part of a larger study under Professor Snezhnevski at the Psychiatric Institute, USSR. At the Leningrad center under Professor Mnukhin, one group was interested in residual damage to the central nervous system and its correlation with various psychiatric disorders. Another group was studying pyknolepsy and petit mal epilepsy. At the Bekhterev Institute in Leningrad, Professor Abramovich was continuing to investigate epilepsy with its specific childhood features. In Kiev, a chair of child psychiatry was just established in January 1969, although the center had been receiving trainees for four years. Professor I. A. Polishchuk and his staff were interested in endocrine disorders and their psychic characteristics in children, cerebral palsy, treatment of neuroses and neurotic-like syndromes, and phenylketonuria of children and adults.

Cycle of Specialization: Psychoneurology

While I was visiting Professor Kovalev and his co-workers at the Kafedra of Child Psychiatry associated with the Psychoneurological Hospital for Children and Adolescents in Moscow, they were teaching the cycle of specialization in psychoneurology to a group of about 40 pediatricians. This four-month program with 70 days of instruction ran from January 3 to April 26, 1969. It was run by the Kafedra of Child Psychiatry, the Kafedra of Clinical and Experimental Physiology, the Kafedra of Military Medical Preparation, and the Kafedra of Child Neuropathology, all associated with the Central Institute for the Increased Qualification of Physicians in Moscow. Nine instruction days were taught by the staff from military medicine. I have no information about the contents of this aspect of training or whether it is included in all of the cycles offered. The students were pediatricians learning the specialty of psychoneurology.

The teaching facilities were in a building shared by the Moscow City Psychoneurological Dispensary for Children and Adolescents, with Hospital. There was a large lecture room with many wall charts containing information about the organization of psychiatric services, a small library, and several offices for individual doctors and practical clinical work. Case material was abundantly available from the hospital, supplemented by outpatient material at the polyclinics of Moscow. The daily program consisted of a two-hour lecture in the morning, followed by an illustrative case presentation. Afternoons were devoted to the examination of patients by students in pairs, followed by a group discussion with an instructor. Special parts of the program were given in other places: lectures in general psychopathology were offered at the Psychoneurological Hospital named for Kashenko for adults: lectures on oligophrenia were given at the Home for Invalids.

The curriculum for this particular cycle is presented in Table 11 in simplified form, to show the subject matter taught to doctors expecting to work in children's polyclinics that receive both psychiatric and neurological cases. The physiology of the nervous system and neuro-pathology occupied 10 days and were taught by the cooperating kafedras. The emphasis on the functioning and pathology of the nervous system is consistent with the physiologically based, monistic psychiatry characteristic of the Soviet system. The general psychopathology at Kashenko occupied 7 days, relatively little considering these were pediatricians who had limited experience with mental illness. Distributed throughout the 70 teaching days were 8 mornings devoted to Marxism-Leninism, showing the importance attributed to this subject. I have no idea what the content of these lectures was and consider this one area where more information is needed. The afternoons of these days and Saturday mornings were scheduled at the polyclinics, totaling 12 practical exercises in examining ambulatory patients. This emphasis on the practical seemed entirely appropriate to me in terms of the job these doctors were being trained to perform. Speech disturbances were given 5 days, the same amount of time devoted to reactive states and personality disorders. Oligophrenia and epilepsy each received four days. Treatment was deemphasized in the formal lecture series: psycho-pharmacology 2 days, psychotherapy 1 day, and pedagogy 1 day. However, treatment of specific conditions appeared in 6 days of the program of practical exercises: neuroleptic drugs, psychopathy, oligo-phrenia, and cerebral palsy.

Some areas we considered important in the United States were either deemphasized or missing: the theme of the doctor-patient relationship, in its real and irrational aspects, its use as a therapeutic tool, and explicit instruction in interview technique (with parents or children) were conspicuous by their absence. No techniques of expressive therapy were included. Although the importance of the collective is recognized as a therapeutic tool, there were no efforts to teach group process or dynamics. Family assessment and work with families of disturbed children were not explicitly discussed. Developmental tasks of childhood and adolescence as they relate to psychopathology were discussed to some extent in the psychology lecture but not sufficiently emphasized. Social problems as they relate to the psychopathology of childhood were not considered.

Three formal lectures in the program were attended, each one by a different instructor. They were clear, well-organized presentations. Dr. K. S. Lebedinskaya's lecture followed the series on general psychopathology and served as an introduction to the special psychopathology of childhood. She talked on infectious psychoses, drawing a distinction between symptomatic psychoses accompanying general toxic states and infectious psychoses due to disease of the brain or meninges. She added that this distinction is not so clear-cut in childhood, since the brain is often affected in general toxic states, such as dysentery. While these psychoses are seen more in general pediatric hospitals than in psychoneurological practice, they still are part of child psychiatry. Dr. Lebedinskaya described disturbances in several spheres, characteristic of these states: disturbances of consciousness, memory defects, anxiety and excitement, emotional lability and hyperesthesia. Individual infections have special identifying features. For example, she mentioned the schizophrenic-like picture frequently accompanying dysentery in early childhood.

Professor Kovalev's lecture on residual encephalopathy introduced some key concepts in Russian diagnostic thinking, elaborated above in Chapter III. Professor Kovalev referred to the work of Mnukhin and credited Freud with study of cerebral paralysis in children and recognition of the role of intrauterine trauma and birth trauma. Kovalev also mentioned the role of prenatal toxoplasmosis. He referred to a study at the Bekhterev Institute where half of a series of unspecified psychiatric syndromes were attributed to postnatal infections in the first year of life. In a discussion of pathogenesis, he said that varying etiological factors can produce a similar clinical picture, depending on several variables:

1. The age reactivity of the brain: the older the child, the milder the damage to global functions.
2. Localization of the brain damage: One example given was diencephalic damage due to basilar arachnoiditis causing affective disturbances, psychopathic-like states, and cerebrasthenia.
3. Massiveness of the brain damage.

Table 11. Cycle of Specialization in Child Psychiatry: Four-Month Program

Number of Days	Subject of Lecture	Practical Exercises
5	Physiology of higher nervous activity———	
9	Military medicine———	
1	Introductory lecture	Introductory practical information
7	General psychopathology	Characteristics of delusions in children: 2 days Affective disturbances Obsessive phenomena Motor disturbances Disturbances of consciousness Intellectual disturbances
2	Psychology: psychic characteristics of children: pathopsychology of childhood	Methods of psychological study of children
2	Psychopharmacology	Methods of Psychiatric Study: 1 day Neuroleptic drugs: 1 day
1	Medical genetics: inheritance*	Hereditary illnesses of childhood
3	Psychic disturbances with infections (acute infectious disturbances, syphilis, cerebral rheumatism)*	Psychic disturbances in grippe: 1 day Psychic disturbances in children's infections: 1 day Cerebrasthenic states during brain infections: 1 day
1	Psychic disturbances in general somatic illnesses of childhood	Clinical conference
1	Psychic disturbances in cerebro-endocrine disorders	Psychic disturbances in brain infections
1	Postnatal brain trauma	Psychic disturbances with brain trauma
1	Birth trauma and asphyxia: Residual neuropsychic disturbances	Psychic disturbances with brain trauma
4	Epilepsy	Clinical conference Clinical picture of epilepsy in early childhood; personality

		changes with epilepsy; treatment of epilepsy in childhood
3	Schizophrenia	Clinical features of schizophrenia in early childhood Clinical conference Neurotic-like states with schizophrenia
5	Reactive states	Clinical conference Neuroses in children Monosymptomatic neuroses in children Neurasthenia Pathological development of character
3	Psychopathies	Clinical conference Epileptoid psychopathy Psychasthenia and other forms of psychopathy
1	Psychotherapy	Treatment of psychopathy
1	Therapeutic pedagogy	Clinical conference
4	Neuropathology of childhood————	
4	Oligophrenia	Clinical picture of oligophrenia in early childhood; clinical forms of oligophrenia; differential diagnosis of oligophrenia; treatment of oligophrenia
5	Disturbances of speech————	
2	Cerebral palsies	Treatment of cerebral palsies
1	Legal and forensic psychiatry	
1	Organization of psychiatric help for children and adolescents	Organization of extramural help
8	Marxism-Leninism	Polyclinic: 8 days
4	(No morning lecture)	Polyclinic: 4 days (Saturdays 9:00–3:00)
1	Consultation and preparation for examination	
1	Examination	

Source: Adapted from mimeographed schedule of program: January 1–April 26, 1969.

* A change handwritten into this part of the schedule indicates more time to be given to genetics, less to infections than shown here.

Kovalev then introduced the concept of an original residual defect following a brain insult evolving into a disease process, depending on subsequent environment factors. Such a process is believed by Sukhareva and others to occur in one kind of epilepsy and in some periodic psychoses. This means the Russian concept of organic residual is not necessarily a static one. In the second part of the lecture, a classification of the type of neuropsychic disturbances resulting from residual damage to the brain was outlined (Chap. III). More detailed descriptions were given of cerebrasthenic, psychopathic-like, and neurotic-like syndromes. Kovalev particularly emphasized that the differential diagnosis of these from what he termed true neurosis was important, since psychotherapy will not work in the case of the symptoms produced by organic residual. He felt this question had not been sufficiently studied in the Soviet Union and even less abroad. After the lecture, a case was presented to show the kind of neurotic-like picture these doctors were being taught to regard as predominantly an organic disturbance.

Fedor, a ten-year-old boy in the third class, was readmitted to the Psychoneurological Hospital for Children and Adolescents three months previously because of headaches, emotional instability, and easy fatigability, affecting school performance. The family history revealed the mother and father had separated because of the father's alcoholism and irritability. The boy was living with his mother, who was working as an engineer.

When Fedor was two, he had severe grippe, followed by persistent severe headaches and dizziness. At three years, stuttering and enuresis began. He became so hyperactive, restless, and unable to concentrate that he was admitted at three and one-half years to the psychoneurological hospital. He was placed on dehydration therapy and chlorpromazine and discharged, to be followed by a doctor in his local polyclinic. When he began school, Fedor was so distracted by strong stimuli that he was unable to work well. He constantly complained of headaches and dizziness. He had to repeat the first class.

Because of all of these difficulties, Fedor was sent to the sanatorium for neurotic children, where he at first adapted poorly to the regime. He returned to regular school in the third class and now began to show behavior problems: he took 10 rubles ($11.00) from his mother. In school he was not motivated to do his work.

When he returned to the hospital, physical examination was not remarkable except for general pallor and poor nutrition. Neuro-

logical examination revealed some minimal signs: slight hydrocephalus, slight facial asymmetry, and a bit of unsteadiness when
carrying out voluntary acts such as hopping. Mental status revealed tics of the face, mild stuttering, and several neurotic complaints. Fedor complained of headaches and episodes of dizziness
lasting about ten minutes. He mentioned an episode in school when
everyone's voices seemed very far away. In the hospital, he was
often tearful and unable to sleep well. He expressed fear of grippe
and conflicted feelings about his parents. He loved both mother and
father, in spite of father's behavior. In the hospital environment,
Fedor's behavior improved but the deep disturbance of ability to
do sustained school work continued.

In his discussion of this boy, Professor Kovalev said the leading
syndrome was cerebrasthenia. The headaches, dizziness, and sensitivity to sound suggested a diencephalic disturbance after the grippe
infection. The moodiness and tearfulness, he said, were consistent,
too, with a diencephalic residual lesion. The tics and enuresis he
placed more in the category of neurotic-like disturbances. The behavior problems and emotional instability suggested some elements
of the psychopathic-like syndrome. The diagnosis was postinfectious
residual organic state with cerebrasthenic syndrome. Fedor was able
to go to school only with supplementary periods of sanatorium or
hospital care but the ultimate prognosis was favorable because of
his intact intellect. Treatment recommended was dehydration
therapy and neuroleptics: levomepromazine for the affective disturbances and librium for anxiety and restlessness, with some
medication-free periods. If behavior problems worsened, chlorpromazine and propericiazine could be used.

The case shows how the psychoneurologist is trained to see
the organic components in a chronic neurotic clinical picture. He
is discouraged from trying to influence psychotherapeutically symptoms diagnosed as the manifestations of organic residuals. The
social factors in Fedor's case were not explored. However, the
child's vulnerability to stress was recognized. He would continue
to require medication and perhaps the intermittent protection of a
sanatorium-type regime. American psychiatrists might have
dwelled on the family situation to the exclusion of assessing the
grippe and its aftermath.

The psychology lecture was given by S. Ya. Rubenshtein. It was
a marathon four-hour lecture, first defining terms of general psy-

chology: sensation, perception, consciousness, and so forth. These mental processes were described as reflections of the external world. Character formation was described in general terms with emphasis on the role of social relationships. Stages of child development were given, utilizing some of the concepts of Piaget in depicting stages of intellectual development and characteristics of play at different ages. A second psychology lecture was to outline "pathopsychology" in childhood.

The procedure for examining a patient and summarizing the findings was taught in the early practical sessions. Dr. Lebedinskaya was kind enough to go through the procedure for my benefit with the following case.

> Lara, a 15-year-old girl, was transferred to the Psychoneurological Hospital for Children and Adolescents from the Fifteenth Psychoneurological Hospital (for older adolescents) because she was felt to be too immature for the older setting. She had been originally admitted because of intense preoccupation with her body, fear of fatness, weight loss, and moodiness. This had all culminated in a suicidal gesture and increasing uncooperativeness with the psychiatrist in the psychoneurological dispensary.
>
> She was the only child of an army officer and a mother who was working as an engineer. During the pregnancy with Lara, the mother, who at the time was working in chemical production, had some seizures. The medical history was not remarkable except for a head trauma at nine with loss of consciousness for some period with no sequelae. Lara's physical development was slow. In early childhood she played well and was fond of dolls. Her first school years were not unusual. She was a responsible student and developed an interest in being a detective.
>
> In the sixth class, Lara began to be moody and irritable. In the seventh class, she became critical of members of the family, especially her mother and grandmother. She fought with contemporaries and complained that they were "hooligans." She began to be preoccupied with deeper questions of life and its meaning. She read a lot, showing particular interest in nineteenth-century writers such as Tolstoi. Specific preoccupations with body size and shape began to dominate Lara's thoughts. She felt her mother was too fat and blamed both parents for bad inheritance. She complained her thighs were too fat, her eyes were the wrong color, and her hair was not nice. She kept looking at herself in

the mirror and began to reduce her food consumption to avoid being fat. During the summer, she became thin while attending Pioneer Camp but did not enjoy herself and lost her taste for food. In the eighth class, she continued to be preoccupied with the meaninglessness of life and with her body. She did gymnastics and asked the advice of a physical culture instructor about her figure. She was taken to a psychiatrist and cooperated initially in taking medicine because she believed it would help her figure. Then she became increasingly depressed and uncooperative, expressing wishes to kill herself by jumping off a balcony or throwing herself under a streetcar. An actual suicidal gesture led to her hospitalization.

Physical examination revealed an unusually pale, slender, pubertal girl, but no other remarkable findings. Her first menstrual period came shortly after hospitalization. She was tearful, complained of feeling unattractive. She believed her nose was shaped poorly and complained she had a bad figure; she especially disliked her legs. She saw no sense in living, but did not regard her state as illness and demanded discharge. She smiled inappropriately at times and expressed the fear that she would get fat if she stayed in the hospital.

Lara became calmer under treatment with levomepromazine, amitriptyline, and trifluoperazine. She read a lot and became interested in drawing. Her mood shifted and she became euphoric. She frequently smiled inappropriately, seemed indifferent to her state, and was somewhat manneristic. Her body preoccupations and lack of insight into her condition continued. Five days after transfer to the children's psychoneurological hospital, she became suddenly excited, hostile, demanded consultation with a physical culture specialist, and demanded discharge. When we saw her, she was still in a similar state: She was a thin, pale girl, defensive, smiling inappropriately, denying her illness, dismissing her suicidal wishes as foolish.

Students are encouraged to keep notes on their cases as follows: *psychic status, physical status,* and *neurological status,* with regard to the *course of the illness,* the *premorbid picture,* and *inherited factors.* From these data, the analysis, as outlined by Dr. Lebedinskaya, is illustrated here with the case of Lara.

The *basic syndrome* was described as dysmorphophobia, common in adolescence, suggestive of schizophrenia, or in some cases, anorexia nervosa. Lara's preoccupations, characteristic of dysmorphophobia, were her bodily preoccupations and her delusional ideas about ugliness. *Additional symptoms* were affective disturbances and altered personal relationships, with some paranoid ideas. Her *neurological status* was not remarkable. *Physical findings* were infantilism, including delayed sexual development.

The *onset of the illness* was gradual at puberty with moodiness and "philosophical intoxication," another common adolescent symptom. The *course* was gradual, with some periods of exacerbation. Lara's *premorbid personality* had a paranoid tinge. She was also described as formally punctual and self-critical. *Physical characteristics* of importance were the history of head trauma and delayed development. A possible *genetic factor* was indicated in the description of the father's character.

Dr. Lebedinskaya diagnosed Lara as schizophrenic but included a reactive state in the pubertal period in the differential diagnosis. Students are expected to complete the case analysis by discussing *therapy* and the *literature* on the subject.

I also observed an oral examination, conducted by Dr. Lebedinskaya just after the trainees had completed their series of lectures on general psychopathology at Kashenko. The questions were conducted in such a way that the session was a learning experience as well as a test of knowledge. Basic definitions of key concepts constituted most of the examination: illusions, hallucinations, delusions, fantasy, obsessions, compulsions, phobias, and so on. One group of questions had to do with typical adolescent syndromes. The content of the examination was based on formal psychopathology, as it is presented in a standard psychiatric text.

Ancillary
Personnel

A variety of personnel besides doctors is involved in the care of Soviet psychiatric patients. The educational background of the teachers, educators, and speech therapists who work with children was briefly described in Chapter IV above. The restricted role of psychologists in clinical settings was considered in Chapter III. *Feldshers* and nurses also work with psychiatric patients.

The feldsher attends a "medical technicum" after ten years of secondary school education. Victor Sidel, an American, studied the role of feldshers in Soviet medical practice (2). He learned that in rural areas, feldshers are admitted to the technicum after an eight-year education. In this event, their program at the technicum lasts a year longer so they can learn basic subjects: history, literature, mathematics, physics, chemistry, and foreign language. The duration of the program, then, depends on how much secondary school education the student has completed before entering: two and one-half or three and one-half years. Subjects taught include Marxism-Leninism, Latin, basic medical sciences, and clinical specialties, as well as nursing technique, physiotherapy, and physical culture. Dr. Romanova at the adult Psychoneurological Hospital named for Kashenko explained the psychiatric training of feldshers. In the technicum, there is a six-month course in psychiatry. After graduation, the feldsher can enter a two-year program at a psychoneurological hospital such as Kashenko. The student learns about typical psychiatric states, handling disturbed patients, and giving medication. Examinations are given after the first and second year. Graduates work in psychiatric hospitals (largely doing nursing type of work), in psychiatric emergency services under the supervision of doctors, and in psychoneurological clinics. Further inquiry is needed about what role feldshers play in a psychoneurological hospital for children.

A nurse enters training in a nursing school after eight years of secondary education. I was told the program lasts two years, but the First US Mission reported three years (1, p. 69). At the Psychoneurological Hospital for Children in Moscow, the following series of lectures was being given by a child psychiatrist for first-year students in the field of psychiatry:

1. History of psychiatry, the work of a nurse in a psychiatric hospital, the work of the educator and of the upbringer who assists the educator.
2. Initial psychiatric help, uncooperative patients with medical complications, bleeding, etc., sterile procedures (two lectures).
3. Diagnostic methods: Analysis of blood, cerebrospinal fluid, pneumoencephalogram, psychological investigation, examining the vegetative nervous system.
4. Structure of the central nervous system, conditioned and unconditioned reflexes, excitement and inhibition, regulatory functions, psychoses, etiology and characteristics of childhood disorders.

5. States of consciousness, confusion, delirium, amentia, twilight states.
6. Hallucinations, visual and auditory, distinction from illusion, delusions.
7. Speech disturbances, excitement, psychopathic-like behavior, fantasy formation.
8. Disturbances of intellect: memory, attention, thought; disturbances in the emotional and volitional sphere; impulse disturbances.

The following series was being offered by the same psychiatrist to second-year students:

1. Schizophrenia (two lectures).
2. Epilepsy (two lectures).
3. Infections, toxic psychoses.
4. Brain trauma.
5. Behavior difficulties in children.
6. Neuroses, reactive states.
7. Concluding lecture.

Some Implications for American Training

One of the positive features of the Soviet system is the way in which it encourages continuing education and increasing professional qualifications. Advanced training is rewarded by better positions and by salary increases. Many nurses and feldshers enter medical institutes to become full-fledged doctors after several years of work.

The multiplicity of levels in the training of doctors has some advantages worth our consideration, especially at a time when American medicine seems particularly open to exploring new ways to approach training. In psychiatry, a multileveled system allows more people to become eligible to work in the mental health system where the need for increased numbers of trained personnel is great. An expanded range of levels at which a psychiatrist might work could be one alternative to further development of ancillary mental health professionals outside medicine. Higher academic degrees in medical science may stimulate those with ability to advanced study and preparation for careers in research.

Our tendency to associate medical schools with universities seems healthier to me than the Soviet practice of usually keeping them separate. One of the results on the Soviet side is the persisting isolation of medical psychology from psychiatry. However, I believe we should have even more interchange than we do between academic departments in related disciplines and psychiatry.

We might consider requiring control work or preparation of written assignments as a prerequisite to enter a training program. The value of reading, periodically reviewing the literature, report writing, and organizing a body of material receives too little consideration in our programs.

More specifically related to the problems of training in child psychiatry, pediatric training could be required for those who wish to enter child psychiatry. Psychiatric residents need more instruction about minimal brain damage and associated psychiatric syndromes, without losing psychodynamic understanding, to achieve diagnostic sophistication. It is just as serious to misjudge what is not modifiable in a child as to overlook reversible disturbances amenable to individual psychotherapy. To expect a child to change in ways in which he cannot is an error psychiatrists often ascribe to parents and teachers and one to which we can ill afford to contribute ourselves. Finally, it may well be that relationship therapy individually or in groups could be carried out by workers with far less training than our full-fledged child psychiatrists or clinical psychologists at the doctoral level.

VII

Research

Research activities of the late fifties and sixties continued traditional Soviet interests in the problems of childhood schizophrenia, epilepsy, and syndromes that result from residual organic brain damage (17, 8). To these, however, were added some new lines of inquiry. Genetic studies became a legitimate field of inquiry, acknowledging the possibility of inheritance of acquired characteristics through environmentally caused gene mutations. Our department of the hospital associated with the Psychoneurological Dispensary for Children and Adolescents in Moscow was exclusively devoted to the study of genetic syndromes. In another direction, this interest has led to further work in the field of oligophrenia with definition of the syndromes associated with chromosomal abnormalities. Sukhareva tried to refine a classification of oligophrenia, according to the etiological agent and the developmental stage of the organism at which the damage occurs. Forms of retardation, too, associated with toxoplasmosis and immuno-biological incompatabilities, have aroused considerable interest. The refinement of the classification of retardation has led to the recognition that there are many kinds of delays in intellectual development of a reversible nature which must be differentiated from oligophrenia. Medical people and educators have focused on the etiology of school failure and poor achievement. The importance of differentiating these reversible states from true oligophrenia is well appreciated but made complex by the avoidance of testing.

Finally, more studies have been done in the whole field of "border-line states" in the Soviet sense. T. P. Simpson's work with preschool children led to the recognition of many neurotically based somatic symptoms at this age: anorexia, vomiting, coughing, shortness of breath, enuresis. There is great interest in speech pathology, particularly stuttering problems approached from the diagnostic and educational point of view. V. V. Kovalev and his co-workers in Moscow have been conducting studies of the anxiety neurosis in children, pathological character development, and ways of differentiating various types of speech disorders. This increased interest in the milder psychiatric disorders is beginning to lead Soviet investigators toward the problems of systematizing knowledge and forming a theoretical base for educational approaches and psychotherapy but, as yet, these fields have been little explored.

Some Studies of Childhood
and Adolescent Schizophrenia

To illustrate the Soviet approach to research in childhood schizophrenia, I have chosen several studies from the Clinic for Childhood Psychoses of the Psychiatric Institute, Academy of Medical Sciences, USSR. Investigators whom I knew personally were extremely cooperative in making reprints of their work available to me.

The first is a multidimensional study of 60 schizophrenic children in adolescence (and a smaller group of 15 with "infectious psychosis") published as a monograph in 1959 by V. A. Gilyarovski et al. (5). Gilyarovski, discussing the Soviet attitude of that time toward hereditary factors in psychiatric disorders, said psychiatrists are trying to conduct their work in accordance with I. V. Michurin's teaching about the possibility of hereditary transmission of acquired characteristics, an approach which allows for preventive intervention. He cited work in the West, particularly recognized by Soviet psychiatrists in the field of childhood schizophrenia: Charles Bradley, Loretta Bender, Louise Despert, and Leo Kanner.

His research group consisted of 60 schizophrenic children and adolescents: 47 girls and 13 boys, a reversal of the usual sex ratio.

However, the age distribution of these patients may be significant, for 40 of them were either 15 or 16 years of age at the time of the study and only 4 were under 12. It is consistent with the general trend I have observed for the number of females with schizophrenia to increase in relation to males during adolescence.

The multidimensional approach included both clinical and laboratory studies. There was investigation of the family histories of the patients for psychosis and deviant character traits. External precipitating factors of both an organic and a psychogenic nature were studied. Clinical description of the patients, both before and during the illness, was undertaken. Among physiological correlates with the clinical picture were studies of unconditioned reflexes by means of pneumograms and plethysmograms to measure, respectively, fluctuations of respiration and peripheral blood volume. Especially interesting were EEG studies, correlating type of electrical wave activity and length of illness. Immunological activity was also studied, although the exact type was not defined. A lowering of complement titer was correlated with a slow, insidious course of schizophrenia. Sharp fluctuations in the level of complement titer were correlated with clinical states of excitement.

Chemical indicators of protein metabolism, oxidative processes, and adrenocortical activity were also studied. In the blood, determinations were made of total nitrogen, residual nitrogen, coefficient of proteolysis, Weltmann's reaction, thymol turbidity, the albumen/globulin ratio, and the cholesterol level. In the urine, the following determinations were made: the Buskin-Kimbarovski test, the oxidation coefficient, the ammonia coefficient, amino-nitrogen, and 17-ketosteroids. In going over the details of these tests, I felt the results were confusing and inconclusive. Gilyarovski's group made attempts to correlate these variables with changes in the clinical state and also with chlorpromazine treatment. They studied a subgroup of 30 patients following discharge from the hospital.

The conclusions of the authors were as follows. There is reason to believe in the congenital predisposition toward schizophrenia, because a family history of psychosis was found in 27 cases and of pathological character traits in 14 cases. The history of possible intrauterine damage was also thought to play a role in the occurrence of schizophrenia in children and adolescents. There was no evidence of infection as a cause of schizophrenia, but repeated and prolonged infections could hasten the appearance of an acute attack. Mild psychic trauma could not be considered a single cause of schizophrenia, but prolonged traumatizing situations could be significant. No evidence was found for a conflict in the mother-child relationship as a cause of schizophrenia. Endocrine activity in puberty was considered to play a significant role in establishing the schizophrenic process.

The developmental histories of the patients showed that half had been withdrawn and isolated before the illness, but a quarter were friendly, active, alert, and in no way disturbed. Fourteen patients had psychotic episodes in the prodromal period one to three years before the acute attack as a reaction to mild psychic trauma or somatic illness, or without any provocation. These abortive attacks lasted a day to two weeks and resembled the abortive episodes observed in remissions. There were gradual changes in behavior and emotional reactivity, particularly headaches, daytime sleepiness, and night fears. The commonest forms of schizophrenia in the patients studied were hallucinatory-paranoid and catatonic forms. When the process began in early childhood, the first manifestations were usually obsessions and delusion-like fantasies. A special feature of schizophrenia appearing in puberty was that the clinical picture resembled the infectious psychoses in the acuteness of the symptomatology, which included disturbances of consciousness, the presence of visual illusions, sexual disturbances and fears, disturbed interoceptive sensations.

In a preponderant number of cases, there was a correlation between psychological, EEG, biochemical, and immunological signs. At the height of the illness, there was a tendency toward diminution of the refined functions of the cortex, lack of reactivity in the plethysmographic curve, diminution to absence in the EEG of the alpha rhythm, dominance of the beta rhythm, a lowered immunological reactivity, and pathological biochemical signs in protein metabolism and oxidative processes. With improvement in the clinical state, all signs tended to reverse. There was also a trend toward normalization of conditioned inhibitory reflexes and unconditioned reflexes; concurrently, the alpha rhythm tended to return. The complement titer showed a rising trend, and the reactivity to cold stimuli, as measured by the plethysmogram, increased.

Because in some patients there was a discrepancy between laboratory signs and clinical improvement, a group of 30 were studied after discharge, and it was found that pathological EEG and plethysmographic characteristics reappeared in patients about to have a recurrence of psychotic symptoms. In the subcompensated group, these latter signs remained pathological though improved. Recurrences were favored by overfatigue, psychic trauma, and recurrent infections, and sometimes occurred for no demonstrable reason. The instability of the compensated state in these patients was underscored by the presence of abortive attacks. The authors believed schizophrenic patients require prolonged study to determine the conditions of remissions and whether supportive medication might prevent recurrence of overt psychosis. The resemblance of the abortive recurrences of the psychotic phase and larval psychotic episodes in the prodromal period may be significant in working out measures for the prevention of the first manifest psychotic outbreak or severe exacerbation.

A study by M. S. Vrono was the subject of a doctoral dissertation and several articles, published in the sixties (21, 22, 23). Vrono reviewed the admissions to the children's department of the Psychoneurological Hospital named for Kashenko from 1945 to 1959. Out of 1,380 schizophrenics aged 7 to 15 years, he selected 200 without defining his criteria. (Unfortunately, the exact method by which the study was done was not described, beyond the use of the term "catamnestic.") Half had experienced the onset of schizophrenia in childhood before 12 years, 45 below 5 years. The remaining half were adolescents when the illness began. The study is particularly valuable because of the length of the observation: ten years or more in 125 cases. The duration of the schizophrenic process, too, was prolonged: over ten years in 140 cases. There were twice as many boys as girls with onset below 10 years of age and an equal number of boys and girls with onset at 15 years. Vrono found that schizophrenic children under 12 were six to seven times less frequently admitted to this hospital than adults with schizophrenia. Further, the schizophrenic children's admissions were four times less frequent than schizophrenic adolescent admissions. From this, Vrono concluded that schizophrenia in childhood is a relatively rare disorder.

The author described the age factor in its relationship to type of onset of schizophrenia. A gradual onset was commoner in childhood, but an acute onset was nearly twice as frequent in adolescence. The characteristic insidious onset in childhood included the following symptoms: diminished closeness to the parents, unusual, one-sided interests, strange, solitary games, pathological fantasy formations, autistic trends, and changes in the emotional and intellectual spheres. The changes were subtle at first and only became more obvious as the disease progressed. Delusions and hallucinations were lacking. The symptoms resembled both those of a schizoid personality and some characteristics of healthy children: favorite games, fantasy formations, motor activity and grimacing.

The age factor was also studied in relation to the type of course of the schizophrenic process. A slow, progressive course was most characteristic of onset in childhood. The intermittent course with recovery in the interval periods was seen more in adolescence. A mixed course was also identified, characterized by slow progression of the disease with periods of acute flare-up.

The age factor was also related to the symptomatology. The younger the patient was, the simpler and less structured the symptomatology. As intellectual development progressed, there was an increasing variety and complexity of the symptoms. Vrono was particularly interested in symptoms he described as catatonic in children: posing, unusual movements, and passive submissiveness. Including speech symptomatology with catatonic symptoms, Vrono reported echolalia, verbigeration, neologisms, and mutism.

The quality of the fear the children experienced was distinctive. At first, it might be like ordinary childhood fear (fears of the dark, of being alone or of new situations). Gradually, the fears in the schizophrenic children lost their connection with reality, becoming ill-defined forebodings of death, of the end of the world, and so on, which the patients were reluctant to discuss. Some children in later childhood and adolescence had hypochondriacal fears. Delusions were rare in early childhood and tended to begin in prepuberty, at first without systematization. Among the affective disturbances, mania and depression were not seen in childhood. Obsessive and compulsive syndromes were common, as were tics and rituals. Pathological fantasy formations were also characteristic but with a peculiar quality, emphasizing numbers, maps, machinery, and travel routes.

Vrono reported 56.5 percent of his 200 patients were unable to work (22); 35.5 percent needed supervision. The younger the patient at the time of onset, the poorer the outcome. When the onset was in preschool years, there tended to be an intellectual defect resembling oligophrenia. Of 60 patients with a childhood onset, 43, or 71.6 percent, were unable to work. Of 29 with an onset under five years, an unfavorable outcome was observed in 25. However, even with an adolescent onset, 32 percent still needed supervision.

The second factor in the outcome was the malignancy of the schizophrenic process. The group of patients was divided into those with a malignant process through the whole course of the illness, a mild process for the duration of the illness, and a mixed group where the disease seemed progressive but with exacerbations in the malignancy at some point during the course.

A third factor in the outcome was hereditary predisposition. A study of the family history revealed positive factors (not further defined) in 59 percent, greater with childhood onset and an unfavorable course of the illness.

Vrono concluded that there was no direct relationship between pathology during pregnancy, birth trauma, asphyxia, postnatal infection or trauma, and the course of schizophrenia in these children. He did find that unfavorable life conditions were twice as frequent in patients with an unfavorable course as in patients with a favorable course, although he did not elucidate these. He found psychic trauma and infectious illnesses were related to the onset of the schizophrenia when there happened to be an acute or subacute type of onset. Finally, Vrono believed psychotherapy, education, and other forms of treatment all affected the course and outcome of the illness.

V. M. Bashina published a study in 1963 concerning the ability to work and the social adaptability of patients with an onset of schizophrenia in childhood and adolescence (1). Bashina's research group, also patients admitted to Kashenko in 1947–1951, consisted of 148 patients—70 females and 78 males—who had been observed over a period of 10 to 18 years. One hundred twenty-three or 83 percent were living at home at the time of the study. Of the remaining 25, some were in colonies, some were in the hospital, and 1.7 percent of the total were dead. These figures show how few patients remain hospitalized under Soviet conditions and how their maintenance in the home is more dependent on conditions at home than it is on the severity of the illness. Of the 123 who were living at home, 43 were not working, or 34.9 percent. This left 80 patients working or 65.1 percent. The work activities in these 80 were as follows:

1. Work shops and work cooperatives—3
2. Industry: low-level qualifications—29
3. Industry: middle-level qualifications—17
4. Middle technical education—5
5. Higher education—19
6. Higher and middle institutions—7

Bashina's figures agreed closely with Vrono's—Bashina's population: not working, 55.3 percent; Vrono, not working, 56.5 percent.

Since Bashina's series contained only 8 patients with a childhood onset and Vrono's series contained 60 patients with a childhood onset, the two patient populations were not the same, even though they came from the same hospital. Of Bashina's 8 cases of childhood schizophrenia, 5 had severe defects and were not working, or 62.5 percent; of Vrono's 60 cases, 43 patients were not working, or 71.6 percent.

In 1968, Bashina published a study of catatonic symptoms in children with schizophrenia and their change with age, confirming Vrono's findings (2). This study was of 52 schizophrenic patients, 34 males and 18 females. Among these was a group with a very early onset of one to three years at which time Bashina found it hard to distinguish catatonic symptoms from other diseases of the central nervous system. She described a syndrome of underactivity with emotional illness, inattentiveness and loss of acquired personal habits, indifference to the presence of parents, to wet clothing, and so forth. In the speech realm, the children would tend to repeat one word and to be completely mute or to lose what speech they had. Pavlov's symptom was observed: the children were mute in the daytime, talked to themselves at night, but stopped if adults approached. Echolalia was also seen. Another type of disturbance was alternating states of excitement, usually accompanied by muteness and restless jumping and running in circles. Full stupor and waxy flexibility does not appear at a very early age, although by three to six years, some patients were posturing, grimacing, and spinning. In some children, excitement reached a state of exhaustion, resembling a toxic state. These children experienced a particularly malignant course with deep defect formation. In Bashina's patients six to eight years old, stuporous states with maintenance of poses up to two or three months were already observed. I felt the major contributions of this study were careful clinical description and the conclusion that modification of motor and speech symptoms depends on age characteristics at different stages of development of the motor system as well as on the schizophrenic process itself. Maturation of the central nervous system permits increasing complexity and variety of symptoms with advancing age.

There is considerable interest among Soviet psychiatrists in early childhood schizophrenia. I. A. Kozlova published a study in 1967 describing the clinical course of schizophrenia in 57 patients with an onset in early childhood up to five years; 45 were male and 12 were female (10). Twenty-seven of the children were observed at four to six years of age; the rest were older. Kozlova described a congenital schizophrenic process in accordance with Loretta Bender's concept of a distortion in the maturation of the nervous system, especially those functions which appear latest in evolutionary development. Disturbances of the "instinctual life" were manifest in infancy: these children were unresponsive at a behavioral level to hunger, wetness, or change in body position. They demonstrated disturbances in rhythm and depth of sleep, poor appetite, and unusually long persistence of uncoordinated movements. Yet the infants seemed to have frozen, immobile faces. Speech development usually appeared at the expected time, but vocabularies failed to increase at the normal rate and sentences would appear late by Soviet standards—between two and three years. The infants tended to be underactive. Kozlova described a malignant course in 24 patients, including 6 of the congenital type. These patients displayed transitory mutism, withdrawal, outbursts of motor excitement, unmotivated mood swings. Those with speech development frequently had echolalia, verbigeration, and rhythm disturbances. If the children had acquired the use of the first person, they frequently lost it. As they grew older, they were left with deep defects, emotional dullness, and diminished reactivity.

It was rare for the psychotic process to begin acutely in this group of early childhood cases. Usually, there was a prodromal phase, characterized by silence, sluggishness, crying without reason, avoidance of people, tendency towards aimless running around, eating disturbances, sleep disturbances and enuresis; this preceded the psychotic phase. However, some children in the four-to-six-year age group were observed in hypomanic states, characterized by a euphoric mood and a tendency to fooling and meaningless play. One rare child from the age of two and one-half years on had hypomanic and depressive attacks.

In two studies, O. P. Yureva focused on insidious schizophrenia beginning in early childhood (25). She chose a series of 78 schizophrenic children (56 males and 19 females) with a history of a slow course or a mixed course with progression and intermittent exacerbations. In agreement with Kozlova, Gessell, and Bender, Yureva found signs of a congenital schizophrenic process.

In infancy, there were disturbances of the gastrointestinal tract, particularly the appetite. The sleep rhythm was upset, with an indistinct boundary between sleep and wakefulness. The first manifestations of the social contacts seemed disturbed, and there was a deficit in the energy level with a tendency towards underactivity, sluggishness, and insufficiency of adaptive mechanisms. Many of the patients had enuresis until puberty. As young children, these patients were limited in their emotional contact with others, though sometimes they became excessively close to one person. In preschool years, they rarely spoke or would only speak to themselves rather than to adults. They preferred to play alone at primitive, idiosyncratic activities. They were clumsy, particularly in fine, singular movements. They had difficulty in learning how to feed and dress themselves. Frequently, they would refuse solid foods. At three to five years, the usual age of questioning either did not appear, came late, or concerned abstract questions with a very unchildlike quality, revolving around expectation of death or the end of the world or of life on earth.

The age of stubbornness was unrelated to real issues and real people, not amenable to usual corrective measures, and likely to disappear as rapidly as it appeared, seemingly without reason. Creative activity in fantasy in these children was less related to real life than it is in normal children. Fantasies and drawings tended to be one-sided, repetitive, for months or even years, and contained fearful ideas related to death: war, fires, skeletons, graves. These children preferred to play by themselves, or, if a companion was present, he would be treated like a thing or an attribute of the play. Yureva concluded that one group of patients demonstrated a congenital schizophrenic process, the second group showed a schizoid constitution, and in the third group, the process appeared to start later in life. She thought that these three groups really formed a unity.

In a second study, Yureva described the manifest period of slow, insidious schizophrenia, using 18 patients (14 males and 4 females) who had a history beginning in early childhood (24). The family histories of 12 of these patients showed schizophrenia. This is a 2:3 ratio, in contrast to the nearly 1:1 ratio of patients with a positive family history of schizophrenia in the first study reported by Gilyarovski et al. Yureva found that 16 of her 18 patients had a history of toxicosis during the pregnancy. This compares with 10 out of 60 in the Gilyarovski study. Four had relatives with schizoid traits and tendency to fearfulness and suspiciousness.

One group at four to five years showed precocious intellectual development and an unusual interest in archaeology, history, mechanical construction. These patients tended to ask deep philosophical questions, to have well-developed speech and underdeveloped motor functions, particularly the fine movements of the fingers. They had trouble learning how to write. In personal relationships, they tended to be cold and kept people at a distance. Some showed a very highly developed sense of responsibility, and some were excessively frank. They showed both awareness of inadequacy and a tendency to feel superior to contemporaries which made them ill-natured and arrogant. They were unable to modify their behavior in the face of protest from other children. They were excessively sensitive and easily wounded in human relationships but unable to appreciate analogous feelings in others. Gradually, they became more and more isolated and withdrawn.

Night fears and nightmares appeared early and intermittently, often consisting of an ill-defined presence of danger or fear of attack. Fear of common environmental phenomena like the change from day to night would appear. These children were hesitant to reveal their fears or to seek help. Yureva's patients were less severely ill than many reported in the literature. These children could still be included in other kinds of activity which did not have to do with their personal preoccupations. They always maintained their ability to tell fantasy from reality.

At puberty, the rich fantasy life was replaced by an empty, flat state. Obsessive thinking appeared, with a loss of the emotional component and a gradual reduction of work capability in school. Their good memories enabled these patients to retain old knowledge, but they became less attentive to the demands of the school regime. The thought content took on an increasingly delusional quality and the mood tended to be chronically depressed with suicidal thoughts, despair, fear or simple boredom, withdrawal, and silence. In addition to strange behavior, isolation, and irritability, these patients sometimes began to have visual and auditory hallucinations.

In conclusion, Yureva stated that the roots of these slowly progressive forms of schizophrenia go back to early childhood, and there are disturbances in development dating from the first year of life. Particularly characteristic were emotional coldness, the lack of correspondence between sometimes high but one-sided intelligence and motor insufficiency and an absence of the social ability to evaluate situations correctly in relationships with people. Yureva picturesquely described these patients' fragility as the quality of "wood and glass."

Her comparisons with the similar developmental stages of healthy children showed many qualitative differences between normal development and schizophrenic development in questioning, play activities, and fantasy life. The study seemed to be of great value because it gave a picture in time of a slowly developing, insidious process. It also demonstrated quite convincingly that Soviet psychiatrists may be right when they diagnose schizophrenia in some young people with pseudo-neurotic symptomatology.

A descriptive study of periodic schizophrenia in adolescence by V. A. Lupandin was reported in 1965 (12). The research group contained 30 patients (23 girls and 7 boys). Lupandin distinguished three clinical subgroups. The basis for the grouping was not clear but appeared to include premorbid characteristics and course of illness in spite of the fact that the study was supposed to consider only the periodic form.

The first group he called the "oneiroid-catatonic form" (13 females and 2 males). The symptoms resembled the clinical picture in adults, although with more catatonic symptoms, sensory disturbances, and hypochondriacal complaints. Auditory hallucinations were not uncommon. There were brief periods of excitement and frozen stupor. Other catatonic symptoms were grimacing, absurd laughter, echolalia, and echopraxia. Clouding of consciousness with perplexity and disturbances of orientation were present. There were also disturbances of body image and alterations in the affective sphere. A prodomal period lasting weeks to a year was identified in this group with the following symptoms: seemingly unmotivated mood fluctuations, social withdrawal, diminished success in school, fears of some impending catastrophe, psychopathic-like traits, and brief episodes of confusion with disturbed orientation or freezing speechless in one posture. In remission, some residual disturbances were noted.

Lupandin's second group (3 females and 2 males) had transitory attacks of delusions and fears: delusions of reference, with depression and guilt. Other symptoms were hallucinations of smell, depersonalization, perplexity, hypochondria, diminished activity, brief stupor or excitement. The attacks would begin with mood disturbances and last two or three weeks. In remission, some disturbance was noted in this group, too, particularly in the affective sphere.

The third group (7 females and 3 males) was characterized by schizoid personality traits before the manifest psychosis and the development of schizophrenic personality traits after the acute psychotic episode. Only three patients had no family history. Since none of the patients in the study were completely free of residuals in the state of remission, it must be difficult to decide when to classify a given case as an example of periodic schizophrenia or a case of intermittent schizophrenia with progression.

An educator and a psychiatrist published a collaborative study in 1967 of the drawings of preschool schizophrenic children, as they related to the clinical state (3). Sixteen hundred drawings of 42 children (10 females and 32 males) five through eight years were reviewed and related to clinical data. The drawings were stereotyped and repetitive. The children resisted drawing any other subject. They would cry, stamp their feet, break their pencils, try to leave or tear up their drawings. They were impervious to teaching or demonstration and would not correct their errors. They appeared to live in a world of fantasy.

A clinical subgroup of 19 patients contained the sickest children, who showed negativism, autism, disturbance of play activity, as well as regression in the motor and speech spheres. In addition to outbursts of excitement, tension, and impulsiveness, they were rigid, and ritualistic and showed much discomfort over any changes in routine. Their drawings were extremely primitive. Fourteen just scribbled, sometimes tearing the paper. Five made simple, stereotyped drawings resembling productions of children three or four years younger. One eight-year-old repeatedly drew houses with many windows (some in the roof), surrounded by several tractors, each with a patient sitting on it. When the boy became worse, he scribbled heavy black lines over crude human-like forms, calling the drawing a storm, airplanes, and the whole earth and recalling a frightening experience at six of falling. When his clinical state improved, his drawings became better proportioned, richer, more varied with better use of color.

The second subgroup of 10 patients had a slow, insidious form of schizophrenia. These children sometimes had early precocious development. One six-year-old boy from this group had for years been drawing light bulbs. He made a picture of a steam engine with two enormous light bulbs on the front. The light bulbs were done with remarkable detail and accuracy, especially of the screw base and the filaments, while the car was done crudely and schematically. When this child grew worse, he drew random lines and called them light bulbs. Many patients were enthusiastic about their drawing sessions but showed poor self-control and an unwillingness to follow instructions or fulfill assigned tasks. The authors recognized the patients were drawing the subjects of their autistic fantasies, special preoccupations, and fears, and that the drawings had symbolic meaning. I watched Kudryatseva and Boldyreva working with patients in the hospital and felt their handling of the children was skillful and sensitive. They seemed more interested in the cognitive and intellectual aspects of the drawings than in the symbolic and expressive aspects.

The final subgroup was 13 patients whose course was mixed, with acute psychotic manifestations and varying degrees of remission. The regressions in the clinical state of these patients were closely paralleled by regressions in the drawings; in severe cases the patients became unable to draw. Even in a favorable clinical state the patients' drawings showed primitive perspective and spatial distortions. Sometimes fantastic creatures, drawn in psychotic states, would be preserved in drawings during remissions. Symbolism and neologisms appearing in the drawings sometimes expressed fear not evident in external behavior or verbal expression.

A subsequent study, published by Boldyreva in 1969, dealt with expression of hallucinatory experiences in drawings of preschool children (4). In a series of 70 children aged five through seven years suffering from schizophrenia, only five drew the content of their hallucinations. Two others showed a manifest change in the quality of their drawings under the influence of hallucinations. These children all had a progressive course with exacerbations. Their drawings were idiosyncratic, reflecting internal preoccupations rather than the external world.

One six-and-one-half-year-old boy had begun one year previously to see large green monsters which would call to him. He drew a great creature with burning eyes and another caterpillar-like monster with a witch in some kind of vessel close by. When he talked about these experiences, the youngster would become pale with fright, whispering, "Although I knew these things I saw were not real, all the same, I was afraid."

Boldyreva concluded that the artistic productions of schizophrenic children could be used as a diagnostic aid. However, she also recognized the psychotherapeutic value of drawing in establishing contact with the children, explaining to them the disturbances in their sensory experiences, helping them to criticize their psychotic experiences and to evaluate them correctly.

A final study, published in 1969 by Yu. I. Polishchuk and V. L. Shenderova, is part of an investigation of the genetic aspects of schizophrenia by Professor Snezhnevski and his co-workers at the Psychiatric Institute, Academy of Medical Sciences, USSR, in Moscow. Professor Vrono and his associates were working on the cases of childhood schizophrenia. Since they kindly permitted me to sit in on case presentations, I know the care and thoroughness of their interviews with patients and families, going back several generations. The part of the project reported by Polishchuk and Shenderova concerned the family background of 70 patients with early onset of unbroken schizophrenia who at the time of the study were 17–35 years old and had been ill 3–22 years (15). The essential facts about the research group may be summarized as follows:

	Malignant Course Group I	Insidious Course Group II
Number of patients	40	30
Number of relatives studied	507	278
Absence of pathological character traits in relatives	239	33
Presence of psychosis in relatives	17	28

Personality types were broken down into three groups: Schizoid, hyperthymic with schizoid traits, and mixed, each with three grades of severity. In the first category were essentially healthy people; in the second were people whose personalities might clinically fall in the group of psychopathies (in the Soviet sense); in the third category were people whose anomalies were severe enough to raise the question of a latent schizophrenic process.

Schizoid personality types of the three grades ranged from unfriendly people, described as individualists, to people with deep schizoid defects. They were hostile, suspicious, and limited in their interests. Others characterized them as cold, yet they were sensitive and easily wounded. Among the hyperthymic personalities with schizoid traits were people who seemed normal, though with elevated mood, narrow, one-sided activity patterns, and rigidity. In the third category were hyperthymic personalities with emotional defect. These people were unable to appreciate the complexity of human feelings. They would overlook illness and serious personality change in their children. They were argumentative, physically and psychically juvenile. Many may have been suffering from a latent schizophrenic process.

The mixed personality types included those with hysteria, epileptoid and psychasthenic psychopathy, and a mixed group with schizoid traits and expansiveness, energy, and psychic rigidity. They were hard working, serious, intolerant of foibles, yet unsure of themselves and indecisive. They were compliant in relationships outside of work. Their emotions lacked depth. They had intermittent mild depressions.

Table 12 summarizes a comparison of the family characteristics of the patient group with insidious schizophrenia and the patient group with malignant schizophrenia. The relatives of patients with insidious schizophrenia had statistically significant increases in the number of

Table 12. Distribution of Basic Types of Personality and Psychoses in Families of Patients with Schizophrenia

| | Relatives of Patients | | |
Personality type	with malignant course (40 families)	with insidious course (30 families)	t^*
Absence of pathological traits	239 (47.1%)	33 (11.9%)	> 12
Schizoid	110 (21.7%)	87 (31.3%)	> 3
First category	50 (9.8%)	25 (9.0%)	
Second category	17 (3.4%)	30 (10.8%)	> 3
Third category	43 (8.5%)	32 (11.5%)	
Hyperthymic with schizoid traits	106 (20.9%)	46 (16.6%)	
First category	44 (8.6%)	18 (6.5%)	
Second category	43 (8.5%)	25 (9.0%)	
Third category	19 (3.8%)	3 (1.1%)	> 2
Mixed	14 (2.8%)	46 (16.6%)	> 6
Other personalities with pathological deviation	21 (4.1%)	38 (13.6%)	> 4
Psychoses	17 (3.4%)	28 (10.1%)	> 3
Total	507 (100%)	278 (100%)	

Source: Adapted from data of Yo. I Polishchuk and V. L. Shenderova, "O tipakh lichnosti v semyakh bolnykh shizofreniei s rannim nachalom i nepreryvnym techeniem zabolevaniya" (On the Types of Personality in Families of Schizophrenic Patients with an Early Onset and Continuous Course of the Disease), *Zhurnal nevropatologii i psikhiatrii im Korsakova,* 69:113–119 (1969).

* The t test was used as a criterion of statistical significance. When t is > 2, the probability that the relationship is not chance is 95% or higher. Where t is not given, it was < 2 and not statistically significant.

personality abnormalities and psychoses in comparison to the relatives of patients with malignant schizophrenia. Among the relatives of the insidious schizophrenics, the second category of severity of the schizoid personality type was especially numerous. In contrast, the relatives of malignant schizophrenics had significant numbers of hyperthymic personalities with emotional defect, falling in the most severe category.

Polishchuk and Shenderova concluded that there is a genetic influence on the course of schizophrenia. Both groups in the study had an unbroken course, but they varied in the degree of malignancy. The age factor was excluded, since all of the patients had an onset of the illness in adolescence or youth. The study does not exclude the possibility of other factors influencing the malignancy of the schizophrenic process.

Although I was impressed with the care and thoroughness of the research I saw in process, I noted the lack of a control group of non-schizophrenic patients. There was no way to consider the factor of raising the child who later becomes schizophrenic in a psychically sick environment. Yu. F. Polyakov, psychologist at the laboratory of Kashenko Psychoneurological Hospital, told me about his studies of the psychological characteristics of adult schizophrenic patients and their relatives. He found the same disturbances of thought and perception in the families that he found in the patients. Although both groups tended to have a big fund of information, there was poor selectivity of relevant information. To what extent do these patterns of thinking represent genetic blueprints and to what extent are they identifications with significant people in the child's early environment? I was surprised by the statistically significant difference between the higher number of relatives with personality disorders of all types in patients with insidious schizophrenia and their diminished number in patients with malignant schizophrenia. Could this mean we are placing together two or more different illnesses? Of does it suggest environmental influences may greatly increase the malignancy of a genetically based schizophrenic process, as the study by Gilyarovski et al. suggested?

Some Studies of Childhood Epilepsy

Epilepsy is of considerable interest to Soviet psychiatrists. The studies described below show how the approach to the psychopathology of epilepsy resembles the approach to schizophrenia, with detailed observations on the symptomatology and attention to the onset and course of the illness.

Sukhareva conceived of epilepsy as a unitary disease process with a progressive, though variable, course (18, 19). Symptomatic seizures were excluded: fits with cerebral palsy, severe anomalies of the brain with feeblemindedness, progressive, degenerative brain diseases (amaurotic idiocy, tuberous sclerosis, Schilder's disease, etc.). Fits accompanying acute brain trauma and some posttraumatic fits were labeled respectively "epileptic reaction" and "epileptic syndrome" when there was no evidence of a continuing pathophysiological process. The form of attacks in childhood she considered more characteristic of the maturity of the central nervous system than of the pathological process.

Sukhareva classified epilepsy in childhood on an etiological basis. Endogenous factors include hereditary predisposition, as well as congenital and early-acquired brain damage. Exogenous factors are influences which can bring out the epileptic predisposition later in life. Since childhood attacks may be changeable and/or polymorphous, Sukhareva found the nosological position of any given case more defined by the interparoxysmal characteristics in the affective, intellectual, and volitional spheres. In other words, she identified specific "epileptic personalities."

In endogenous epilepsy, changes in the affective and volitional spheres include tension, irritability, hostility, outbursts of aggression, and mood fluctuations. Depression and gloom may predominate in some, alternating with euphoria or even ecstasy. The patients show an interesting bipolarity: obsequiousness with superiors and hostility to equals and underlings. The intellectual changes are not marked. The patients are concrete in their thought processes, have a long attention span, and can persist doggedly to assigned tasks.

In exogenous epilepsy, the intellectual changes are more evident: recent memory difficulties, short attention span, restlessness, overactivity; in short, the organic brain syndrome. Emotional changes are present too: Lability, tearfulness, excitability, proneness to outbursts of rage. Thought processes are concrete, rigid, and perseverative.

Sukhareva proposed the following classification based on the relative distribution of internal and external factors:

1. Endogenous epilepsy.
2. Exogenous epilepsy.
3. Mixed form: the pathological process leads to a mixed picture, with affective changes resembling the endogenous form and in-

tellectual changes suggestive of later superimposed pathology, interacting with the epileptic predisposition.

In studying the development of the illness in an individual, Sukhareva mentioned the following factors (18):

1. The interval between the first attack and regular attacks.
2. The type of attack, the time, known reason for appearance.
3. The "dynamics" of the individual attack: single type, polymorphic.
4. Transformation of attacks: time interval, complexity.
5. Frequency of attacks; when does polymorphism appear? Status epilepticus; remissions.
6. Phenomena during seizures: twilight states, automatisms, paralyses.
7. Neurological picture: Postictal and interparoxysmal period.
8. Psychopathology of the interparoxysmal period.
9. EEG.

Sukhareva found a correlation between the type of onset, the type of course, and the psychopathology of the interparoxysmal period. Changes in the emotional and volitional spheres predominated in epilepsy with a gradual onset and a slow course, while intellectual changes predominated in the more rapid forms. A catastrophic, rapid course was associated with massive postnatal damage. Sukhareva proposed the following schema to describe the course:

1. Gradual onset with benign or mild course.
2. Subacute onset with progressive course.
3. Acute onset with rapid progression.
4. Mixed type: gradual onset with progressive course.

Foci in the limbic system tended to be associated with disturbances in the emotional and volitional spheres. Foci on the medial surfaces of the temporal lobes gave a picture more typical of endogenous epilepsy. In her conclusion, Sukhareva emphasized the need for interdisciplinary study of epileptic disease. The psychologist, excluded from her list, could in my opinion make a valuable contribution to the refined study of the psychopathology of the interparoxysmal period.

L. Ya. Visnevskaya, a co-worker of Sukhareva, did a dissertation, published in 1967, on the psychopathology of school-age epileptic children (20). She studied 100 children (43 males and 57 females). Sixty-two were 7–12 years of age and 38 were 13–16 years. The average length of the illness was six to seven years. Each had clinical interviews, physical and neurological examinations, skull x-ray, and EEG. Half also had cerebrospinal fluid examinations. Visnevskaya delineated three groups based on the psychopathological features and related them to predominantly hereditary (or congenital and early acquired) causes or predominantly acquired, external causes.

The endogenous form was characterized by a gradual or mixed course with disturbances mostly in the volitional and emotional spheres. Intellectually the children were concrete and unimaginative. They demonstrated a polarity of attitudes. The exogenous form was characterized by a picture of organic brain damage and a catastrophic course. There were gross intellectual defects and dissociation of intellectual functioning.

The mixed group showed signs of minimal brain damage with affective-volitional disturbances characteristic of the endogenous group. In a discussion with Visnevskaya, I mentioned the conviction of some Western psychiatrists that emotional conflict could increase the frequency of seizures in predispensed people. She agreed it was easier to achieve control of the seizures in the relatively neutral hospital environment, but she had not studied the emotional factor. She expressed a great interest in the psychic characteristics of temporal lobe epilepsy.

There were briefer opportunities to discuss epilepsy with other investigators. At the children's Psychoneurological Hospital in Moscow where the above studies were done, there was also a group interested in the genetic aspect of epilepsy. These investigators were doing twin studies of epilepsy and oligophrenia on 72 families: premorbid characteristics, age of onset in the case of epilepsy, type of attack, changes in the type of attack, reactions to treatment, type of course, and somatic characteristics, including EEG. One conclusion was that in familial epilepsy, the age of onset is not usually progressively younger over a time span of several generations. The investigators believed the type of course was genetically influenced, but there were other factors operating. They believed epileptics with a genetic predisposition had a specific kind of focal attack. The type of attack, however, was also related to age factors, since petit mal was more characteristic of younger patients and grand mal more frequent in older children and adolescents. The outcome was related to both genetic and age factors. They believed the EEG pattern was genetically determined but found EEG changes in only 60 percent of epileptic patients. There were also many nonepileptic syndromes with EEG abnormalities, especially migraine, epileptoid psychopathy, and some kinds of alcoholism. Trance-like states with automatisms in an altered state of consciousness were also considered epileptic equivalents.

G. B. Abramovich at the Bekhterev Institute in Leningrad seemed in basic agreement with Sukhareva that heredity and exogenous factors operated together to varying degrees. He considered Jacksonian and psychomotor seizures characteristic of childhood. In his study of the pathogenesis of epilepsy, histories and follow-up information were placed on cards for statistical analysis. Abramovich mentioned some of his conclusions: He saw no single dominant cause of epilepsy but a chain of factors operating together. Infection of the brain was not to him a dominant factor, but disturbances in brain development during the prenatal period and birth trauma can cause vulnerability to postnatal insults. He described the pathogenesis of epilepsy as a nonspecific process. He defined specificity as the formation of an epileptic focus, the result of this process. He felt the location of a focus was not genetically determined, and thus he may be in some disagreement with the Moscow group. Rather, he preferred to think the propensity to form an irritable focus was genetically determined, with the localization dependent on exogenous factors. Abramovich claimed that in the majority of cases a focus is present, even in diffuse damage to the brain. The surgical approach is rarely possible because of the inaccessibility of the focus or its proximity to vital centers. Treatment to Abramovich was a decisive factor in the course of the epileptic illness. The illness can be arrested or degeneration can be slowed down.

S. S. Mnukhin in Leningrad, has also been interested in the problem of epilepsy. He agreed with the concept of an epileptic illness, defining it as episodes with clouding of consciousness and the development of stable psychic changes (13). He saw the benign or malignant type of course as dependent on the "type of higher nervous activity in the patient": the patient with a "weak nervous system," characterized by inertness and inhibition, is more likely to have a malignant course, with pathology of the temporal lobes and subordinate structures in the hypothalamus and the limbic system. He felt epilepsy should be distinguished from epileptiform equivalents, such as migraine and narcolepsy. He commented that the search for foci has diverted attention from the study of epilepsy as an illness with stable personality changes.

I had the impression that the workers in the major centers were in basic agreement with Sukhareva. Some have been more interested in the delineation of types of attack characteristic of childhood. For example, G. K. Poppe, a co-worker of Mnukhin, differentiated the syndrome of pyknolepsy from pykno-like epilepsy in children (16). The former is characterized by more numerous, very brief absences, with no motor component or personality changes. The small absences of epilepsy are less numerous, have associated automatic movements, and are accompanied by definable personality changes. Other workers, following Sukhareva, have dwelt more on descriptive psychopathology. None of the investigators denied the importance of heredity. There may be some disagreement about its role in localization.

Some Studies of "Borderline States"

The studies described below show a trend in Soviet research toward increased interest in the lesser psychiatric disturbances. Some illustrate typical Soviet interests, and two are problems about which little has been published.

L. I. Golovan in 1961 published a study of the neurodynamics of compulsive states in children which illustrates how Pavlovian principles are applied, using the conditioning method of Ivanov-Smolenski, to the investigation of the mobility or flexibility of nervous processes (6). Her research group consisted of seven children aged 8–14 years with compulsive neuroses and a control group of ten normal children the same age. After giving illustrative case examples, Golovan compared the compulsive symptoms of her patients to the normal movements of young children, which can sometimes be single and repetitive, especially when they are in an excitable, volatile state. She noted six of the seven compulsive patients had vegetative disturbances such as sweating, tachycardia, bradycardia, lability of somatovegetative reactions. The experimental part of the investigation was carried out by the method of motor and speech reinforcement. Positive conditioned reactions were formed to stimuli of the first and second signal system (light, sound, and words). The responses so established were then inhibited through differentiation, conditioned inhibition, extinction, and delayed conditioned response.

There were no differences in positive conditioning between the experimental and control groups. Five of the seven compulsive patients showed an unusually rapid generalization to several other "analyzers" (modes of perception). This generalization of the excitatory process was not present in the healthy children. Conditioned inhibition was rapid in both patients and controls. Differentiation of the response to blue light of a different intensity and stabilization of the differentiated response was significantly longer for the patients than for the controls. Extinction of the conditioned reactions to light, sound, and words and restoration of the extinguished response were both achieved in the patient group with significantly more difficulty than in controls. In the formation of delayed conditioned reflexes, longer time intervals were required for the compulsive patients than for the controls. One patient was an exception, forming rapid conditioned inhibition. It was discovered that the symptom of obsessive counting had accidentally facilitated the child's response.

Golovan concluded that the results indicated both "weakness and inertness" of nervous processes. The weakness, demonstrated experimentally in the process of active inhibition, was manifest clinically in symptoms: tearfulness, inability of the patients to correct their behavior, irascibility, lack of perseverance in school assignments or in work therapy. She felt the treatment should be devoted to strengthening cortical inhibition through medication and psychotherapy. Compulsive symptoms she found to be related to general characteristics of motor development and to the immaturity of the second signal system in childhood. The disturbances experimentally demonstrated lay not in positive conditioned responses, but in active internal inhibition. Golovan related this experimental finding to several symptoms the patients showed: the stability of the compulsive formations, the lack of control and concentration difficulties in school tasks or work therapy.

I thought Golovan's study illustrated the rigidity and resistance to change so prominent in the clinical picture of even young compulsive neurotic patients. Although the results may not be statistically significant, the reported differences in the published tables seemed convincing. These patients showed concentration difficulties which interfered with school success. My clinical impression is that compulsive neurotics are often good in school, even overachieving. Perhaps there is a difference between the compulsiveness (with perseveration, distractibility, and concreteness) of some organically brain-damaged patients and the kind of compulsiveness we believe to be rooted in constitutional predisposition and internal psychic conflict.

Problems of inhibitions of intellectual development and school
failure have received increasing attention of Soviet psychiatrists, educators, and psychologists. I hear much discussion of how to distinguish
true oligophrenia from temporary or reversible delays in intellectual
development and psychic infantilism. S. S. Mnukhin wrote in 1968
about the disorders Americans call neurotic learning inhibition, ego
restriction, and learning problems secondary to passive-aggressive character disorders, immaturity, and minimal organic brain damage (14).
Mnukhin was critical of the point of view which would attribute social
causes to oligophrenia and other neuropsychic disturbances, though he
asserted that capitalist and underdeveloped countries have cases of
delayed development due to neglect. He also considered it unjustified
to say psychopathic behavior causes inhibitions of intellectual development, because many of these patients do well in school. Rather, the two
syndromes can both be caused by residuals of organic brain damage.
He saw the sequelae of debilitating physical illness (somatic asthenia)
as related to psychic infantilism. Asthenic patients, he said, frequently
lose previously acquired habits such as walking and talking, and the
reversibility of these losses is variable. Some children are left with the
emotional, volitional, and intellectual defects.

Mnukhin went on to describe an asthenic form of oligophrenia. These
children show a clear, stable intellectual defect on an asthenic base.
They are very slow in mastering reading, writing, and arithmetic, poor
at abstract generalizing; they also have deficient temporal and spatial
orientation. They show right-left disturbances and difficulties carrying
out sequential tasks. Emotional responsiveness may be dulled, but the
rest of development is relatively unimpaired. Mnukhin saw the cause
of this disturbance as residuals of diffuse brain-stem damage, involving
the reticular formation. He recognized, too, a group of delays in intellectual development which lie outside the boundaries of oligophrenia
where the defect may be reversible with maturation. The group is important in educational planning, because such children should not be
placed with oligophrenics and yet they need longer periods of specialized help than are offered in the sanatoria.

A symposium sponsored by the Academy of Pedagogical Sciences
was held in February 1969 at the Institute of Defectology to consider
the problems of children not succeeding in school because of temporary
inhibitions of intellectual development. There were papers by psychiatrists on the clinical characteristics and neurological status of such children and the relationship of the intellectual syndrome to behavior dis-

turbances, as well as work by psychologists and educators on the psychological characteristics and school performance of such children. Of 30 papers presented, only 7 were from places other than Moscow. I was able to make a tape recording of one paper by V. V. Kovalev on school maladaptation and behavior disturbances in which he emphasized psychogenic factors. These children with school maladaptation he tentatively placed in three groups within the framework of borderline states: true neuroses, pathological character development, and true pathological development of the personality. He gave case histories illustrating the transition of a neurotic reactive state into a more internalized pathological character formation.

Kovalev's ideas were further elaborated in a paper published in 1969 on pathological development of the personality in children (9). He said the term had been introduced into Soviet psychiatry in the thirties, and since then there had been divergent views. Some considered these cases to be a form of true psychopathy. Others separated the cases into two groups: a psychopathic form and an environmentally caused form. Still a third view was that these were reactive states, occupying an intermediary position between psychogenically caused disturbances and psychopathy. Kovalev distinguished a group of pathological development of the mature personality from a group of pathological formations of the personality during the course of development. In the childhood group, he distinguished three main types. The first was character development associated with unfavorable upbringing and psychotraumatizing situations in the microenvironment, usually the family. Among these were several varieties with case illustrations.

As an example of the excitable variety, Kovalev described a boy, brought up without difficulty until the age of seven in children's institutions, who was returned to a desperate family situation where the father had a history of alcoholism and arrests for drunkenness and hooliganism. The mother and sister drank and beat the boy. The child underwent a gradual personality change. He began to be rude to his mother and would run away after punishment. He developed sleeplessness, night fears, and enuresis. In school, he was rude to the teacher, resisted school discipline, and fought with the other children. In the psychoneurological hospital the child improved, but his symptoms returned when he was sent back home.

Other varieties described by Kovalev were the fearful, inhibited child who has been subjected to excessive punishment, a condition to be differentiated from neurotic development. The hysteroid variety is characterized by striving for personal attention and lack of concern for others. Finally, there is the pathologically formed personality following severe psychic trauma. Kovalev's illustration is interesting, since it has many features of a reactive depression, in my opinion.

An eleven-and-one-half-year-old boy was admitted to the sanatorium because of pathological jealousy of his mother and conflicts with other children and teachers. The child had been very close to his father, especially during the latter's terminal illness. After the father's death, the boy had a strong overt grief reaction. He cried, spent much time at the grave, saying he saw his father. After half a year, the grief subsided, but he became excessively jealous of his mother. He forbade her to meet or to talk with other men and followed her around to try to enforce his will. He even threatened to kill her if she did not do as he wished. In the sanatorium he was suspicious and distrustful of the doctors and educators. Though he improved somewhat, his suspicions and jealousy persisted.

Kovalev's second major type of pathological character formation is that secondary to longstanding neurosis. In childhood this may be an asthenic state, a mixed neurosis, or a neurosis of fear. Neurotic symptoms and moods, first appearing as reactions to psychotraumatizing situations, gradually merge into pathological traits of the personality, losing their connection with the external life situation. In American terminology, this is a process of internalization present in neuroses as well as neurotic character disorders.

Kovalev's third type of pathological character formation is secondary to physical defects and generalized somatic illness. Cardiac patients may be excessively inactive and dependent because of the restrictions placed on them, especially if the environment responds with too low expectations. Another example was the patient responding to cerebral palsy with strong feelings of inadequacy, compensatory fantasies, and a tendency to "autization" of the personality.

The conclusions of the study were that some psychogenic character disorders are reversible and some are not and can lead to "pathological deviation of higher nervous activity." These disorders Kovalev would place in an independent position among the borderline states. Although they are psychogenic, they are to be distinguished from other psychogenic states. They are very important from the point of view of preventive and therapeutic measures.

Kovalev's study of the psychic characteristics of congenital cardiac patients was the subject of a doctoral dissertation. Some of the results were published in 1959 (7). The research group was 86 patients, of whom 54 were children 3–16 years of age and 32 were adults 16–36 years. The type of cardiovascular anomaly described was Tetralogy of Fallot, 29 cases; arterial anomalies, 15; septal defects, 9; "Azenmenger complex," 5; other defects, 29. Forty-two patients were cyanotic; 44 were acyanotic. Other physical defects were found in 36 patients: microcephaly, dysplastic skull structure, high palate, underdevelopment of the external genitalia, cryptorchidism, hypospadias, anomalies of the teeth. Nonspecific neurological deviations were present in 64 patients: mild deviations in the cranial nerves, mild pareses.

The psychic disturbances of the patients were of three kinds: asthenia, mental retardation, and pathological character traits. Eighty-two patients had asthenia in some form. In 32, there was no other disturbance. The fatigue was most prominent in the morning on arising and in the evening. There were sleep disturbances and nightmares with sensations of being pressed on or strangled. Mood disturbances included mild euphoria or apathy and were correlated with oxygen hunger. The patients showed less hypochondriasis and fear of death than patients with acquired heart disease or other somatic states. In children, physical fatigability and weakness appeared early, but psychic asthenia usually did not appear until the school years and gradually increased, running an intermittent or continuous course. The uninterrupted course was more characteristic of the cyanotic patients. Twelve of the 54 children showed neurotic traits: fears, enuresis, sleep disturbances, nightmares, motor restlessness, and transitory obsessional states.

Thirty-six patients, 21 of whom were children, showed intellectual retardation. This was more frequent among the cyanotic patients. Some form of physical retardation was frequently present, too. Seven did not show intellectual backwardness until they were 10–12 years old.

Nine patients had pathological character traits, of whom three had the Tetralogy of Fallot, two had arterial anomalies, and four had complex, mixed anomalies. Four were cyanotic and five were acyanotic. The main types of deviation were excitability or hysterical traits. Aggressive outbursts, present in a few, would usually end in an asthenic state of tears and exhaustion. The hysterical patients, in contrast to the majority (who underestimated their condition), overdramatized their suffering and state of health. Kovalev attributed the deviations in these cases to psychogenic factors, particularly unfavorable family circumstances, or excessive catering to the child's whims.

Kovalev concluded that the mood disturbances, asthenia, and mild intellectual changes in memory, attention, and judgment were due to hypoxia. Although he stated the oxygen saturation of the blood was studied, figures were not included. The retarded patients he believed to have congenital insufficiency of the nervous system in addition to the cardiac lesions. He found no organic etiology for the character changes.

In 1969, K. S. Lebedinskaya, E. S. Kuznetsova, and T. I. Buraya wrote on "Psychic Characteristics of Children with Congenital Dysfunctions of the Adrenal Cortex" (11). The specific defect, found in both sexes, was a blocking of the synthesis of glucocorticoids, leading to excessive production of androgens, the male sexualizing hormone, by the adrenal cortex. The growth rate is accelerated, the musculature is overdeveloped, and there may be premature closure of the epiphyses. If the patients are started on treatment before two years of age with glucocorticoids to suppress the secretion of androgens, normal development will result. When treatment is begun later, virilization is stopped.

The research group was 36 patients aged 4–16 years. The psychic characteristics were generally more prominent in females. Even by three and one-half years, the children began to show self consciousness about undressing and about speaking, if there had been lowering of the voice. During school years, the awareness of difference increased, leading to withdrawal, isolation, and depression, favoring pathological development of the personality. Protests against the feminine role occurred in girls mistakenly brought up as boys who later underwent corrective surgery of the external genitalia. At all ages, the patients showed fear of ridicule. They were rejected by adults, who feared they would be sexually aggressive. Sometimes they were therefore isolated from other children.

Two main motor patterns predominated in the group. The first was the male pattern, regardless of actual sex. These children were strong, active, alert, with jerky movements, lacking in grace and rhythm but good at sports. They showed an unchildlike evenness of mood, judiciousness, and lack of aggression. Intellectually, they seemed advanced for their age, although psychological study showed them to be average, not superior. They had good memory and attention and applied themselves better than most children. Their interests included physical work, technical games, and typically masculine professions. The second group was described as inhibitory. These children were passive, slow moving, inactive, with poor memory and a poor fund of information. They seemed retarded but actually were not. They required more than the average stimulation for intellectual development. Since they were not good at imitative play and were socially isolated, their defects gradually increased. In adolescence they showed chronic depression and remained at a primitive level.

The sexual behavior of the patients was increased beyond what the investigators considered age appropriate. Masturbation was noted especially in the boys and adolescent girls. The treated girls who required corrective surgery showed changes in their sexual orientation to more feminine interests and preoccupation with self-beautification.

The psychic changes were reversible if hormonal therapy was begun early. The masculinizing motor pattern was reversible, too. The girls, especially, became more feminine in their movements as well as their appearance. Interests were reoriented along more sex-appropriate lines. The good motivation and activity level of the first group tended to persist. The second group was only reversible if treatment began before puberty.

An eight-year-old girl had been considered a boy at birth with hypoplasia of the external genitalia and hypospadias. At two years, she developed hair on the external genitalia, and a low pitch of the voice was present by three years, along with an accelerated growth rate. At five and one-half, the correct diagnosis was made. A genitourinary sinus ended at the root of the clitoris which resembled a penis. Chromosomal study showed her to be female. Treatment with prednizone resulted in breast development and feminization of the body contours. At seven, the child underwent surgical correction of the genitalia. The patient, who had been brought up as a boy, now became officially female.

The child's psychic development had been along masculine lines. She was active, played with boys, was interested in machines and liked to ride a bicycle. She fantasied herself captain of a whaling vessel. She never fought with other children. During treatment, she cried in protest against the change in her sexual orientation. She continued to behave as a boy with her contemporaries. She became stubborn and began to stutter. Her family moved to another city, following the surgery; the patient assumed her feminine identity and adapted. She began to play with dolls and to sew, but still preferred the company of boys and retained an interest in travel. At eight years, her physical development was like that of a girl twelve or thirteen years. She was emotionally controlled, hypermature in her manner. She retained boyish gestures and intonations but blushed if this was called to her attention. She was still interested in travel and liked Tom Sawyer. Her interest in sports diminished as she found now she was not as strong as formerly. She wanted to become an airline stewardess. Emotional lability and sensitivity were increased. The authors presented the case as a reaction of protest, a reversible psychic change which had been corrected with appropriate therapy.

Lebidinskaya et al. believed the psychoneurologist should play a role in the management of these patients. Medication such as mellipramine may be indicated for depression, and the inactive group may require stimulants. Librium or levomepromazine may be useful in preparing patients for surgery. Supportive psychotherapy is important, too, in helping the patient find compensatory areas of competence and in interpreting the need for hormonal treatment and corrective surgery. Sometimes the change in sexual identification may turn out to be unrealistic if the necessary reconstruction of the personality is not possible. In concluding, the authors stressed the need for working with parents around such specific issues as their fear of the patient's sexual aggressiveness, the social isolation of the patient, the need to stimulate patients of the second group and the need for strict adherence to the medication regime.

Conclusions

In the development of Soviet research during the fifties and sixties, there has been a gradual broadening of research interests to include investigation of "borderline states." Genetic studies became important. Syndromes associated with known chromosomal anomalies, genetic predisposition in epilepsy, and studies of familial incidence of psychoses and character anomalies in patients with schizophrenia are some areas of research. More needs to be done to separate the environmental from genetic factors in schizophrenia, in both Soviet and American research.

In general the studies indicated a strong interest in the descriptive aspects of the onset and course of an illness and in age characteristics as they relate to psychopathology. The studies of schizophrenia made very convincing the Soviet claim that much mild schizophrenia exists in latent and pseudoneurotic form with symptoms of anxiety and depression often dominating the clinical picture. The concept of a process is particularly evident in the work on schizophrenia and epilepsy, but it is a pathophysiological process. I find lacking the concept of a *psychic process* (in distinction to a purely reactive state, with no idea of movement or change in the clinical picture).

Various research methods were used in the studies reviewed. These included a multidimensional approach with attempts to establish psychophysiological correlations. There were many clinical-descriptive studies of psychopathology and an attempt to correlate drawings of patients with clinical data. The only study to use statistical devices was the research on the families of schizophrenics. The study of higher nervous activity by the method of Ivanov-Smolenski illustrated a more experimental Pavlovian approach; this was the only study of its type reported here. Pavlovian concepts have exerted far more influence on treatment methods observed than on the research studies reviewed. The study of higher nervous activity by conditioning methods seemed to be decreasing in the sixties. Neither did the investigators with whom I talked emphasize this approach. If there has been a real shift, I wonder why this is so. Dr. Mark G. Field too, in personal communications, expressed the opinion that Pavlovian concepts were diminishing in importance in Soviet thinking.

VIII

Conclusions

The organization of the Soviet psychiatric care system is praiseworthy, because it is planned on a rational basis with stress on delivery of service and prevention. Long-term hospitalization is discouraged, and regional outpatient care and follow-up are emphasized. Partial hospitalization is a feature Soviet and American planners might expand to advantage: day care for psychotic children, night care for some disorders such as anorexia nervosa. The Soviet care system has already exerted some influence on American psychiatry, because several prominent American psychiatrists have reported, for the most part favorably, on organizational aspects.

Soviet diagnostic thinking has been less stressed in previous American reports. I found a tendency, in accordance with the German medical model, to equate psychiatric illness with a pathophysiological process in the brain. While the medical model may be overdone in Soviet psychiatry, it should not be abandoned in American psychiatry. Soviet diagnostic formulations were detailed and thorough and excelled at the descriptive level. Of particular interest to me was the study of the course of the illness over a period of time and the distinction between a process and a state. Soviet formulations were deficient with respect to the recognition of a psychodynamic process. The concept of involvement of the central nervous system in a rheumatic process with psychiatric syndromes was a surprise. It would be of interest to know whether these claims can be confirmed in the United States. The Soviet concept of pseudoneurotic schizophrenia might be useful to American psychiatry in the diagnosis of conditions where anxiety and depression for no apparent reason dominate the clinical picture. The Soviet experience impressed me with the need to reassess the place of diagnosis in my own practice and work with trainees.

Treatment practices showed the influence of Pavlovian concepts of higher nervous activity. The general aim of treatment was to promote calm and relaxation. Tranquillity was achieved by medication, physical therapies, the sanatorium regime, work therapy, and suggestive psychotherapy. These measures desensitized the patient to environmental stress, in contrast to much American therapy, which is devoted to sensitizing patient and family to the human environment. Suggestive therapies were thought to be good for stuttering, enuresis, and other monosymptomatic neuroses, while character disorders were thought to be more amenable to rational psychotherapy. Makarenko's influence and Marxist-Leninist teachings were most evident in the second aim of treatment, promotion of the child's adaptation to the collective through the special educator's group work. While I did not consider the sanatorium regime necessary for neurotic children, it might be valuable in managing children with characterological problems and psychopathic traits in the United States. The model of a limited hospitalization and outpatient follow-up might be considered in American clinics for many symptoms. Suggestive techniques might find a greater place in the treatment of American children and adolescents.

While the Soviet and American systems both recognize the need for continuing education, the Soviet system offers more tangible rewards for advanced study. Nurses and feldshers not infrequently become doctors, and doctors return to become specialists. The multiplicity of levels of training and the flexibility this lends to the system reward those who wish to increase their qualifications and allow more to serve in the psychiatric care system. At higher levels, the Soviet system encourages advanced study and research but discourages collaboration between psychiatry and psychology or other academic disciplines. The training of American child psychiatrists could benefit by a required six-month pediatric internship before psychiatric training, followed by a choice in concentration, either in neuropsychiatry or in psychotherapy. The Soviet experience of combined training in neurology and psychiatry might meet a need for the management of children with behavior disorders associated with minimal cerebral dysfunction who require neurological examination and pharmacotherapy and do not respond to psychotherapy. This is not to deny the need for well-trained individual and group psychotherapists, but to realize that this is only one type of training needed. The middle medical worker could be developed in new professional roles, within the framework of medicine, to staff mental health clinics. A combination of medical subjects, public health nursing, and social work techniques could be taught to candidates for a bachelor's degree, preparing them to work in preventive psychiatry and treatment in the community of disadvantaged and socially deprived people.

Research could be encouraged in the American system by making more demands on trainees for preparatory reading and written reports. An advanced psychiatric degree, a Ph.D. in Medical Sciences (those relevant to psychiatry), could be offered to encourage a high level of creativity and career training in research. The Soviet research studies reviewed showed a broadening of interests in the fifties and sixties to include genetic problems, reversible educational handicaps, and other "borderline states." Statistical methods were just being introduced. Studies of higher nervous activity by Pavlovian conditioning techniques were on the decline. Studies of epilepsy and schizophrenia continued, with interest in careful clinical description, course of illness, and age characteristics. The expressive and therapeutic aspects of children's drawings in mental illness were just beginning to be recognized. There was no systematic study of the effect of psychotherapy on the course of an illness. In the study of the family background of schizophrenic patients, there was insufficient attention to the problem of differentiating between genetic and environmental factors contributing to the characteristic thought patterns and psychopathology of the child patients. Psychologists contributed in innovative and ingenious ways to diagnosis of cognitive functioning, but remained isolated from many clinical and research areas where they might have made valuable contributions.

In the area of psychiatric theory, an effort could be made to apply the Marxian principles that quantitative changes lead to qualitative changes at a higher level of integration and that phenomena at a higher level cannot wholly be reduced to the terms of a lower level. The levels of organization most relevant to the understanding of children's psychiatric disorders are the physiological, the psychological (intrapsychic), the social-psychological (interpersonal), and sociological (personal-cultural) levels. More rarely, even the biochemical level is crucial. Much of our failure in child psychiatry may come from incorrectly assessing the level at which the modifiable aspects of a given disturbance lie. At lower levels, this principle is more clearly understood than at higher levels. Phenylpyruvic oligophrenia cannot be successfully treated by means of an intrapsychic method such as play therapy. The treatment must be directed to the metabolic defect. But some aspects of the symptomatology may be at a very different level and will continue to operate unless correctly assessed. A family's inability to accept the retardation of one of its members may call for intervention at an interpersonal level with family case work or family therapy, in order that the retarded one can develop as fully as possible within his limitations.

At a higher level, the problem becomes more complex. In the United States, I have frequently seen efforts to treat social pathology with intrapsychic methods. When the child fails to improve, there is a tendency to abandon the method as outmoded and useless. Actually, it has merely been misapplied. Individual psychotherapy is as effective as it ever was for intrapsychic disturbances. Sharper definitions of levels in the spectrum of intrapsychic, interpersonal, and personal-cultural interpretations and some consensus about terminology might contribute to both theoretical understanding and practical effectiveness.

Suggestions for Further Study

Some concrete suggestions for further study arose from my observations. First, I would like to see a joint Soviet-US project on schizophrenia. Collaborative studies could be set up to investigate the genetic factors and the psychically determined identification patterns within the family of the designated patient so that these two main variables in the pathogenesis of schizophrenia might be separated. Further, it would be extremely valuable if such a study could be designed so that comparisons could be made between Soviet and American case material. I was pleased to learn that a proposal had been submitted in 1971 to the Soviet government by the National Institute of Mental Health for Soviet-US investigation of schizophrenia.

A second area for mutual cooperation might be comparative statistics on the incidence and prevalence of various psychiatric disorders. It would be of particular interest to find out whether Field's assertion can be substantiated that the incidence of major psychiatric disorders in the two countries is comparable. Then it would be of further interest to find out whether differences might be found in a more refined analysis of the incidence of various "borderline states" (in the Soviet sense), since these are the disorders most affected by socio-cultural factors.

A third area might be further transcultural studies of the type initiated by Bronfenbrenner. It would be interesting to compare approaches of children from different cultures to childhood dilemmas and developmental tasks encountered in all industrialized civilizations. An instrument which would lend itself well to such a study is the Task of Emotional Development (TED), a test developed by Geraldine Rickard and Haskel Cohen (6). In its use of the projective principle, the test resembles the Thematic Apperception Test. The TED is a series of photographs depicting children in easily identifiable situations, representing areas of conflict. One picture shows two children arguing; another shows a child standing separate from his peers; there is a picture of a child about to enter or leave with his mother standing next to the door; a fourth shows a child by himself reaching for an ambiguous object on a table. The children are asked to tell a story about each picture. The first two commonly elicit stories about peer relationships and the child's handling of aggression. The third usually stimulates stories about separation between mother and child. The fourth as a rule encourages stories about the temptation to steal. There is a separate series with boy subjects and girl subjects at two age levels (school-age children 6–12 and adolescents). The test has been standardized on a large, urban American population of children in public schools.

Although the TED is mostly used in clinical settings, it presents rich possibilities for the study of cultural questions: At what age in different cultures does internalization of the prohibition against stealing take place? Rickard, in personal communication, expressed surprise that American children of ten to eleven years would tell stories in response to the "temptation card" in which the decision about stealing was motivated more by the fear of outside punishment than by a truly internalized sense of right and wrong. She had expected evidence of an internalized conscience at an earlier age because of the psychoanalytic formulation that the superego forms in the process of the resolution of the oedipus complex, with the beginning of the "latency period" at around six years of age. I wondered at what age an internalized sense of right and wrong appears in Russian children. Bronfenbrenner's studies, reviewed in Chapter I, suggest there might be a significant difference between Russian and American children. The TED might also shed some light on the problem of dealing with age-appropriate separation between mother and child in the two societies. I had the opportunity to show several Soviet psychologists photographs from the test. In most instances, they were able to grasp the problem in child development. This suggests that the problem of misunderstanding the test material might be less than one would expect, although validity would have to be considered.

There are specific areas in Soviet child psychiatry I was unable to cover in the present study which I feel are important. Facilities under the Ministry of Health which I did not see were psychiatric emergency services under the administration of general pediatric hospitals, psycho-neurological hospitals for chronic psychotic patients, and hospitals or departments for older adolescents 16–18 years of age. Adolescent services are particularly important in terms of questions I have raised about identity crises, the formation of masculine and feminine identities, and problems in alienation. Neither was I allowed to see psychiatric facilities in outlying rural areas, if they exist at all, or in eastern non-Russian parts of the country. It would be most interesting to observe the pilot training programs for psychoneurologists offered in Tashkent, Riga, and other cities.

Also under the Ministry of Health, training and research in psycho-therapy could be further studied: Professor V. E. Rozhnov's program associated with the Twelfth Psychoneurological Hospital in Moscow, Professor I. Z. Velvovski's program in Kharkhov, and the Consultation and Training Center under the Leningrad City Health Department are the specific ones about which I know. Further observations could be made on suggestive techniques and their application to older children and adolescents.

Aspects of outpatient practice which I could not observe included the community activities of the psychoneurologist. Consultations held in nursery centers, kindergartens, and schools, work with parents, home visiting, and educational work are examples.

There were facilities under the Ministry of Education related to child psychiatry which would interest Americans. These include schools with a special regime for children with behavior problems, speech schools and kindergartens which deal with problems in learning, dyslexia, and spoken speech, and colonies for delinquent young people. Further, there was no opportunity to study research in child psychiatry at the Institute of Defectology, or to learn more about the allied field of medical psychology as it is developed in the institutes of psychology and the psychological departments of institutes of philosophy and universities. Another allied discipline is pedagogy: training programs exist for teachers who work with children with psychiatric disorders. Some of the studies of the family in departments of sociology are relevant to the understanding of the social factors in psychiatric illness.

Finally, there were sanatoria for neurotic patients and perhaps other unknown psychiatric facilities administered by trade unions.

The Social Environment
and Psychiatric Disorders

In the beginning, some broad questions were raised about character formation, culture, and psychiatric disorders, problems relating to the formation of an internalized, social, collectively oriented conscience, adolescent identity crises, and patterns of sexual identification. Personal observations of the social environment surrounding the Soviet child and comparison with observations of others led me to some preliminary ideas about the relationship between common child-rearing practices and character formation.

A warm, solicitous, strict upbringing with early demands for toilet training and continued, consistent demands for controlled behavior and obedience characterize Soviet child-rearing practices. Early childhood training at home and in the collective stresses altruistic concern for others. My conclusion is that these practices foster a certain cluster of character traits. Soviet adults tend to be warm, genuine in their emotional expression, and sensitive to the needs of others, especially children. They are also concrete and compartmentalized in their thinking or in more extreme cases, rigid and obsessional. These traits make it difficult to generalize, to synthesize experience in different areas into a new whole. When combined with a high degree of outward conformity and obedience, they are not conducive to original, creative thought. The adults also have well-internalized ethical values, self-confidence, and a sense of belonging. They value achievement and wish to contribute to the society. As this cluster of traits (warmth, obsessive concreteness, rigidity, and dedication to work) emerged, I recalled the study by Polishchuk and Shenderova (reported in Chap. VIII) describing traits of the families of schizophrenic children. There was the combination of hyperthymic with schizoid traits which had just this blend of warmth, industriousness, and obsessional rigidity. Some of these people were considered within the normal range; others were diagnosed a form of psychopathy or even latent schizophrenia. There is no attempt to say the Russian national character is schizophrenogenic. Rather, a Soviet study of a large number of Soviet people comes up with the same character type I have described in relation to the child-rearing practices of the culture.

Additional Russian traits noted in personal observations are a certain freedom from preoccupation with sexual identity and lack of conflicts regarding masculinity and femininity. Some of the hardships of day-to-day living, as they still existed in 1969, fostered manipulativeness and opportunism. The national focus on the importance of health and its linkage with rest and recreation I felt could enhance the secondary gain of somatic symptoms and therefore increase their frequency. The historical review showed that recognition of increasing numbers of functional somatic complaints in the outpatient clinics was precisely the stimulus which led to the development of suggestive psychotherapy.

Can any connection be discerned between common Russian characterological patterns and psychiatric disorders appearing in the children and adolescents? Children's psychiatric disorders encountered in hospitals and outpatient facilities in the Soviet Union did not differ markedly from those the American clinician customarily sees, with the exception of severe drug problems, which have become prevalent in the United States. In particular, organic brain damage, minimal cerebral dysfunction, and childhood schizophrenia showed no differences in symptomatology.

However, in lesser psychiatric disturbances, most sensitive to the influence of psychosocial factors, there may be differences only detectable by refined statistical techniques. Future studies might confirm the following suggestions.

1. A rigid, internalized conscience might be expected to be associated with a high incidence of obsessive-compulsive character disorders and neuroses. Obsessive and compulsive syndromes actually were frequent in the Soviet case material observed and reviewed in the literature. Stuttering, so emphasized in the Soviet psychiatric care system, is frequently symptomatic of an obsessional character structure.

2. Phobic states might also be frequent in a society where only children are not uncommon and where cultural values foster oversolicitousness. However, if the conclusion is correct that the problem of separation between mother and child is made less traumatic in Soviet society because of the early development of a collective mother image, it might turn out that the psychodynamic structure of a Soviet school phobia would differ from an American one.

3. The high value placed by Soviet society on outward conformity, controlled behavior, and matters of health might create the conditions

for an increase in psychogenic somatic symptoms. Both Sukhareva and Simpson stress these in their writings, particularly about early childhood. Although not preponderant in hospitals, they may be frequent in outpatient practice.

4. In older children and adolescents, the same factors promoting externally controlled behavior and discouraging overt rebelliousness might heighten the incidence of depressive reactions. I was unable to get figures on suicide in children and adolescents in the Soviet Union.

5. Among the character disorders, Soviet conditions might discourage the formation of primitive, chaotic personalities unfortunately seen in urban areas of the United States. Soviet conditions would rather foster the development of a more organized character deviation of a manipulative kind. While the child's exposure to many different mothering figures may ease the impact of separation, there is the possibility of conflicting value systems in the different people mothering the child. The babushka represents old traditional values not acceptable to the modern urbanized Soviet mother. Some of the cases observed had the element of a power struggle on the part of the adults for the child's affection and, on the child's side, playing one adult against the other in a manipulative way.

6. A particularly stressful time in the life of the Soviet child is entrance into school with the abrupt increase in demands for concentration and conformity. This factor is explicitly recognized in the writings of Sukhareva and Simpson. The last year of school is stressful, too, because of the stiff competition for admission to universities and institutes for advanced study, combined with the high value the culture places on learning and achievement.

Psychiatry
and Culture

One of the benefits of the privilege of making extended observations of child psychiatry in the Soviet Union was that the new perspective led me to certain ideas about the relationship of psychiatry to culture in the US as well as in the USSR.

THE ROLE OF THE CHILD PSYCHIATRIST

There are significant differences between the professional role of the child psychiatrist in the Soviet Union and in the United States. Seely, a sociologist, wrote on the problem of the relationship of sociological theory to psychodynamic theory. He summarized eight functions which a psychiatrist fills in American society (7, pp. 41–44). Five of these help to differentiate the role of the Soviet child psychiatrist from that of the American.

1. Refinement, elaboration, and extension of theory.
2. Illustration and enrichment of theory.

Child psychiatrists in the United States, particularly psychoanalysts, have been concerned with research problems in normal development and psychopathology. Findings of the studies in child development have diffused into related disciplines of education and psychology. Other studies, investigations of specific syndromes in children and adolescents, are examples of the illustration of theory. In the Soviet Union, both of these functions are filled by senior scientific workers and professors. Usually, the professor elaborates the theory and his co-workers undertake to illustrate the theory with clinical studies of one entity or age group. But there is a much sharper division between normal child development and psychopathology. The former is the concern of psychology, far removed from clinical settings.

3. Education. American child psychiatrists frequently lecture to parent groups and educators. Education, too, is emphasized in the Soviet system at all levels, from the professor lecturing in an academic setting to the psychoneurologist working with parents and teachers in the community. However, the subject matter is more limited to medical matters than it is in the United States, where psychoanalytic principles have diffused into child-rearing literature for parents and into preschool and educational institutions.

4. Practice of psychotherapy. The child psychiatrist's traditional training in the United States has been individual, psychodynamically oriented psychotherapy within a team which offers casework to the parents. One typical American attitude toward psychotherapy was expressively stated by Seely when he called the therapeutic alliance "infinitely generalizable" (7, p. 45). He further described it in almost religious terms as "beneficent encounters in the authentic" (7, p. 46). The implication that all ideal human relationships should be cast in the therapeutic model places a tremendous burden on the psychotherapist and an expectation of the unattainable on the part of the public. For the Soviet psychiatrist, the practice of psychotherapy is limited and conceived as a medical discipline.

5. Planning public policy. Here too, the expectation of the American public that insights and research findings will be immediately translated

into public policy leaves the American child psychiatrist and his colleagues in related disciplines in the unenviable position of failing to fulfill unrealistic expectations. The reaction of disappointment, inevitable when demands are not met, is frequently to go to the other extreme and to exclude the child psychiatrist from planning. Recently, American psychiatrists have been encouraged to engage in political action as individuals and through their professional organizations. The Soviet child psychiatrist might be expected to make recommendations to the Ministry of Health about additions of special services to the psychiatric care system, but the more diffuse American expectation of some expertise which will cure the whole society is lacking.

Thus there are three aspects of American culture which are related to both the frustrations and the successes of the child psychiatrist.

1. Permeability. On the positive side, this leads to flexibility and openness. To the American, but not to the Russian, eclecticism is acceptable. We have many approaches to therapy and a willingness to try new things. My interest in undertaking this study itself is an example of American permeability. On the negative side, permeability may lead to instability. As outlined in Chapter I, the Russian rejection of eclecticism may be related to Marxian theory requiring the study of man-in-his-environment as a dynamically operating system with its own internal characteristics and rules appropriate to the particular level of integration.

2. Diffusion. Ideas taken into the American culture spread through many areas of life. Most striking is the diffusion of Freudian ideas from professional circles to nonprofessional people. Families and peer groups indulge, not always constructively, in analysis of each other's motives and behavior. Contemporary literature, theater, television, and movie productions show a similar preoccupation with self-awareness. Group sensitivity training is widespread in educational circles as well as business and industry. Further, role diffusion leads to a sense of being lost with respect to one's function in family life and professional life. Endless discussions go on in mental health faculties about "what our function is." I never heard this in the USSR. The professional people with whom I talked *knew* what their function was. A more positive aspect of diffusion is the ability to generalize experience from one area to another in a creative or innovative way.

3. The escalation of expectations. One American attitude in the fifties was that if the psychotherapeutic relationship based on the psychoanalytic model has elements of an authentic interpersonal relationship, shouldn't everyone have the benefit of such a one-to-one

relationship? Another, perhaps more characteristic of the sixties, was: If psychiatric expertise and the research findings of behavioral science show that certain deprivation syndromes and chaotic personality disorders can be prevented by bringing up a child in a loving, stable environment with firm discipline, then why cannot this knowledge be translated immediately (if not yesterday) into public policy at all levels?

PSYCHIATRY AS A REFLECTION OF CULTURE

The second idea which emerged from the transcultural comparison was that psychiatry is a reflection of culture. The background for my own thinking about the characteristics of Soviet child psychiatry as they are related to social patterns is the significant contribution of Field and Aronson. Their central thesis is that the psychiatric system, both theory and practice, must be regarded as a reflection of the culture and the social structure. They defined a psychiatric system, one of the maintenance mechanisms of a society, as "the multiplicity of practices, social supports, and facilities that are essential to permit the psychiatrist and psychiatric personnel to carry out their functions" (2, p. 306). The people operating within the system tend to remain unaware of the cultural values implicit in their theory and treatment. In making cultural comparisons, we become aware of our own values, formerly unconscious and implicit. We may also be able to learn about new methods applicable to our own practice.

In later works, Field characterized the Soviet social system and the background of Russian culture from which the psychiatric system emerged (3, 4). Characteristics of Russian culture which Field considered most important are collectivism, humanitarianism, denial of sexuality, and isolation of the culture from the rest of the world. While these cultural attributes characterize Soviet society, they were also present in pre-Revolutionary Russia. Field's thesis that psychiatry reflects culture is particularly applicable to Soviet and American attitudes toward Freud and psychoanalysis. *There are cultural determinants both to the Soviet rejection of Freudian ideas and to the American embracement of them.* Too many American discussions of these matters totally leave out the second half of this proposition.

To examine the Soviet side of the question first, with great consistency the Soviet psychiatrists I met denied psychoanalytic theory; they would begin a conversation by remarking, "You know, we don't believe in Freud." Not one showed the slightest understanding that psychoanalysis has several meanings: a theory of personality, a theory of neurosis, a treatment method, a research method, and a method of training psychiatrists and other mental health workers. Although I tried to explain this several times, it is not at all certain that I was really understood. Neither was there much awareness of post-Freudian developments and changes in psychoanalytic theory, although there were a few exceptions. Erikson, Hartmann, and Kris were almost completely unknown to my Soviet colleagues, as was the shift in emphasis from instinct theory to ego psychology.

Soviet objections to Freud form a striking feature of Soviet psychiatry. As we saw in Chapter I, psychoanalytic ideas were initially accepted in the atmosphere of experimentation of the early twenties. Increasing criticism appeared after the introduction of the structural theory of personality: the id, the ego, and the superego. Man's social relationships, according to Marxian theory, are based on economic relationships. Social relations in turn form the basis of character formation. Psychic illness was conceived as the conflict between the social environment and the needs of the individual. In Freudian structural theory, by contrast, illness is conceptualized as a conflict between structural regions of the personality; neurosis is seen as a conflict between the biologically based instincts of the id and the prohibitions of the superego.

A widespread Soviet criticism of psychoanalysis, previously referred to, is that it overemphasizes sexuality. This Soviet attitude toward sexuality in Freudian theory can be directly related to traditional Russian shyness about sexual matters. It is not so much that the role of sexuality is completely denied in the etiology of some neuroses, but the external behavioral manifestations of sexuality are suppressed, especially in adolescence. (Compare Myasishchev's formulation of conflicts in Chapter I, e.g., ethical demands versus sexuality.)

Another common criticism of Freud is the overemphasis on unconscious motivation. Again, I did not see a total denial of the unconscious, since Soviet psychiatrists repeatedly said in discussion of psychotherapy that patients are unaware of the "real cause" of their neurosis. But Soviet society as a whole places high value on maintaining conscious control over everything. Our theories of the unconscious are threatening because they represent a victory of the irrational and the uncontrollable. To assign unconscious thought processes an important role would be to collide with the Soviet ideal of conscious control, social planning, and the building of New Soviet Man. But to deny them completely would be overly simplistic. The Russian doctors I met were not naïve.

As for the Soviet criticism that Freud unduly emphasized the past, there is again not a complete denial of the importance of childhood and early conflicts. Rather, there is a shift of primary emphasis to the present life situation of the patient along with willingness to investigate the past *as it relates dynamically to the present,* true of the best American psychotherapy as well. However, one aspect of Freud's emphasis on the past is poorly understood: the role of transference in the doctor-patient psychotherapeutic relationship and the development of the transference neurosis in the psychoanalytic relationship. The Soviet understanding is that the doctor unwittingly creates an iatrogenic disturbance with the doctor himself the focus of the patient's intense feelings. Soviet psychotherapists overlook the therapeutic leverage in utilizing the patient's inappropriate behavior toward the doctor to show how this resembles the behavior toward others in the patient's life and how both stereotypes are automatic repetitions of past conflicted relationships no longer adaptive in the present.

Soviet doctors, as we have seen in Chapter I, also complain that Freud failed to evaluate correctly the role of social factors in the development of personality and in the etiology of psychiatric disturbances. The claim is not so much that Western theorists totally leave out social factors; rather, only a Marxist-Leninist orientation can give social scientists or therapists a correct orientation toward these problems.

Other Soviet criticisms have been enumerated by Field (1, 4):

1. The unverifiability of psychoanalytic hypotheses by scientific methods.
2. Therapeutic ineffectiveness of psychoanalysis.
3. Deemphasis of prophylaxis.
4. Conflicting Marxist and Freudian attitudes toward work.
5. Blind, illogical voluntarism.
6. Pessimism and fatalism.
7. Emphasis on man's aggressive instincts: seeming justification of war.
8. Attributing a decisive role to the great men of history.

Western critics, too, have attacked psychoanalysis for overemphasizing sexuality, for cultural naïveté, for spawning too many untestable hypotheses, for creating a cumbersome, costly psychotherapeutic method which only works well on patients who are basically healthy anyway, and finally for the theory of the death instinct. So the Russians are not alone in their criticism.

However, here we are less interested in whether psychoanalytic theory is "the truth"; the focus is rather on the ways in which Freudianism is incompatible with values important in Russian culture. Soviet cultural values have already been introduced in the preliminary discussion of child psychiatry and Soviet culture in Chapter I. In Table 13, these

Table 13. Soviet Values, Child Psychiatry, and Anti-Freudian Attitudes

Cultural value	Corresponding aspect: child psychiatry	Corresponding aspect: anti-Freudianism
Humanitarianism and the perfectibility of man	Warmth, kindly treatment	Pessimism and fatalism Therapeutic ineffectiveness of psychoanalysis Deemphasis of prophylaxis
Family the basic social unit	Emphasis on outpatient care, short-term hospitalization	
Socialized medicine	Centralized system of psychiatric services for children	Long, expensive treatment, available only to the privileged, who are able to pay
Scientific method	Emphasis on descriptive classification	Unverifiability of psychoanalytic hypotheses
Monism	Physiologically based psychiatry closely tied to medicine	Error of idealism
Collectivism	Treatment aim: to adapt child to productive life in collective	Psychoanalysis too individualistic as a therapeutic method
Building communism	Treatment aim: to enable child to help build communism	
Dependence	Aspect of collectivism	
Submission to authority	Aspect of collectivism	
Work as basis for social relationships	Work therapy	Deemphasis on gratification of work
Control of overt expression of sexuality and aggression	Drug to control behavior	Overemphasis on sexuality Overemphasis on aggression

Acceptance of inner emotional states	Deemphasis of expressive therapies	
Conscious control and planning	Centralized system of psychiatric services for children	Undue emphasis on unconscious, on past, on irrational aspects of doctor-patient relationship; blind, illogical voluntarism
Isolation of the Soviet system	Shielding from foreign influence	Unawareness of development and change in Freud's thought; unawareness of post-Freudian developments

values are brought into relationship both with aspects of child psychiatry and with anti-Freudian attitudes. It is possible to show that each criticism of the Freudian position, outlined from Field's work, can be related to a significant value:

1. The unverifiability of psychoanalytic hypotheses violates the value of scientific (Marxist-Leninist) methods.

2. Therapeutic ineffectiveness violates the values of mass medical care and humanitarian faith in man's plasticity and perfectibility.

3. The deemphasis of prophylaxis again violates the value of mass medical care.

4. Marxism values work as a key human activity, gratifying in its own right. Freud regards work as a necessity rather than as a means of fulfilling needs.

5. Blind, illogical voluntarism violates the cherished Soviet ideal of conscious planning and control.

6. Pessimism and fatalism are incompatible with the Soviet view of man as perfectible.

7. To emphasize the inevitability of aggression seems to justify war and to devalue the possibility of conscious control.

8. If the Freudian position does indeed give individual man a decisive role in history, the Russians would say it introduces the error of personalism.

PSYCHOANALYSIS AND AMERICAN CULTURE

Since there is clear evidence of correspondence between common Soviet criticisms of psychoanalysis and commonly held Russian values, it is necessary to ask ourselves the parallel question concerning the role of psychoanalytic theory in American culture. The remarks in this concluding section are offered as a preliminary attempt at this kind of analysis. This discussion does not explain why our pro-Freudian bias is present, but it does begin to describe our beliefs in this area in relation to our cultural values. The same is true of the foregoing discussion of Soviet anti-Freudian attitudes. Some readers may object to the assertion that American culture readily embraces Freudian ideas, since strong forces in American medicine and within the field of psychiatry oppose psychoanalytic thought. American culture is pluralistic, irreconcilable points of view coexist.

Nevertheless, it seems to be beyond question that psychoanalysis has found more ready acceptance in the United States than in any other country, with the possible exception of England. To illustrate the permeability of American culture to psychoanalysis, Freud received his first official and international recognition in the professional circles of the United States. The beginning of the international psychoanalytic movement was the series of lectures delivered by Freud at Clark University in Worcester, Massachusetts, in 1909, at the invitation of G. Stanley Hall (5, pp. 53–54).

Equally significant is the relative ease with which the ideas not only diffused into the culture but molded it and changed it. Seely described how psychoanalytic ideas had "become something imminent in American life, interfused with all thought and activity" (7, p. 13). This comment fits well with my observation of the permeability of our society to psychoanalytically oriented thinking. It has spread, as we have seen, into education, psychology, sociology, cultural anthropology, public planning, and child rearing, to mention only a few fields of endeavors. This tendency contrasts with the compartmentalization of social science and psychiatric thought in Europe (7, p. 13). This trend, along with concreteness and limitation of the capacity to generalize or transfer experience from one area to another, was one of the chief features of the Russian character previously described. Now it remains to add my observation that the same compartmentalization characterizes Soviet child psychiatric theory, which plays a much more restricted role than the psychoanalytically based theories of child psychiatry in the United States.

To carry the analysis of our receptivity to psychoanalytic ideas one step further, the question can be restated: What are the key concepts of psychoanalytic thought? How are they related to American values? The psychoanalytic concepts which I consider most unique and im-

Conclusions

portant are described below briefly, roughly in order of their historical development. Each one is brought into relationship with corresponding American values. In this way I hope to expand on the second half of the proposition that there are cultural determinants both to the Soviet rejection of Freudian ideas and to the American embracement of them. Table 14, a companion to Table 13, summarizes this discussion.

Table 14. American Values and Pro-Freudian Attitudes

Cultural value	Psychoanalytic concept
Permissiveness	Unconscious and preconscious determinants of behavior
Free speech	Method of free association Method of expressive play therapy
Parental care of children and informal parent-child relations	Infantile sexuality; pregenital libidinal zones Oedipus complex; incestuous fantasies
Child-oriented society	Decisive importance of early childhood
Rebellion and revolution Independence	Transference and countertransference
Diffusion	Structural theory: id, ego, and super-ego
Personal responsibility Individualism and self-realization Protestant and Jewish ethic	Ego psychology

1. Preconscious and unconscious determinants in the motivation of all behavior were first identified in the studies by Freud and Breuer of hysteria, using the hypnotic method. American attitudes are permissive with respect to behavior and encourage expression of hostile and negative feelings. These attitudes may foster recognition of unconscious and preconscious determinants in the motivation of behavior in so far as they are hostile or negative. However, Americans are more reluctant to express love or tender feelings or to acknowledge feelings of guilt. The reluctance to confront children with anything that might make them aware of guilt feelings fits well with one early but now outmoded psychoanalytic attitude toward personal responsibility, which held that the individual cannot be made accountable for his behavior if it is determined by forces outside his awareness.

2. The method of free association soon replaced the hypnotic method. The basic rule to say anything which comes to mind without conscious editing is converted in child work to free play with verbal expression. Both methods ideally give permission to express ideas, feelings, and fantasies only within the therapeutic hour. No permission is given to *act* on them outside the therapy (an overlooked part of the theory). Both free association and expressive play therapy certainly fit well with the most treasured of American values: the right to free speech.

3. The concept of infantile sexuality evolved as the method of free association was applied, enabling patients to express inner thoughts and fantasies. The concept of sexuality was broadened to include pregenital libidinal zones (oral, anal, urethral) as well as phallic and genital. The object of the instinct was also considered, as well as the course and the aim. All of the sexual instincts were claimed to operate in an infantile form in early childhood. The vicissitudes of the instincts were considered decisive in the formation of the male and female identities. American acceptance of infantile sexuality may have been facilitated by American child-rearing practices. First, there is the deeply held conviction that the parents, particularly the mother and no one else, should take care of the children. Secondly, in the United States, informal relations between parents and children prevail, with few nannies and outside child-care centers. Since mothers, even in the upper classes, personally care for their children, they are in a position actually to see infantile behavior, and it is harder for them to deny libidinal pleasure in sucking, bowel movements, masturbation, and other forms of instinctual expression.

4. Along with the idea of infantile sexuality, the concept of the oedipus complex evolved, first as the result of Freud's self-observations during his own psychoanalysis. The idea of incestuous fantasies, sexual drives, and murderous impulses in the young child was so unacceptable to early twentieth-century society that the pioneer psychoanalysts saw the cultural shock reaction as the major motive for the ridicule of psychoanalytic theory. But in America, with its permissiveness and previously described child-rearing practices, the acceptance of the oedipal myth as a key factor in infant psychology was facilitated.

5. Psychoanalysis came to stress the decisive importance of early childhood in the formation of personality and the neuroses. Quite early, the notion of actual sexual trauma was abandoned when Freud understood that so many of his patients with hysteria were reporting sexual traumata that it was highly unlikely all their recollections could be of

actual events. The focus shifted to early object relations, internal fantasies, childhood misconceptions, and other experiences. We have already seen how child-oriented American society is, so there would be little resistance to a theory stressing the importance of childhood. It might be added that Catholic teaching, a strong influence in America, has also stressed the role of early childhood in character formation and to this extent has supported psychoanalytic theory, although in other respects it has exerted influences in the service of repression.

6. The concepts of transference feelings, the transference neurosis, and countertransference emerged as psychoanalyses became longer, with more ambitious goals, after the sexual-trauma theory had been abandoned. Particularly important is the idea of using both transference and countertransference for exposure and working through of conflict. Rebelliousness, the revolutionary tradition, independence, and openly abrasive attitudes toward authority are deeply held American values. Perhaps this tradition makes the idea of working out conflicting feelings in the transference more acceptable to us than to people who are more accepting of authority.

7. With the appearance of the structural theory of the id, ego, and superego, psychopathological states became categorized in terms of various combinations of conflict between internalized moral imperatives, demands of external reality, and instinctual strivings. The previously noted American tendency toward diffusion makes us receptive to opportunities to generalize, to transfer knowledge from one field of inquiry to another. Although there may be other not-yet-identified factors in the ready American acceptance of the structural theory (id, ego, and superego have become household words), there is probably less resistance here to a theory claiming to encompass both normal personality and psychopathological states.

8. The structural theory led psychoanalysis in a new direction to the development of ego psychology. One important consequence was a shift in the attitude toward personal responsibility. The earlier theory tempted society to conclude that no one is responsible for everyday behavior and decision-making, since these are determined by unconscious drives to repeat infantile experiences and gratifications. The later theory tended to push at least the educated, knowledgeable segment of society to the opposite extreme: everyone is potentially responsible for everything he does, because through psychoanalytic treatment, the unconscious drive derivatives, ego defense mechanisms, and archaic superego prohibitions can be made conscious and therefore subject to rational control. This process is believed to bring about structural

changes in the personality so there is a healthier content and balance of the id, the ego, and the superego. The result is supposed to be an increase in the range of freedom of choice and in the capacity to act rationally, realistically, and compassionately.

The high value Americans place on individualism and self-realization makes it possible for the more informed and privileged in our society to accept long-term treatment with far-reaching goals of personality reconstruction and optimal creative functioning. We have seen how these values seem highly questionable to Soviet doctors committed to serving the collective interests of the society and helping their patients as quickly as possible to resume their place in the collective.

The Protestant and Jewish ethic of hard work and personal responsibility have also helped many accept long, demanding analyses which not uncommonly last five years or more, particularly the analyses of trainees in psychiatry and psychoanalysis. An ethic which emphasizes personal responsibility is receptive to the attitude developed with the growth of ego psychology that the individual can be freed to act in accordance with reality and at the same time humanely, while still meeting his instinctual needs.

This analysis of Soviet and American attitudes toward psychoanalysis shows clearly the need to be more aware of the cultural determinants in our respective ideologies. I conclude that healthy skepticism is necessary with regard to all theory. Further, it would be most constructive to arrange a Soviet-American exchange, in the form of a parallel lecture series or an international symposium, so that each could become more aware of the other's theory, particularly points of development and change. Specifically, Americans should be exposed to Soviet thinking on the application of Marxist-Leninist theory to psychiatry and Russians should be exposed to post-Freudian developments in the psychoanalytic movement. Only through such an exchange can I see any possibility of beginning to allow for cultural bias in our basic assumptions and theorizing. At the least, we can be more informed and sophisticated than we have been about what we criticize in each other. In short, I propose that the dialogue between Marxism and psychoanalysis which began in the twenties and was abandoned in the thirties be reopened.

The transcultural comparison has taken us a step beyond the assertion that psychiatry is a reflection of culture to the last conclusion. Psychiatry in its theorizing and in its practice develops in such a way as to meet certain needs of individuals within the culture for survival and adaptation. Particularly with respect to treatment practices, psychiatry at least partially corrects for or compensates for certain cultural deficiencies and incompatibilities. Table 13 summarizes how Soviet child psychiatry developed in accordance with commonly held Soviet values stressing collectivism, submissiveness to authority, control of external behavior, conscious planning, humanitarianism, warmth, materialism, and cultural isolation. By way of contrast, American child psychiatry developed in accordance with individualism, rebelliousness with respect to authority, permissiveness in regard to external behavior, pluralism, permeability, diffusion, and escalation of expectations, to mention only a few differences.

Against this background, I have come to see a major cultural difference in the overall aim of treatment in the two societies, as it pertains to psychiatric disorders. Treatment in the USSR acts to desensitize or perhaps to insulate the patient from a frustrating environment, occasionally to give some temporary respite by removing the patient to more tranquil surroundings, but there is little or no attempt to change the environment.

The forms of treatment growing out of the psychoanalytic movement in the United States have acted to sensitize the patient and his family to the interpersonal environment, to experience and to work through conflict, and in some instances to modify the environment. The stress on sensitivity seems to me to be related to a paradox in our society: severe communication difficulties in the land of free speech. This particular cultural deficit may be connected with the melting-pot features of American society, which require a much higher degree of awareness of the other fellow's point of view and more expertise in communication for effective functioning than is necessary in more homogeneous societies. Being a good American requires flexibility and tolerance of diversity. Other components of the deficit may be egocentricity fostered both by individualism and by permissiveness with respect to behavioral excesses. Also, there is the curious cultural restriction in our freedom of speech which forbids expression of love, warmth, tenderness, and, lately, patriotism. Russians do not need psychotherapists to help them find acceptable expression of love feelings, but Americans frequently do. So my investigation ends with the somewhat surprising conclusion that we have developed expressive therapies because we need them and have evidently needed them more than Soviet society. To each his own, then, but one hopes with some understanding of the other.

Appendices
References
Index

Appendix I

Institutions
Visited

MOSCOW, 1968–69

Medical Institutions

1. Ministry of Health, USSR
   Rokhmananovski, Pereulok,·Dom 3
   Department of Foreign Relations
      Representatives: Mikhail Victorovich Borisov
         Alexander Alexandrovich Sazanov, Lev Ivanovich Malyshev

2. *Hospitals*

   Clinic for Childhood Psychoses
   Moscow Institute of Psychiatry, RSFSR
   Pyaty Donskoi Proezd, Dom 21A
      Professor: Grunya Efimovna Sukhareva

   Clinic for Childhood Psychoses
   Institute of Psychiatry, Academy of Medical Sciences
   Pyaty Donskoi Proezd, Dom 21A
      Professor: Moisei Semenovich Vrono

   Psychoneurological Hospital named for Kashenko
   Zagorodnoe Shosse, Dom 2
      Chief Doctors: Nataliya Stepanovna Maslaeva
         Nataliya Grigorevna Romanova

3. *Dispensaries*

Psychoneurological Dispensary for Children and Adolescents with Hospital
Pyaty Donskoi Proezd, Dom 21A
   Chief Doctor: Vera Alekseevna Kolegova

Regional Psychoneurological Dispensary
Leningrad Region of Moscow
   Senior Child Psychiatrist: Ya. M. Bardenshtein

4. *Children's Polyclinics*

Children's Polyclinic No. 32
Sverdlovski Region of Moscow
Psychoneurological Office

Children's Polyclinic
Leningrad Region of Moscow
Psychoneurological Office

5. *Training Institutes*

Chair of Child Psychiatry
Central Institute for the Increased Qualification of Physicians
Pyaty Donskoi Proezd, Dom 21A
   Professor: Vladimir Victorovich Kovalev

Chair of Psychotherapy
Central Institute for the Increased Qualification of Physicians
Ploshchad Vosstaniya, Dom 1
   Professor: Vladimir Evgenevich Rozhnov

6. *Research Institutes*

Institute of Psychiatry, Academy of Medical Sciences, USSR
Zagorodnoe Shosse, Dom 2, Corpus 3
   Research Secretary: Maya Germanovna Shirina

Moscow Psychiatric Institute, RSFSR
Ulitsa Poteshnaya, Dom 3
   Deputy Director: S. F. Semenov

7. *Sanatorium*

Children's Psychoneurological Sanatorium No. 44
Otkritkoe Shosse, Dom 30
Moscow B-143
   Director: Vladimir Andreevich Gamza

Institutions
Visited

Educational Institutions

1. *Schools*

Middle School No. 739
Leningrad Region of Moscow

Special Boarding School No. 103 (for Mildly Retarded)
Ulitsa Kazakova Dom 13
   Director: Nina Sergeevna Ivanova

Special Boarding School No. 31 (for Children with Central Nervous System Disease)
Ulitsa Pogono-Losinostrovskaya Dom 29
   Director: Elizaveta Fedorovna Popova

Forest School-Sanatorium No. 9 (for Children with Neuroses)
   Director: Vasily Akimovich Khaustov

2. *Kindergarten*

Specialized Kindergarten No. 468 (for Retarded Children)
Kvartal 38 Corpus 186
Moscow B 421
   Director: Mariya Nikiforevna Olekhovskaya

3. *Research Institutes*

Institute of Defectology
Pogodinskaya Ulitsa Dom 8

Cooperative Education Department
Academy of Pedagogical Sciences
Bolshoi Tomachevski Dom 3
   Representative: Zoya Malkova

Institute of Preschool Education
Lemontovski Periulok Dom 1

Miscellaneous

Children's Militia Room

Moscow Police Department

Appendix I

LENINGRAD, 1969

Medical Institutions

1. Leningrad City Health Department
   Mala Sadovaya Ulitsa, Dom 1
      Chief: Avetis Airapetovich Asaturian

2. *Hospitals*

   Children's Psychoneurological Hospital
   Pesochnaya Naberezhnaya, Dom 4
   Leningrad P-22
      Chief Doctor: Polina Vasilevna Mashlakova

   Psychoneurological Institute named for Bekhterev
   Ulitsa Bekhtereva, Dom 3
   Leningrad S-19
      Director: Modest Mikhailovich Kabanov
      Secretary: Rafael Alexandrovich Zachepitski
      Child Department: G. B. Abramovich
      Medical Psychology Department: Yusif Mikhailovich Tonkanogi

3. *Dispensary*

   Regional Psychoneurological Dispensary
   Moscow Region of Leningrad
   Vozdukhoplavatilnaya Ulitsa, Dom 13
      Chief Doctor: Emanuil Anatolevich Breslav

4. *Training Institutes*

   Chair of Psychiatry
   Pediatric Medical Institute of Leningrad
      Professor: Samuil Semenovich Mnukhin

Educational Institution

1. *School*
   Sanatorium-Forest School for Nervous Children No. 2
   Ulitsa Dekabristov, Dom 14
   Pavlovsk
      Director: Ludmila Alexandrovna Moiseeva
      Pediatrician: Rima Grigorevna Ivanova

KIEV, 1969

Medical Institutions

1. Ministry of Health, Ukrainian SSR
   Ulitsa Kirova, Dom 7
   Department of External Affairs
      Special Medical Services for Children:
      Valentina Constantinovna Blazhievskaya

2. *Hospitals*

   Specialized Clinical Children's Hospital
   Ulitsa Kosyura, Dom 28
      Chief Doctor: Tatyana Petrovna Novikova
      Psychoneurologist: Ekaterina Efrermovna Vasilyuk

   Psychoneurological Hospital Named for Pavlov
   Ulitsa Fruize Dom 103
      Chief Doctor: Anatoli Denisovich Rebenok

3. Children's Polyclinic
   Pecherski Region
      Chief Doctor: Natalya Ivanovna Soloveva

4. *Training Institutes*

   Chair of Child Psychiatry
   Kiev Institute for the Increased Qualification of Physicians
   Ministry of Health
   Ukrainian SSR
      Professor: Yusif Adamovich Polishtuk
      Assistant: Svetlana Nikolaevna Zinchkina

5. *Research Institutes*

   Kiev Scientific Research Institute of Pediatrics, Obstetrics, and Gynecology named for Bulko
      Director: Ivan Aleksandr Germanovich
      Department of Childhood Psychoses, Senior Scientific Worker:
      Elvira Constantinovna Gur

6. *Sanatorium*

   Children's Psychoneurological Sanatorium
      Chief Doctor: Kapitolina Aleksandrovna Brilliantova

Appendix I

Educational Institutions

1. *School*

     Special School No. 1, Oktyabraskaya Region (for mildly retarded)
     Deputatskaya Ulitsa, Dom 1
          Director: Gregori Ulyanovich Gilchenko
          Pediatrician: Mariya Igorevna Makarenkova
          Psychoneurologist: Valeriya Kuzminichna Kuzmina

2. *Research Institute*

     Kiev Institute of Psychology, Ukrainian SSR
     Ulitsa Pankovskaya, Dom 2
          Director: Academician Gregori Silovich Kostyuk

Miscellaneous

1. Children's Nursery No. 20 (for normal infants)
   Leninski Region

2. Central Pioneer Palace

3. Darnitsa Children's Home (for retarded: imbeciles)
        Director: Giorgi Fedorovich Tishchenko

Appendix II

History of Child's Development

(Adapted from Clinical Record Form No. 112,
published by the Ministry of Health, USSR, 1954)

Micro-region (*Uchastok*) No.
Name
Address
Date of birth
Date of discharge from maternity home after birth
Date of first visit: Nurse at the home   at age _____
                         Doctor at the home   at age _____
                         Consultation with doctor   at age _____
Attends Nursery No. _____   Date of entry   Date of leaving _____
     Kindergarten No. _____   Date of entry   Date of leaving _____
     School No. _____   Date of entry   Date of leaving _____
Left observation of Polyclinic:
     Age _____   Date _____   Reason _____
Observations of child during first and second year of life:
     Doctor of Micro-region: In Polyclinic   Date ___ months of life
                         At home
     Visiting Nurse: At home
Information about the parents at the time of the child's birth:
     Mother: Age _____ Place of work _____ Occupation _____
     Father: Age _____ Place of work _____ Occupation _____
     History of mother's pregnancies:
         Total number of pregnancies _____
         Full term deliveries _____ Premature births _____ Abortions _____

Live births ———— Still births ————
Number of children in the family at present ————
Information about the birth of the child:
Full term ———— Premature ———— Multiple birth ————
Child born in maternity home ———— At home ————
Birth—normal ———— pathological ————
Operative intervention ————————
Weight at birth ———— at discharge ———— length ————
Living conditions in the family ————————————
Illnesses in the family (tuberculosis, syphilis, alcoholism, etc.) ————
——
Illnesses in the apartment ————————————————————
Early feeding history: From (age) to (age)
Breast ———— Mixed ———— Artificial ————
Development
Sitting ———— Standing ———— Walking ———— Talking ————
First teeth ————
Number of teeth at 1 year ————
Anthropometric data

	Birth	Month 3	6	9	12	Years 2	3	4	5	6	7
Weight in grams											
Height in centimeters											
Circumference of head											
Circumference of chest											

Acute infectious illness: Date ———— Age ————
Measles
Scarlet fever
Diphtheria
Whooping cough
Chicken pox
Dysentery
Chronic illnesses   Age of onset ———— Outcome, at what age ————
Hypotrophy
Rickets
Tuberculous intoxication
Vaccinations and revaccinations: Date ———— Age ———— Reaction ————
Tuberculosis
Small pox
Diphtheria
Tuberculous specimens ———— Worm specimens ————
Inoculations: Date ———— Age ————
Subsequent observations
Date; Polyclinic or home
History; Data about physical development
Clinical observations
Results of tests

History of Child's
Development

    Conclusions of specialists
    Diagnosis, Disposition
    Signature of doctor
    Observations of visiting nurse (initials of supervising doctor)
Weight Chart

Appendix III

Grouping of Psychiatric Disorders

(After G. E. Sukhareva, *Clinical Lectures in Child Psychiatry*.)

VOLUME I, MAJOR PSYCHIATRY

I. Symptomatic psychoses: infectious or postinfectious

    A. Malaria
    B. Virus grippe
    C. Diphtheria
    D. Measles
    E. Scarlet fever
    F. Enteritis
    G. Typhoid, paratyphoid
    H. Pneumonia

II. Acute infections of the brain and meninges

    A. Meningitis
        1. Serious meningitis—typhoid fever, pneumonia, grippe, parotitis, etc.
        2. Tuberculous meningitis
    B. Encephalitis
        1. Encephalitis

           a. Poliomyelitis
           b. Japanese form
           c. Rabies
           d. Epidemic
           e. Virus
       2. Secondary encephalitis
           a. Infectious
           b. Choreiform
           c. Pertussis
  C. Atypical forms, abortive forms (virus)
  D. Residuals
       1. Dementia
       2. Epileptiform seizures
       3. Psychopathic-like syndromes
       4. Cerebrasthenia

III. "Rheumatism" of the central nervous system

  A. Rheumatic cerebrasthenia
  B. Epileptic seizures
  C. Rheumatic cerebropathia with dementia
  D. Rheumatic psychoses
       1. Depressive form
       2. Oneiroid form
  E. Neurotic-like syndromes
  F. Rheumatic chorea

IV. Syphilis of central nervous system

  A. Congenital central nervous system syphilis
       1. Progressive form
           a. Pseudoparesis
           b. Epileptiform
           c. Apoplectiform (vascular)
           d. Meningoencephalitis
       2. Stationary form
  B. Juvenile progressive paresis

V. Brain trauma

  A. Psychic disturbances accompanying acute brain trauma
       1. Open trauma
       2. Closed trauma
  B. Residual encephalopathy after brain trauma
       1. Traumatic cerebrasthenia

2. Motor disturbances
   a. Apathy, underactivity syndrome
   b. Hyperkinetic syndrome
3. Psychopathic-like behavior
4. Traumatic intellectual defects
   a. Disturbances of memory, attention
   b. Aphasia, other speech disturbances
5. Traumatic epilepsy

VI. Epilepsy

A. True epilepsy (endogenous)
   Hereditary predisposition
B. Symptomatic (exogenous)
   1. Traumatic
   2. Syphilitic
   3. Associated with encephalitis, meningitis
   4. Rheumatic
C. Epileptic illness caused by brain damage (mixed)
   with characteristic features of "true epilepsy"

VII. Schizophrenia

A. Forms
   1. Childhood form
   2. Adolescent form
B. Classification by type of onset and course
   1. Insidious, progressive
   2. Acute onset with intermittent course and no residual
   3. Mixed: intermittent with progression

VIII. Manic-Depressive Psychoses

A. Manic form
B. Depressive form
C. Mixed form

IX. Periodic psychoses (nosological status still questionable)

A. Disturbances of affect
   1. Depressive form
   2. Manic form
B. Motor disturbances—without negativism
   1. Inhibition
   2. Excitement
C. Sensory disturbances
D. Disturbances of consciousness

VOLUME II, MINOR PSYCHIATRY: BORDERLINE STATES

I. Reactive states—neuroses and psychoses

    A. Acute shock and subshock reactions
        1. Fear with motor excitement
        2. Twilight states
        3. Stupor
        4. Monosymptomatic forms
            a. Speech disturbances—stuttering mutism
            b. Paralysis, paresis
            c. Hyperkinesis
            d. Functional disturbances of the internal organs
            e. Sleep disturbances
    B. Subacute psychogenic reactions
        1. Depression
        2. Paranoia
        3. Asthenia-neurasthenia
            a. Increased fatigability
            b. Increased excitability
        4. Anxiety neurosis
            a. Panic state
            b. Twilight state
            c. Phobic state
        5. Hysterical neurosis
        6. Reaction of protest
            a. Passive form
                1. Elective mutism
                2. Suicidal attempts
                3. Vegetative-somatic disturbances
            b. Active form
                1. Aggressive acts
                2. Tantrums
        7. Vegetative-somatic disturbances (organ neuroses)
            a. Psychogenic anorexia
            b. Habitual vomiting
            c. Enuresis, encopresis
            d. Nervous cough
        8. Speech and motor disturbances—monosyptomatic neuroses
            a. Sleep disturbances, night fears
            b. Stuttering
            c. Tics
        9. Pathological reactions at transitional growth periods
    C. Chronic reactive states (Myasishchev: Neurosis of development)
        1. Obsessional neurosis
        2. Hypochondriacal, asthenic, and hysterical development

3. Distorted character formation (changes of character)
—unfavorable conditions of upbringing
   a. Aggressive-defensive type
   b. Passive-defensive type
   c. Infantile type

II. Neuropathy (nervousness, nervous predisposition)

   A. Congenital
   B. Acquired

III. Psychopathy (pathological development of the personality)

   A. Infantilism: inhibitions of development
      1. Instability
      2. Excitement
      3. Hysteroid
      4. Pseudologia
   B. Disproportional (distorted) development—genetically determined
      1. Cyclothymic personality
      2. Schizoid (autistic) personality
      3. Psychasthenic personality
      4. Paranoid personality
      5. Epileptoid personality
   C. Damaged development—intrauterine or postnatal brain damage
      1. Failure of inhibitory controls
      2. Impulsive excitement

VOLUME III, OLIGOPHRENIA

   I. Levels of retardation
      A. Idiot
      B. Imbecile
      C. Moron

  II. Etiological grouping

   A. Endogenous—genetic
      1. Langdon-Down disease
      2. True microcephaly
      3. Enzymopathic forms with hereditary disturbances of lipoid, carbohydrate, and albumen metabolism
         a. Phenylpyruvic oligophrenia
         b. Oligophrenia with galactosemia, sucrosuria
         c. Other enzymopathies

4. Oligophrenia with diseases of the bones and skin
   a. Dysostosis
   b. Ichthyosis
   c. Angiomatosis
B. Oligophrenia acquired in embryonal or fetal period
   1. Viruses: German measles, grippe, parotitis, infectious hepatitis, infectious mononucleosis
   2. Toxoplasmosis, histoplasmosis
   3. Congenital syphilis
   4. Hormonal and toxic agents
   5. Hemolytic disease of the newborn
C. Exogenous oligophrenia—acquired by damage at birth or early in life
   1. Birth trauma and asphyxia
   2. Brain trauma in early childhood
   3. Encephalitis and meningitis in early childhood
D. Atypical forms of oligophrenia
   1. Progressive hydrocephalus
   2. Localized defects in the development of the brain
   3. Endocrine disturbances

Appendix IV

Case Studies

1. SASHA: A PROBLEM IN THE DIFFERENTIAL DIAGNOSIS OF PSYCHOSIS

Sasha, a nine-and-one-half-year-old boy, presented a problem in differential diagnosis which illustrates the distinction between a process and a state in Russian diagnostic thinking. He was seen in consultation by Professor Sukhareva during his second admission to the psychoneurological hospital because of exitement and severe behavior problems. Also, he had been calling himself a girl.

Family history and early development were not remarkable except for toxicosis during the pregnancy and several illnesses during the second year: chicken pox, virus grippe, otitis media, and sore throat. At three, Sasha went to kindergarten and began to show signs of disturbance. He cried frequently and did not achieve full bladder training for the next year and a half. He preferred to stay close to his mother or to play alone and showed an interest in construction in his choice of play materials. An obsessive wish to spit appeared at this time, and Sasha began calling himself by a girl's name, believing girls were preferred.

At five, he was hospitalized for an illness diagnosed as encephalopathy. After returning to kindergarten, Sasha showed improvement in his relationship with other children through a new interest in playing chess, but he began looking through calendars in an obsessive way. At seven and one-half, he said his mother did not love him and turned more to his father. In kindergarten, compulsive activities were noted, along with increasing irritability and excitability.

When chlorpromazine failed to control his symptoms, Sasha was admitted to a psychoneurological hospital, where at first he cried and ate poorly, blaming his behavior on his grandmother. Although he said he loved her, he complained she would not let him eat alone. On the ward, Sasha's behavior was infantile and his contact with other children was poor. He showed an interest in singing and evidence of good development of speech and intellectual functions. He claimed one little girl was his wife, embraced her, and tried to kiss her, although she cried out and objected to his advances. After three months in the hospital on trifluoperazine and chlorpromazine, Sasha was discharged to his home.

During the next three years, Sasha received home tutoring. He worked particularly well with his music teacher. He began saying he was an editor and a journalist. After about two months, the obsessive preoccupations shifted to an interest in newspapers. He read about international events and began saying he was president of one or another country, becoming increasingly restless and agitated. As the obsessions increased, Sasha gave up most normal activities except for chess, in spite of treatment with trifluoperazine and librium.

Because of the persistence of symptoms, Sasha was hospitalized again. He showed rapid movements and speech, with much gesticulating. His mood was euphoric, with a great deal of joking and laughter. He referred to himself as the prime minister, the president of the communist party, or an ambassador of the USSR in various world capitals. The newspaper preoccupation continued. He recalled his previous hospitalization, knew his age and that his father was a rocket engineer and his mother was a doctor. He had no insight into his illness. Except for his perseveration on newspapers, his attention span was poor. He had only the most superficial contact with other children.

With treatment (chlorpromazine and "milertzine"), Sasha became calmer, less euphoric, and more able to work with the teacher in the third class. But his only relationship with other children was through playing chess. During the month before the presentation, Sasha had begun to shout compulsively, "I am finished: I am finished!" (*Konchalsya! Konchalsya!*) He said this was because at home, his father would say the president (presumably his preoccupation with the president) was finished; or if he had been bad, it was finished.

Physical examination revealed undernourishment and positive Babinski signs bilaterally. The skull x-ray showed evidence suggestive of past increased intracranial pressure. No EEG was reported. The psychological report drew a comparison between Sasha's status during the second hospitalization with that two years previously, showing increased fatigability and distractability. His obsessive thought processes were considered to be deeply disturbed.

Sasha entered the room to talk with Professor Sukhareva in front of the staff and trainees. He was murmuring to himself, "Konchalsya! Konchalsya!" He spoke in a low, throaty voice about newspapers. He was a thin, wiry boy with a black crewcut. He wore especially baggy pants. When asked why he was saying "Konchalsya, konchalsya," he replied it was because there was an election for president and he cannot forget. He knew Richard Nixon had been elected president in America and that the latter was preceded by Lyndon Johnson. He mentioned that the Americans were bombing "the People's Republic of North Vietnam." He did not know whether he was president or not, but acknowledged wanting to become president. When asked why, Sasha could only repeat "Konchalsya! Konchalsya!"

Professor Sukhareva told Sasha that if he kept saying "Konchalsya, konchalsya," he could not possibly learn in class and this was bad behavior. After he announced he would soon be going home, she appealed to him strongly, telling him first, he must give this up. Sasha declared he did not want to because he is interested in endings and wondered whether the doctor, too, might be interested in endings. He added that he wanted to find out about the presidents in various countries and when he was big, he would be president. By this time, he was speaking quite rapidly in a loud, deep voice. He seemed not the least embarrassed by being the focus of attention of a roomful of people. Nor did he show any awareness of the confusion his utterances betrayed. After a brief physical examination, he was allowed to have a newspaper, but when asked to read aloud, he said nothing. He showed intact capacity to do simple subtraction and multiplication. His mood was cheerful and his general affective state did not seem remote or withdrawn. Rather, it seemed Sasha was out of contact because he lacked social awareness.

The doctor who presented the case felt this was a schizophrenic process, but with an organic base. She mentioned the boy's lack of emotional contact with other children, the change in the affective state with the present euphoria, the restriction of his normal interests and play activities, and the psychological observations which stressed his fatigability. There were signs of progression which indicated a poor prognosis. Symptoms began at three years and there were two exacerbations. The clinical picture he demonstrated at nine and a half, the time of the consultation, was described as a "manic state with a paraphrenic syndrome."

As the discussion of the case began, the differences in symptomatology between the first and second admissions were stressed. Although Sasha was excited and restless both times, it was noted he was much more sexually attracted to little girls at the first admission. In fact, he was so attached to one girl that he would not eat or study unless she was present. When she was discharged, Sasha cried and showed a severe grief reaction. At the second admission, he was more obsessively fixated, for example, on the question of death.

Everyone agreed that the illness must be described as a process rather than a state. There was an organic residual, as evidenced by the signs of past hydrocephalus, the motor awkwardness, and, in one doctor's opinion, by the euphoric mood and impulse disorder. But it was felt that the whole illness could not be explained on this basis. The differences of opinion and emphasis centered around the fact that there is no room in the nosological schema for a psychosis, distinct from schizophrenia, based on a progressive, degenerative organic brain process, which would have been my own formulation. The lack of EEG investigation only received passing attention from one discussant. Though the change in Sasha's relationship with his mother was noted, there was less attention to the vicissitudes of Sasha's interpersonal relationships than one would hear in a comparable case in the United States and no curiosity about the meaning of the obsessions.

2. IVAN: A CASE OF ADOLESCENT SCHIZOPHRENIA

The case of Ivan illustrates a slowly developing schizophrenic process in an adolescent. When Ivan was 17, he returned to the psychoneurological hospital, where he had previously been a patient, for further consultation because of an exacerbation of his fear and depression.

The history revealed some infantile disturbance, which unfortunately was missed on my tape recording, before six months. Motor development was slower than intellectual development. As a preschool child, he was meticulous, preferred to play alone at home. He learned chess at four years and could read at five. He was impressionable, cried easily, and feared the dark. He had frequent colds and sore throats and one episode of pneumonia.

During school years, Ivan was timid, withdrawn, and fearful of not doing well although he earned good marks. Definite difficulties developed in the eighth class. Other children began laughing and whispering about him. This was verified in reality. Ivan never complained about this but was full of inner fears and tension. He spoke very slowly, took hours to prepare his lessons, and felt very unsure of himself. He feared being left back in school and began to worry about his memory. He read medical journals, trying to find out about his own mental status. At home a hand-washing compulsion appeared, and he demanded that his mother wash fruits several times before he would eat them. He feared crossing the street and also worried that his mother might fall under a street car. He also feared chronic pneumonia and liver disease. Although his teachers considered him competent, he worried so much over lessons that he sometimes even cried. The first definite delusional idea was the thought that people were constantly watching him on the street.

Ivan was first hospitalized in a psychoneurological hospital for three months when he was 15. On admission, he was agitated, tense, and fearful and he cried. One day later, Ivan heard voices of relatives swearing at him and blaming him, particularly when he would hear the personnel talking nearby on the ward. An injection of levomepromazine quickly dispelled the hallucinatory state, although he remembered it clearly afterwards. However, Ivan's obsessive fears and depressed mood remained. He somehow provoked patients to laugh at him and to say he would be a patient forever. Medication included levomepromazine and haloperidol. On discharge, his mood was still somewhat depressed.

At home, he was treated with levomepromazine and librium, later levomepromazine and Mellipramine. When he was 16, he entered the tenth class and continued to do well in his studies, although he was still concerned about his ability. The obsessive thinking continued and once Ivan heard accusatory voices. He withdrew from his mother and his grandmother.

Ivan was hospitalized a second time in a tearful, excited state. He had become more and more depressed, believing his mother and father would fall under a street car, an automobile, or a train. He talked in a soft, monotonous voice and complained of headaches. He was withdrawn and inaccessible. Two days after admission, he began experiencing unknown feminine voices blaming him. During the three days that his hallucinations lasted, Ivan ate practically nothing. He would only talk with the doctors if they sat back to back with him because the voices forbade him to do otherwise. On amitriptyline and trifluoperazine, his hallucinations disappeared but the obsessions continued, as they had during the previous admission. Ivan thought he had gone crazy and would never get better. He began to talk with the doctors but would not associate with other patients and spent most of his time reading, ruminating about insanity. Both his depressed mood and his obsessive fears fluctuated although he became less agitated. When he was seen in conference a month after admission, it was felt that his hallucinatory experiences and certain ritualistic movements indicated a poor prognosis. After two months, Ivan was discharged home to continue trifluoperazine (10 mg a day) and amitriptyline (50 mg a day).

At home, he lay in bed and would not do anything, complaining that he was insane and would never be better. Amitriptyline was increased to 100 mg a day. His mother became afraid to leave him home alone because he expressed thoughts about throwing himself under a streetcar. He also feared some vague catastrophe. After a brief episode of mutism and excitement, Ivan willingly returned with his mother to the hospital for consultation. At that time, he was receiving 15 mg of trifluoperazine and 100 mg of amitriptyline daily.

When Ivan came into the interview, he was tall, pale, neatly dressed, overweight. He moved stiffly and spoke in a soft voice. He said his depressed moods frightened him, and these were accompanied by repetitive thoughts that he would get worse or remain sick. He added that the depressions lasted about six days and were followed by better moods that might last up to ten days. He had not yet given up school, although it was very difficult for him and he doubted his abilities. He had no thoughts about the future and felt his illness prevented him from making plans. He was able to recall the hallucinations during his first hospitalization and said he had none during the last period in the hospital. Professor Sukhareva admonished him to continue his treatment and not to give up taking his medicine, since this helped him. When asked about his relationship with his mother, Ivan acknowledged it was more constrained than it had been before his illness.

Ivan's mother was interviewed briefly. She thought her son was worse now. After he left the hospital, he had no fear at all, but then the fears returned and had become nearly constant. At the present, he was afraid of traffic and public transportation. He also complained of not feeling well.

In the summary of the case, the presenting doctor mentioned the leading syndrome of depression with obsessive fears and thoughts. There had been at least three depressive attacks, one with an hallucinatory episode. The illness had a gradual onset. The first fears formed in early childhood when Ivan was considered very obedient and did not relate well to other children. The diagnosis was schizophrenia with a slow, insidious course and exacerbations of depressive moods and neurotic-like symptoms.

In the discussion, it was considered important to change the medication in an effort to find a way of preventing exacerbations. Unfavorable prognostic signs were the appearance of "psychic automatisms," catatonic manifestations, and the hallucinatory experiences. The obsessive thoughts were felt to have a delusional character and a paranoid tinge. The fears and depression, though resembling psychasthenia, were considered to be part of the schizophrenic process. The course of the illness was mixed, with a slow, insidious onset and progression on which were superimposed episodes of depression. In the early childhood history, Ivan's good intellectual capacity and poor motor development were noted. His inhibited sexual development suggested diencephalic signs and an endocrine component, linked to the serious chronic pneumonia during childhood. Characterologically, it was noted Ivan tended to be emotionally cold yet overly attached to his mother and to remain on an infantile level of development. There was general agreement that the prognosis was not favorable but at present, treatment should continue at home and he and his mother should be encouraged to feel he could continue to attend school. It was recommended that the dosage of amitriptyline be gradually lowered and that he continue trifluoperazine. He was also to receive levomepromazine at times when he was very fearful. There was no consideration of psychotherapy. All of these features were characteristic of Soviet thinking with regard to the diagnosis and treatment of adolescent schizophrenia.

3. IRA: A CASE OF ANOREXIA NERVOSA AS PART OF A REACTION TO PUBERTY

This first case of anorexia nervosa illustrates how the syndrome is sometimes a manifestation of a pathological reaction to puberty. Ira, a 13-year-old girl, was admitted to a psychoneurological hospital because her refusal to eat had resulted in a weight loss from 61 to 42 kilograms (134 to 92 pounds). On admission, she was weak, malnourished, and exhausted.

Ira began to limit her food intake because she was teased about being fat while she was in camp with a circle of friends a little older than she. At the same time, she became increasingly irritable, especially at home with her grandmother and her mother. She began to spend much time looking in the mirror. She continued to do well in school but complained of headaches. Menses, which had begun at ten years, stopped two months before admission. At the time that she was hospitalized, Ira was eating only tea for breakfast, fruit for lunch, and candy for supper.

The family history revealed that the father's drinking led to a separation of the parents, after which Ira continued to visit him. Further details of the family situation were not given. Ira spoke unusually clearly at an early age. Between the ages of eight and ten, she experienced a kidney disorder, pneumonia, and hepatitis. Ira was always bright and conscientious at her studies. She was enrolled in a special school where English was taught, starting in the first class.

On admission to the hospital, Ira was tearful and nervous. She complained that she had been deceived about coming to the hospital and did not consider herself ill or in need of hospitalization. She explained she did not eat because she was afraid of becoming fat. Physical findings were not remarkable except for undernourishment and cool, dry skin. On the ward, she would eat only a third of her food, hiding the remainder and frequently rubbing her stomach after eating. She became overactive and attempted to exercise. She was treated with insulin, librium, and "tizoxine." Her diet was supplemented with intravenous glucose, plasma, gamma globulin, and vitamins.

When we saw Ira in consultation, she was a slender though not emaciated girl in early puberty. She smiled appropriately and did not seem in any way bizarre. She said she was hospitalized because she was ill and at the beginning she had felt weak. Previously, she had denied illness. She had been attending English school, she said, since the first class. During our interview, she spoke some English. She said she had limited her diet because she wanted to become thin and had considered herself fat when she weighed 61 kilograms. All her life, people had teased her about being fat, but this did not bother her much until she was 13. She seemed closely attached in an ambivalent way to her grandmother, who suffered when other girls teased Ira about her weight and worried when the child would not eat. She claimed she loved both her mother and her grandmother and seemed aware of their anxiety over her refusal to eat. She did experience sensations of hunger, but after eating she complained her stomach got very big and heavy and too full. She wanted to gain only 2 kilograms more, but her doctor said she should gain 5 kilograms. Dr. Rotiniyan noted the child did gymnastics on the ward after she ate. Ira realized that she actually enjoyed eating but controlled herself in the presence of hunger. She denied any feelings of depression and said she had friends both in the hospital and at home. She was most anxious to be allowed to go home, but was still worrying about being made to get fat in the hospital. If she did, she asserted she would just get thin again.

Dr. Rotiniyan did not consider Ira to show any sign of a psychotic process. Her total denial of illness and resistance to weight gain are characteristic of the syndrome, as well as the fear of fatness and the appearance of concerns about the body coinciding with pubertal development.

4. OLGA: A CASE OF ANOREXIA NERVOSA AS PART OF A SCHIZOPHRENIC PROCESS

This second case of anorexia nervosa illustrates how the syndrome is sometimes embedded in a more pervasive schizophrenic process. Olga was a 15-year-old girl who was admitted to a psychoneurological hospital because of weight loss and malnutrition after preliminary study in a pediatric hospital.

The family history revealed schizophrenia, alcoholism, and tuberculosis in various relatives. The father was described as active and quick-tempered. The mother had a history of tuberculosis and had been hospitalized recently with an exacerbation. She was a highly intelligent woman, trained as an economist and a specialist in the French language, but was not considered very communicative. She tended to speak in a flat, tangential way, intellectualizing excessively.

Olga, the patient, was an only child. Mother had had a stillbirth and two infants had died. During the pregnancy with Olga, there was slight toxemia. The baby was born prematurely at seven months, for which mother blamed herself. The labor was long, and at birth the baby suffered anoxia and weighed only 2.6 kilograms (5.7 pounds). Childhood illnesses included whooping cough, measles, chicken pox, and frequent sore throats. At ten years, there was a tonsillectomy and adenoidectomy. As a preschool child, Olga was quiet and obedient and learned to read early. She ate well and was plump. At seven, she began school, where she was considered punctual and conscientious. She had girl friends and was accepted by her peer group. In the third grade, Olga was excused from physical culture because of "cardiac symptoms," although she retained an interest in skiing, swimming, and Pioneer activities. She was rigid, serious, and perfectionistic, also stubborn.

When her menses began at 13, Olga was still plump but soon became irritable and began to eat less. She complained there was something heavy in her stomach and would get angry when people tried to urge her to eat. She limited her diet, taking only a little buttermilk and some sour apples. At the same time, she became overactive, doing much exercising and sleeping little. Her weight fell from 38 kilograms to 29 kilograms (83.6 pounds to 63.8 pounds).

When Olga was transferred to the psychoneurological hospital, she was poorly nourished with dry skin and hypertrichosis. Her tongue was coated. Blood pressure was 100/60. She was serious and tense and spoke in a soft voice, giving formal answers. She had no complaints and did not consider herself ill. She said her mother had been in the hospital with tuberculosis, and therefore she had prepared her own meals. Frequently she would skip them because she studied a lot and also did the housework. She denied any wish to become thin. In the summer, she did not eat because she disliked the long lines waiting at restaurants. She failed to notice how thin she was getting but felt a sensation of something heavy in her stomach. She was a solitary girl without friends and claimed she enjoyed being alone. On the ward, she was frequently observed pressing her stomach and pacing around. She was placed on small doses of insulin and stelazine. Her mood remained sullen. She was uncooperative and complained repetitively.

When we saw Olga in consultation, she was a thin, serious girl, preoccupied with the sensation of heaviness in her stomach. She requested enemas and physical care, not psychiatric care, and demanded the services of a pediatrician. She also complained of headaches and said her menstrual periods had stopped completely about six months previously. She complained that the staff did not believe her, that really she wanted to eat but was unable to. Actually Olga's weight had increased from 31 kilograms to 35 kilograms (68 pounds to 77 pounds) in a few days.

Dr. Rotiniyan considered Olga a case of schizophrenia. The ideas of something heavy in the stomach certainly sounded delusional. The child was repeatedly asking for enemas, evidently in the conviction that there was indeed something inside her which was harmful and which she felt the need to be rid of.

5. PETER: A CASE OF PERSONALITY DISORDER

Peter was 14 when he was admitted to the Psychoneurological Hospital, both because of his difficulties in school (including inability to concentrate and do his lessons and conflicted relationships with both teachers and peers) and because of strong persistent sexual urges which included voyeurism and masturbation.

Peter had experienced erection since he was two years old, at the beginning connected with stimulation of the region of the buttocks. When school began, Peter found himself excited in the presence of girls and their clothing. He would lie on the floor and masturbate, though he tried to conceal these activities from other people. While at Pioneer Camp, he secluded himself in the woods with one girl and had sexual intercourse with her. Although she was unwilling, he felt very much attracted to her. Peter tried to free himself from these habits. Somewhere he read in a book if he inhaled gasoline he could hope for relief. He tried this experiment and began to have hallucinations of people and the sea. Peter even began to speak to these human visions and gradually accustomed himself to longer and longer inhalations of gasoline. He also tried acetone but didn't like the visions he saw of dogs and doctors. He was quite guilty about these habits. His doctors tried to calm him and reassure him with the thought that in America, such symptoms were present in 80 percent of all children!

Peter also experienced depression. He began to believe there was nothing to live for. Nothing interested him, not even friends. He seemed never to enjoy life and seldom smiled. He preferred his hallucinatory experiences to real human contacts. He was also plagued by other strong impulses: excessive thirst and wish to eat sweets.

Peter had always experienced difficulty in school, both with the other children and with the teachers. He had no motivation to learn and had to repeat the sixth class. He was particularly handicapped in mathematics. Twice he even ran away from school. In general, he was considered suspicious and stubborn.

Peter's life was one great struggle between his wish to masturbate and his desire to control it. Sometimes, he would go to the showers and try to observe naked women. When he saw one, he would masturbate. He took up smoking with the idea of calming himself and reducing the urge to masturbate.

Peter entered the hospital wishing for help in controlling his impulses. But he was unwilling to talk because of embarrassment about his difficulties. He thought of the sexual problem as an illness but not the urge to consume sweets. He said he remembered being sexually excited since the age of two or three, along with an interest in daydreams. For a long time, he thought he would never marry but during the past year, he changed his mind and began to believe he would marry when he became 18. Physical findings on admission were not remarkable. Skull x-rays revealed a mild, compensated hydrocephalus and the EEG revealed a diffuse dysrhythmia.

Peter received chlorpromazine and began to complain of headaches, dizziness, and pains in the region of the heart. He made no move to get close to anyone and soon began to complain about the medical personnel. No pathological sexual impulses were ever observed, but the child was incapable of engaging in any meaningful activity. As

Peter's discomfort increased, he wanted more and more to go home but agreed to stay if his treatment did not have to be prolonged. At first, although upset and depressed, he noticed he could control the desire to masturbate. As he succeeded, his mood improved. Then he again became depressed and demanded to go home. He promised he would concentrate and obey his mother.

Psychological study revealed that Peter had a good intellect but his performance was uneven, his reaction times were slowed down, and he was unable to keep all the conditions for the solution of a problem in mind. There was no evidence of a degenerative process. (I wonder if the abnormalities noted might be the effect of medication rather than a reflection of Peter's condition.)

When Peter came to the consultation, he was a slender adolescent boy whose voice had already begun to change. He seemed neither very depressed nor very anxious. He thought he had become a bit better since hospitalization. He said he was in the sixth class and liked geography best because of his interest in travel. He liked Russian least. After finishing school, he hoped to go to a technicum where he could learn to be a railroad worker. As a younger child, he had been interested in dogs, hunting, and stamp collecting. He dated the onset of his illness at around three years of age, although he added that a new symptom had recently appeared. Perhaps he was referring to his sexual excitement when he saw women. He realized that it was harmful for him to inhale gasoline, but he had read about it in a book one time.

In summarizing the case, the presenting doctor emphasized the presence not only of the sexual impulses but also the increased appetite for sweets and liquids. The hydrocephalic changes demonstrated by x-ray, the stormy pubertal development, and a history of some anoxia at birth all suggested some "early organic insufficiency." The alternating euphoria and depression, too, pointed in this direction. Pronounced autistic trends were also present, since Peter did not want to have anything to do with people but continued to fantasy about sexual contacts. Intellectual disturbances included the lowering of his ability to do schoolwork and the disturbances noted in concentration and attention.

Peter's personality disorder was considered to be caused by a mild form of early brain damage and was not attributed to social or interpersonal environmental factors. Treatment was directed to lowering the intensity of the sexual impulses with chlorpromazine medication and general supportive psychotherapy. There was no direct prohibition of masturbation. No attempt was made to enter into extensive individual psychotherapy. There was much about Peter's obsessional thinking, his guilt and shame over his sexuality, and his struggle to control it that suggested an obsessive-compulsive character formation, although this was not mentioned in the discussion of the case. The sexual impulse and the patient's struggle with it was believed to cause many of the other symptoms, including the conflicted relationships with his peer group, the retreat into fantasy, the misguided efforts at self-cure, and the difficulties in concentration, which led in turn to his problems with his teachers. It is of interest to note how the rising discomfort and depression immediately replaced the directly sexual manifestations. None of the Soviet doctors commented about this.

6. MARTIA: A CASE OF REACTION OF PROTEST IN ADOLESCENCE

This case shows Soviet thinking in regard to a psychogenic problem in adolescence and is the best example among all the case histories of psychiatric interviewing. Martia was a 14-year-old girl who was first hospitalized in a psychoneurological hospital in Moscow and was subsequently transferred a month before the consultation to Sanatorium No. 44.

The family history and early development were not remarkable. Martia remained with a nurse until she was six and was said to have frequently wandered away from home. At six, it was believed Martia witnessed an act of sexual exhibitionism. In kindergarten, she found it hard to adjust to the routine. She showed an early preference for boys which lasted throughout her later childhood and continued into adolescence. Martia spent two years with her family in Algeria when she was about nine years old. She associated with French and English girls and learned the French language quickly. The child asked many questions about sexual relationships between men and women and how children relate to adults. Mother attempted to satisfy this curiosity by demonstrations with puppies. Martia's parents were strict and she received physical punishment until she was at least 13.

Martia was well developed and large for her age. Her menses began at 12 years and along with her adolescent development, her symptoms started. She began to get poor marks in school and became irritable and moody with frequent crying spells. She was interested in boys three to four years older than she and experimented with drinking and smoking. She was attracted particularly to boys described as "hooligan types" and liked dancing and Beatle-type music. The parents were so upset by her open sexual preoccupations that they placed her under surveillance all the time when she was not in school. So the child fabricated stories about escapades with older boys and her interest in drinking and smoking. The depth of the parents' concern can be measured by the fact that they gained admission for Martia in a mental hospital. They were afraid that the sexual concerns meant mental illness. The doctors played into this by accepting the child in the mental hospital and the sanatorium.

On admission, Martia was found to be a large, well-developed, early-adolescent girl with some facial asymmetry but otherwise negative neurological findings. She was full of typical adolescent concerns. She said she wanted to become a hippie but wouldn't actually because then she couldn't take baths! She had admitted that sometimes she had skipped school and was very much preoccupied with boys. She behaved in a seductive way on the ward and acted as if she felt she had great influence on men, telling exaggerated tales about her escapades.

Psychological study showed that she was willing, cooperative, with intact intellectual processes. Her associations showed a preoccupation with men and some fearfulness. She fatigued quite easily when doing intellectual tasks. She made one interesting drawing of a boy and girl together with a very elaborate guitar covering the genital region of the boy and the girl too. The girl had only half of her left leg and exaggerated eye makeup. Both figures were slender so that feminine contours were deemphasized.

Professor Kovalev held an extremely interesting interview with Martia. Perhaps because of the sanatorium conditions, she was not seductive in her appearance or manner. Martia said she had originally entered because of fatigue. While not complaining about the sanatorium, her attitude seemed less than enthusiastic. She denied missing life at home with her parents. She spent her time with other girls walking, studying, reading stories, and resting. At home she had had headaches, but these disappeared after her admission. She considered herself ill only in the sense of having physical symptoms. At school, she acknowledged difficulty with mathematics, fooling and smoking with other girls, and being fresh with the teacher. However, Martia said she only had one close girl friend with whom she shared activities. She claimed she had five older boy friends whom she had met during the summer at a country cottage. Older boys she found more interesting because they want to become writers of detective novels. She wished to be allowed to accompany these boys back to the summer cottage, but of course was not permitted to do so by her family. Martia was obviously boy-crazy, but she had formed no deep, lasting relationship with one boy.

There were frequent arguments with her mother over boys. Although Martia resented the restrictions placed on her, she would not say her parents were wrong in imposing them. She felt that her mother was much stricter than her father and controlled her free time. She conceded that her relationships with her family were really quite poor; her conflicts were more frequent than other girls'. Martia had always been closer to her father and tended to go to him when she wanted permission to do something. On the other hand, if she had worries about her health, she would be more likely to go to her mother. Perhaps her parents were bringing her up right, even though she didn't like it. If her parents didn't direct her, it might affect her future. Nevertheless she wished only to be left alone to follow her own inclinations. She was allowed to make some choices. For example, her mother would let her choose mini-skirts and other stylish clothes but only on the condition that she do well at school.

After finishing school, Martia hoped she could go to the foreign language institute and study French. Professor Kovalev remarked on how great the competition is to enter such an institute and how necessary it is to study and to do well. Martia thought that after the eighth class, it would be easier for her to study. One of her boy friends told her so. Professor Kovalev disagreed, saying he considered the program in the ninth and tenth classes more difficult. I thought perhaps Martia was trying to say that when she became more accustomed to her own adolescence, it would be easier for her to settle down and organize herself.

Martia was greatly interested in the life of American hippies. She read about this in a magazine called "Around the World." When Professor Kovalev asked her what she knew about the life of hippies and how they spent their time, she said, "They don't wash and they don't shave." I asked Martia what hippie meant, and she said she thought it meant flower children. She said one correspondent had reported conversations he had held with hippies and he had found that they "negated life." Further, anything goes and every day was a holiday. Professor Kovalev laughed and said he thought that what Martia liked was that they were completely without rules or supervision. Then he asked whether there was something else that she might like about them. What about their not shaving or not combing their hair or washing? Martia denied being interested in this aspect of hippie life; she was merely interested in the fact that they were completely free. Professor

Kovalev asked her whether people in the Soviet Union live like that. She replied, not really, though many of our young people would like to imitate the hippies. Martia said that the police sometimes bother these young people and indicated that she had seen them. If she visited America, she would like to watch hippies though perhaps not become one herself. She had discussed these things some with other girls her age on the ward in the sanatorium, but was quite guarded in revealing the content of these conversations. She added that she told her mother and father practically nothing about her activities, interests, and concerns. Professor Kovalev asked her directly about her drinking and smoking experiences, which she acknowledged but minimized, in contrast to the report and the history that she tended to exaggerate. Professor Kovalev commented that Martia was able under sanatorium conditions to behave quite well and wondered why she did not feel like making herself behave at home. At the end of the interview he conducted a brief physical examination, asking a few questions about fatigability and her interest in sports. She did not like most sports but did say that occasionally she would go to the swimming pool. Professor Kovalev encouraged her to be more interested in these activities.

In the discussion of this case, Professor Kovalev judged the sexual drives in this young lady to be normal, though he felt her interest in these matters had been unduly stimulated both by the early environmental factor of the sexual trauma and by the early onset of adolescence. He considered her intelligence adequate but not really high and thought that she would make a good hairdresser rather than a candidate for the foreign language school. He seemed to agree with me that this was "adolescent disease." He said this is not really pathology but "psychological." He did not make a diagnosis of psychopathy, but called her "prepsychopathic" or hysteroid. He felt that the prognosis was favorable and that her behavior was an example of the reaction of protest, a rebellion against excessive parental strictness. Therapeutic recommendations were to increase the dosage of chlorpromazine from 50 mg to 100 mg a day to diminish the intensity of her sexual drives and to help her divert her interest into other channels such as sports. He felt that supportive psychotherapy might be useful, though not on a very intensive individual basis. An important aspect of the case missing in this discussion was what to do about the parents and how to enlist their cooperation in easing up on the child once she returned home.

References

PREFACE

Sources in English

1. Miller, A. D., "The Child Mental Health Care System," *American Journal of Psychiatry,* special section, "Impressions of Soviet Psychiatry," 125:660–665 (1968).

2. Skolnick, A., "Some Psychiatric Aspects of the New Soviet Child," *Bulletin of the Menninger Clinic,* 28:120–144 (1964).

3. Wortis, J., *Soviet Psychiatry.* Baltimore: William and Wilkins Company, 1950.

I. HISTORICAL AND SOCIAL PERSPECTIVES

Sources in Russian

1. Aksarina, N. M., T. S. Babadzhan, M. Yu. Kistoyakovskaya, S. M. Krivna, N. F. Ladygina, and G. M. Lyamina, *Razvitie i vospitanie* (Development and Upbringing). Leningrad: Meditsina, 1965.

2. Kabanov, M. M., and R. A. Zachepitski, "Nauchnaya deyatelnost V. N. Myasishcheva" (Scietnific Activity of V. N. Myasishchev), in *Voprosy sovremennoi psikhonevrologii* (Questions of Contemporary Psychoneurology). Leningrad: Leningradskii Nauchno-issledovatelskii Leningrad: Leningradskii Nauchno-issledovatelskii Psikhonevrologicheskii Institut imeni V. M. Bekhtereva, Trudy Instituta, 1966, pp. 5–14.

3. Kerbikov, O. V., M. V. Korkina, R. A. Nadzharov, and A. V. Snezhnevski, *Psikhiatriya* (Psychiatry). Moscow, 1968, pp. 131–132.

References

4. Kharchev, A. G., *Brak i semya v SSSR* (Marriage and the Family in the USSR). Moscow: Izdatelstvo sotsialno-ekonomicheskoi literatury "Mysl," 1964.

5. Lavrov, A. S., E. A. Shumilin, G. B. Rezniuk, et al., *Ot nolya do semi* (from Birth to Seven). Moscow: Znanie, 1967.

6. Manko, "Osobennyi Sluchai" (A Singular Case), *Pravda,* Nov. 25, 1968.

7. Myasishchev, V. N., "Lichnost rebenka-nevrotika" (Personality of the Child Neurotic), V. N. Myasishchev, *Lichnost i nevrozy* (Personality and Neroses). Leningrad: Izdatelstvo Leningradskogo Universiteta, 1960, pp. 52–67.

8. Myasishchev, V. N., "Nekotorye voprosy teorii psikhoterapii" (Some Questions of the Theory of Psychotherapy), in V. N. Myasischev, *Lichnost i nevrozy.* Leningrad: Izdatelstvo Leningradskogo Universiteta, 1960, pp. 372–382.

9. Myasischev, V. N., "Ponyatie lichnosti i ego znachenie dlya medit- *siny* (Understanding of the Personality and Its Significance for Medicine), in *Metodologicheskie problemy psikhonevrologii* (Methodological Problems of Psychoneurology). Leningrad: Trudy Instituta imeni Bekhtereva, 1966, pp. 25–55.

10. "Otchet o deyatelnosti vospitatelno-klinicheskogo instituta dlya nervnykh detei imeni Akademika V. M. Bekhtereva Psikho-nevrologi- cheskoi Akademii" (Account of the Activity of the Educational Clinical In- stitute for Nervous Children Named for Academician V. M. Bekhterev, of the Psychoneurological Academy), *Voprosy Izucheniya i vospitaniya lichnosti* (Questions in the Study and Training of Personality), 2–3:231– 234 (1926).

11. Semenov, M., "Irinka sdaet exameny" (Irinka Takes Examinations), in N. M. Lariokhina, ed., *Rasskazy Sovietskikh pisatelei* (Short Stories by Soviet Writers). Moscow: Izdatelstovo Moskovskogo Universiteta, 1963, pp. 135–141.

12. Simpson, T. P., *Nevrozy u detei ikh preduprezhdenie i lechenie* (Neuroses in Children, Their Prevention and Treatment). Moskow: Gos- udarstvennoe izdatelstvo meditsinskoi literatury, Medgiz, 1958.

13. Sukhareva, G. E., *Klinicheskie lektsii po psikhiatrii detskogo vozrastra* (Clinical Lectures in Child Psychiatry), vol. I. Moscow, 1955.

14. Sukkareva, G. E., *Klinicheskie lektsii po psikhiatrii detskogo vozrasta* (Clinical Lectures in Child Psychiatry), vol. II. Moscow, 1959.

Sources in English

15. Alt, H., and E. Alt, *Russia's Children.* New York: Bookman Associ- ates, Inc., 1959.

16. Alt, H., and E. Alt, *The New Soviet Man.* New York: Bookman Associates, Inc., 1964.

17. Aronson, J., and M. G. Field, "Mental Health Programming in the Soviet Union," *American Journal of Orthopsychiatry,* 34: 913–924 (1964).

18. Bauer, R. A., "The Conception of Man in Soviet Psychology," Ph.D. diss., Harvard University, 1950.

19. Bauer, R. A., *The New Man in Soviet Psychology.* Cambridge: Harvard University Press, 1959.

20. Brazier, M. A., ed., *The Central Nervous System and Behavior, Transactions of the First Conference,* sponsored by Josiah Macy Foundation, New York, N.Y., and the National Science Foundation, Washington, D.C., 1958.

21. Bronfenbrenner, U., *Two Worlds of Childhood, US and USSR.* New York: Russell Sage Foundation, 1970.

22. Brown, D. R. ed., *The Role and Status of Women in the Soviet Union.* New York: Teachers' College Press, Columbia University, 1968.

23. Cole, M., and S. Cole, "Russian Nursery Schools," *Psychology Today,* October 1968, pp. 22–24.

24. Erikson, E., *Identity, Youth and Crisis.* New York: W. W. Norton and Company, Inc., 1968.

25. *The First US Mission on Mental Health to the USSR.* Chevy Chase, Md.: Public Health Service Publication no. 1893, 1969.

26. Greenacre, P., "The Childhood of the Artist," in *Psychoanalytic Study of the Child,* vol. XII. New York: International Universities Press, Inc., 1957, pp. 47–72.

27. Ivanov-Smolenski, A. G., "Ways and Perspectives of the Development of the Physiology and Pathophysiology of the Higher Nervous Activity of the Child," in *The Central Nervous System and Behavior, Translations from the Russian Medical Literature.* Bethesda: US Department of Health, Education and Welfare, Public Health Service, 1959, pp. 280–294.

28. Kassof, A., *The Soviet Youth Program, Regimentation and Rebellion.* Cambridge: Harvard University Press, 1963.

29. Luriya, A. R., "Verbal Regulation of Behavior," in Brazier, M. A., ed., *The Central Nervous System and Behavior, Transactions of the Third Conference,* Sponsored by the Josiah Macy Foundation, New York, N.Y., and the National Science Foundation, Washington, D.C., 1960, pp. 359–423.

30. Lustig, B., "Therapeutic Methods in Soviet Psychiatry," *ICRS Medical Reports,* Fordham University, vol. 3.

31. Makarenko, A. S., *A Book for Parents.* Moscow: Foreign Languages Publishing House, 1967.

32. Morozov, V. M., "Depth Psychology and Psychiatry," in *The Central Nervous System and Behavior, Translations from the Russian Medical Literature.* Bethesda: US Department of Health, Education and Welfare, Public Health Service, 1960, pp. 654–669.

33. Myasishchev, V. N., "The Problem of Psychological Type in the Light of Pavlov's Teaching," in V. N. Myasishchev, *Personality and*

References

Neuroses, trans. Joint Publications Research Service. Washington, D.C.: US Department of Commerce, 1963, pp. 125–249.

34. Myasischev, V. N., "Problems in Psychology in the Light of the Classical Marxist-Leninist Views of Human Attitudes," in V. N. Myasishchev, *Personality and Neuroses,* trans. Joint Publications Research Service. Washington, D.C.: US Department of Commerce, 1963, pp. 91–115.

35. Pavlov, I. P., "Constitutional Differences and Functional Disturbances (Constitutional Neuroses)," in I. P. Pavlov, *Conditioned Reflexes: An Investigation of the Physiological Activity of the Cerebral Cortex,* trans. and ed. G. V. Anrep. London: Oxford University Press, 1927, pp. 284–289.

36. Pavlov, I. P., "Experimental Pathology of the Higher Nervous Activity," in I. P. Pavlov, *Selected Works,* trans. S. Belsky, ed. J. Gibbons. Moscow: Foreign Languages Publishing House, 1955, pp. 461–480.

37. Perepel, E., "The Psychoanalytic Movement in USSR," *Psychoanalytic Review,* 26:299–300 (1939).

38. Platonov, K. I., *The Word as a Physiological and Therapeutic Factor: The Theory and Practice of Psychotherapy According to I. P. Pavlov.* Moscow: Foreign Languages Publishing House, 1959.

39. Raskin, N., "Development of Russian Psychiatry before the First World War," *American Journal of Psychiatry,* 120:851–855 (1964).

40. Skolnick, A., "Some Aspects of 'The New Soviet Child'," *Bulletin of the Menninger Clinic,* 28:120–144 (1964).

41. Wortis, J., *Soviet Psychiatry.* Baltimore: Williams and Wilkins Company, 1950.

42. Zilborg, G., *A History of Medical Psychology.* New York: W. W. Norton and Company, Inc., 1941.

II. THE ORGANIZATION OF PSYCHIATRIC SERVICES

Sources in Russian

1. *Programmy vspomogatelnoi shkoly: obshcheobrazovatelnye predmety* (Programs of Schools for the Retarded: General Educatinal Subjects). Moscow: Izdatelstvo "Prosveshchenie," 1965.

2. Shanko, G. G., *Preduprezhdenie nevrozov u detei* (Prevention of Neuroses in Children). Minsk, 1968.

3. Smirnova, A. A., "Lektsiya 24" (Lecture 24: Organization of Specialized Services for Retarded Children), in G. E. Sukhareva, *Klinicheskie lektsii po psikhiatrii detskogo vozrasta* (Clinical Lectures in Child Psychiatry), vol. III. Moscow, 1965.

4. Sukhareva, G. E., "Predposylki k organizatsii psikhonevrologicheskoi pomoshchi detyam" Prerequisites for the Organization of Psychoneurological Service to Children), in *Voprosy detskoi psikhonevrologii* (Questions in Child Psychoneurology). Moscow, 1958, pp. 20–29.

References

Source in English

5. *The First US Mission on Mental Health to the USSR.* Chevy Chase, Md.: Public Health Service Publication no. 1893, 1969.

III. DIAGNOSIS

Sources in Russian

1. Deyanov, V. Ya., *Psikhicheskie narusheniya pri revmatizme u detei i prodrostkov* (Psychic Disturbances in Rheumatism in Children and Adolescents). Moscow, 1962.
2. Dimitrieva, I. V., "K voprousu o nevropsikhcheskikh narusheniyakh pri grippe u detei" (On the Question of Neuropsychic Disturbances in Grippe in Children), in *Voprosy detskoi psikhonevrologii* (Questions in Child Psychoneurology). Moscow, 1958, pp. 54–59.
3. Kagan, V. E., "Ob ispolzovanii tematicheskogo appertseptsionnogo testa (TAT) v klinike detskoi psikhiatrii" (Concerning the Use of the Thematic Apperception Test [TAT] in Clinical Practice with Children), in *Rezidualnye nervno-psikhicheskie rasstroistva u detei* (Residual Neuro-psychic Disturbances in Children), vol. 51. Leningrad: Leningradskii Pediatricheskii Meditsinskii Institut, 1968, pp. 141–150.
4. Kerbikov, O. V., M. V. Korkina, R. A. Nadzharov, and A. V. Snezhnevski, *Psikhiatriya* (Psychiatry). Moscow, 1968.
5. Kononova, M. P., *Rukovodstvo po psikhologicheskomu issledovaniyu psikhicheskikh bolnykh detei shkolnogo vozrasta* (Handbook of Psychological Research in Children of School Age with Psychiatric Illness). Moscow, 1963.
6. Kovaleva, T. V., *Revmaticheskie Psikhozy* (Rheumatic Psychoses), Avtoreferat dissertatsii na coiskanie uchenoi stepeni kandidata meditsinskikh nauk (Summary of dissertation for the degree, Candidate in Medical Sciences). Lvov, 1964.
7. Kudryatseva, V. P., "Klinicheskie osobennosti razvitiya detei perenesshikh tyazheluyu (toksicheskuyu ili khronicheskuyu) dizenteriyu" (Clinical Characteristics of the Development of Children who have had Severe [Toxic or Chronic] Dysentery), in *Voprosy detskoi psikhonevrologii.* Moscow, 1958, pp. 72–78.
8. Lomachenkov, A. S., "K voprosu o kartinakh i techenii maniakalno-depressivnogo psikhoza u detei i prodrostkov" (Concerning the Question of the Clinical Picture and Course of the Manic-Depressive Psychosis in Children), in *Rezidualnye nervno-psikhicheskie rasstroistva u detei* vol. 51. Leningrad: Leningradskii Pediatricheskii Meditsinskii Institut, 1968, pp. 259–265.
9. Myasishchev, V. N., "Lichnost rebenka nevrotica" (Personality of the Child Neurotic), in V. N. Myasishchev, *Lichnost i nevrozy* (Personality and Neuroses). Leningrad: Izdatelstvo Leningradskogo Universiteta, 1960, pp. 52–67.

10. Mnukhin, S. S., "Ob etiologii nervno-psikhicheskikh narushenii razvivayushchikhsya na pochve 'detskikh rezidualnykh entsefalopatii' " (Concerning the Etiology of Neuropsychic Disturbances Developing on the Basis of 'Residual Encephalopathy of Childhood'), in *Voprosy detskoi psikhonevrologii.* Moscow, 1958, pp. 99–108.

11. Rotiniyan, N. S., "K voprosu sindroma nevroticheskoi anoreksii" (Concerning the Question of the Syndrome of Neurotic Anorexia), MS, 1969.

12. Simpson, T. P., *Nevrozy u detei, ikh preduprezhdenie i lechenie* (Neuroses in Children; Their Prevention and Treatment). Moscow: Gosudarstvennoe izdatelstvo meditsinskoi literatury, Medgiz, 1958.

13. Simpson, T. P., and V. P. Kudryatseva, "Klinika, etiologiya i patogenez shizofrenii u detei i podrostkov" (Clinical Picture, Etiology and Pathogenesis of Schizophrenia in Children and Adolescents), in V. A. Gilyarouski et al., *Shizofreniye u detei i podrostkov.* (Schizophrenia in Children and Adolescents). Moscow: Medgiz, 1959, pp. 11–52.

14. Sukhareva, G. E., *Klinicheskie lektsii po psikhiatrii detskogo vozrasta* (Clinical Lectures in Child Psychiatry). vol. I. Moscow, 1955.

15. Sukhareva, G. E., *Klinicheskie lektsii po psikhiatrii detskogo vozrasta* (Clinical Lectures in Child Psychiatry), vol. II. Moscow, 1959.

16. Sukhareva, G. E., *Oligofreniya: Klinicheskie lektsii po psikhiatrii detskogo vozrasta,* (Oligophrenia: Clinical Lectures in Child Psychiatry), vol. III. Moscow, 1965.

17. Vrono, M. S., "O vliyanii vozrastnogo faktora na techenie shizofrenii u detei" (Concerning the Influence of the Age factor on the Course of Schizophrenia in Children), *Zhurnal nevropatologii i psikhiatrii im. S. S. Korsakova* (Journal of Neuropathology and Psychiatry named for Korsakov), 65:1039–1044 (1965).

Sources in English

18. Blackwell, A., and N. Rollins, "Treatment Problems in Adolescents with Anorexia Nervosa: Preliminary Observations on the Second Phase," *Acta Paedopsychiatrica,* 35:294–301 (1968).

19. Blitzer, J., N. Rollins, and A. Blackwell, "Children Who Starve Themselves: Anorexia Nervosa," *Psychosomatic Medicine,* 23:369–383 (1961).

IV. GENERAL TREATMENT METHODS

Sources in Russian

1. Avrutski, T. Ya., *Neotlozhnaya pomoshch pri psikhicheskikh zabolevaniyakh* (Emergency Help in Psychiatric Illnesses). Moscow: Izdatelstvo Meditsina, 1966.

References

2. Gamza, V. A., "Instruktivno-metodicheskoe pismo dlya pedagogov detskogo psikhonevrologicheskogo sanatoriya No. 44 mosgorzdravotdela" (Instructive Methodological Letter for Educators at Children's Psychoneurological Sanatorium No. 44, Moscow City Health Department). MS, Moscow, 1968.

3. Grebliovski, M. Ya., *Trudovaya terapiya psikhicheskikh bolnykh* (Work Therapy for the Mentally Ill). Moscow: Izdatelstvo Meditsina, 1966.

4. Korganova, A. N. "Lechenie aminazinom detei i podrostkov, bolnykh shizopreniei" (Treatment with Aminazine of Children and Adolescents Ill with Schizophrenia), in V. A. Gilyarovski et al., *Schizofreniya u detei i podrostkov* (Schizophrenia in Children and Adolescents). Moscow: Medgiz, 1959, pp. 194–202.

5. Sukhareva, G. E., "Lektsiya 25, Lechenie i lechebnaya pedagogika pogranichnykh form psikhicheskikh rasstroistv" (Lecture 25, Treatment and Therapeutic Pedagogy in Borderline Forms of Psychiatric Disturbance), in G. E. Sukhareva, *Klinicheskie lektsii po psikhiatrii detskogo vozrasta* (Clinical Lectures in Child Psychiatry), vol. II. Moscow, 1959, pp. 376–399.

Sources in English

6. Fish, B., "Treatment of Children," supplement to *International Psychiatry Clinics,* vol. 2, no. 4; supplement to N. S. Kline and H. G. Lehmann, eds., *Psychopharmacology,* Boston: Little Brown and Company, 1966.

7. Jablonski, S., *Russian Drug Index,* second ed. Bethesda: US Department of Health, Education and Welfare, Public Health Service Publication, No. 814, 1967.

8. Myasishchev, V. N., "Basic Problems of the Theory and Practice of Work Therapy in Psychoneurological Hospitals," in V. N. Myasishchev, *Personality and Neuroses,* trans. Joint Publications Research Service. Washington, D.C.: US Department of Commerce, 1963, pp. 242–249.

9. Poser, C. M., and V. Osbourn, *International Dictionary of Drugs Used in Neurology and Psychiatry,* Springfield, Ill.: Charles C. Thomas, 1962.

10. Skolnick, A., "Some Psychiatric Aspects of the 'New Soviet Child'," *Bulletin of the Menninger Clinic,* 28:120–144 (1964).

V. SPECIAL PSYCHOTHERAPY

Sources in Russian

1. Drapkin, B. Z., untitled paper on the psychotherapy of stuttering in adolescence, MS, Moscow, 1969.

2. Niss, A. I., "Rezultaty primeneniya gipnoza v lechenii nochnogo enureza u detei" (Results of the Application of Hypnosis in the Treatment of Nocturnal Enuresis in Children), in Banshchikov, ed., *Terapiya psikhicheskikh zabolevanii* (Therapy of Psychic Illnesses), Moscow, 1968.

Sources in English

3. Deutsch, F., and W. Murphy, *The Clinical Interview,* vol. II: *Therapy.* New York: International Universities Press, Inc., 1955.

4. Platonov, K., *The Word as a Physiological and Therapeutic Factor: The Theory and Practice of Psychotherapy according to I. P. Pavlov.* Moscow: Foreign Languages Publishing House, 1959.

5. Schultz, J. H., and W. Luthe, *Autogenic Training: A Psychophysiological Approach to Psychotherapy,* New York and London: Grune and Stratton, 1959.

6. Ziferstein, I., "Direct Observations of Psychotherapy in the USSR," in *Sixth International Congress of Psychotherapy London, 1964: Selected Lectures,* New York: Basel S. Karger, 1965, pp. 150–160.

VI. TRAINING PSYCHIATRIC PERSONNEL

Sources in English

1. *The First US Mission on Mental Health to the USSR.* Chevy Chase, Md.: Public Health Service Publication no. 1893, 1969.

2. Sidel, V. W., "Feldshers and Feldsherism: The Role and Training of the Feldsher in the USSR," *New England Journal of Medicine,* 278:934–940, 981–992 (April 26 and May 2, 1968).

VII. RESEARCH

Sources in Russian

1. Bashina, V. M., "Trudosposobnost i sotsialnaya adaptatsiya bolnikh shizofreniei zabolevshikh v detskom i podrostkom vozraste" (Work Capability and Social Adaptation of Patients with Schizophrenia Who Became Ill in Childhood and Adolescence), *Zhurnal nevropatologii i psikhiatrii im Korsakova* (Journal of Neuropathology and Psychitatry named for Korsakov), 63:1041–1046 (1963).

2. Bashina, V. M., "Dinamika v vozrastnom aspekte katatonicheskikh rasstroistv u detei, stradayushchikh shizofreniei" (Dynamics with Respect to Age of Catatonic Disturbances of Children Suffering from Schizophrenia), *Zhurnal nevropatologii i psikhiatrii im Korsakova,* 68:1549–1553 (1968).

References

3. Boldyreva, S. A., and V. P. Kudryatseva, "Osobennosti risunkov detei doshkolnogo vozrasta bolnikh shizofreniei" (Characteristics of Drawings of Preschool Children Suffering from Schizphrenia), *Zhurnal nevropatologii i psikhiatrii im Korsakova*, 67:1521–1529 (1967).

4. Boldyreva, S. A., "Otrazhenie gallyutsionatsii v risunkakh detei doshkolnogo vozrasta, stradayushchikh shizofreniei" (Hallucinations in the Drawings of Schizophrenic Children of Preschool Age), *Zhurnal nevropatologii i psikhiatrii im Korsakova,* 69:1575–1580 (1969).

5. Gilyarovski, V. A., V. Ya. Deglina, V. P. Kudryatseva, T. P. Simpson, D. D. Fedotova, *Shizofrenia u detei i podrostkov* (Schizophrenia in Children and Adolescents). Moscow: Gosudarstvennoe izdatelstvo meditsinskoi literatury, Medgiz, 1959.

6. Golovan, L. I., "Nekotorye osobennosti neirodinamiki pri nevroze navyazchivikh sostoyanii u detei" (Some Features of the Neurodynamics of Compulsive States in Children), *Trudi Instituta Vyshei Nervnoi Deyatelnosti* (Proceedings of the Institute of Higher Nervous Activity), Seria patofiziologicheskaya, vol. 8, 1961, pp. 96–102.

7. Kovalev, V. V., "Nervno-psikhicheskie narusheniya u bolnikh vrozhdennymi porokami serdtsa" (Neuropsychic Disturbances in Patients with Congenital Heart Lesions), *Zhurnal nevropatologii i psikhiatrii im Korsakova,* 59:986–993 (1959).

8. Kovalev, V. V., "Hauchnye issledovaniya v detskoi psikhiatrii" (Scientific Research in Child Psychiatry), *Zhurnal nevropatologii i psikhiatrii im Korsakova,* 67:1675–1679 (1967).

9. Kovalev, V. V., "O psikhogenykh patologicheskikh formirovaniyakh [razvitie lichnosti] u detei i podrostkov" (On Psychogenic Pathological Formations [Development of the Personality] in Children and Adolescents), *Zhurnal nevropatologii i psikhiatrii im Korsakova,* 69:1543–1549 (1969).

10. Kozlova, I. A., "O formakh techeniya rannei detskoi shizofrenii" (On the Forms of the Course of Early Childhood Schizophrenia), *Zhurnal nevropatologii i psikhiatrii im Korsakova,* 67:1516–1521 (1967).

11. Lebedinskaya, K. S., E. S. Kuznetsova, and T. I. Buraya, "Psikhicheskie osobennosti detei s vrozhdennoi disfunktsiei kory nadprochechnikov" (Psychic Characteristics of Children with Congenital Dysfunctions of the Adrenal Cortex), *Zhurnal nevropatologii i psikhiatrii im Korsakova,* 69:1558–1562 (1969).

12. Lupandin, V. M., "Kliniko-psikhopatologicheskii analiz periodicheskoi schizofrenii u podrostkov" (Clinical Psychopathological Analysis of Periodic Schizophrenia in Adolescents), *Zhurnal nevropatologii i psikhiatrii im Korsakova,* 65:1056–1062 (1965).

13. Mnukhin, S. S., and B. G. Frolov, "O klassifikatsii form epilepsii u detei" (On the Classification of Forms of Epilepsy in Children), *Rezidualnye nervno-psikhicheskie rasstroistva u detei* (Residual Neuropsychic Disturbances in Children), vol. 51. Leningrad: Leningradskii Pediatricheskii Meditsinskii Institut, 1968, pp. 155–165.

14. Mnukhin, S. S., "O vremennykh zaderzhkakh, zamedlonnom tempe

umstvennogo razvitiya i psikhicheskom infantilizme u detei" (On Temporary Inhibitions, Slow Tempo of Intellectual Development, and Psychic Infantilism in Children), *Rezidualnye nervno-psikhicheskie rasstroistva u detei,* vol 51. Leningrad: Leningradskii Pediatricheskii Meditsinskii Institut, 1968, pp. 70–77.

15. Polishchuk, Yu. I., and V. L. Shenderova, "O tipakh lichnosti v semyakh bolnykh shizofreniei s rannim nachalom i nepreryvnym techeniem zabolevaniya" (On the Types of Personality in Families of Schizophrenic Patients with an Early Onset and Continuous Course of the Disease), *Zhurnal nevropatologii i psikhiatrii im Korsakova,* 69:113–119 (1969).

16. Poppe, S. K., "Piknolepsiya i piknopodobnaya epilepsiya u detei" (Pyknolepsy and Pykno-like Epilepsy in Children), *Rezidualnye nervno-psikhicheskie rasstroistva u detei* vol. 51. Leningrad: Leningradskii Pediatricheskii Meditsinskii Institut, 1968, pp. 207–221.

17. Simpson, T. P., "Puti razvitiya nauchnoi mycly v detskoi psikhiatrii v SSSR i za rubezhom" (Paths of Development of Scientific Thought in Child Psychiatry in the USSR and Abroad), *Voprosy detskoi psikhonevrologii* (Questions of Child Psychoneurology). Moscow, 1958, pp. 11–19.

18. Sukhareva, G. E., "Kriterii differentsiatsii epilepsii, po dannym detskoi kliniki" (Criteria for the Differentiation of Epilepsy by the Data of Clinical Practice with Children). MS, Moscow, 1969.

19. Sukhareva, G. E., "K voprosu o kriterii differentsiatsii epilepsii, po dannym detskoi kliniki" (On the Criteria for the Differentiation of Epilepsy by the Data of Clinical Practice with Children), *Zhurnal nevropatologii i psikhiatrii im Korsakova,* 69:1526–1530 (1969).

20. Visnevskaya, L. Ya., "Tipy psikhicheskikh izmenenii pri epilepsii u detei [shkolnyi vozrast]" (Types of Psychic Changes in Epilepsy of School Age Children), Avtoreferat dissertatsii na soiskanie uchenoi stepeni kandidata medistinskikh nauk (Summary of dissertation for the degree, Candidate in Medical Sciences). Moscow, 1967.

21. Vrono, M. S., "O vliyanii vozrastnogo faktora na techenie schizofrenii u detei" (On the Influence of the Age Factor on the Course of Schizophrenia in Children), *Zhurnal nevropatologii i psikhiatrii im Korsakova,* 65:1039–1044 (1965).

22. Vrono, M. S., "Ob otdalennom periode techeniya shizofrenii nachavsheisya v detskom i podrostkom vozraste" (Concerning the Longterm Course of Schizophrenia Beginning in Childhood and Adolescence), *Zhurnal nevropatologii i psikhiatrii im Korsakova,* 66:1053–1057 (1966).

23. Vrono, M. S., "Vozrastnye osobennosti techeniya shizofrenii u detei i prodrostkov" (Age Characteristics of the Course of Schizophrenia in Children and Adolescents), Avtoreferat dissertatsii na soiskanie uchenoi stepeni doktora meditsinskikh nauk. Moscow, 1967.

24. Yureva, O. P., "Materialy k klinike medlenno-tekushchei shizofrenii u detei" (Toward the Clinical Description of Slowly Developing Schizophrenia in Children), *Zhurnal nevropatologii i psikhiatrii im Korsakova,* 65:1048–1055 (1965).

25. Yureva, O. P., "Domanifestnyi period medlenno-tekushchei shizofrenii u detei" (Before the Manifest Period of Slowly Progressive Schizophrenia in Children), *Zhurnal nevropatologii i psikhiatrii im Korsakova,* 67:1511–1515 (1967).

VIII. CONCLUSIONS

Sources in English

1. Aronson, J., and M. G. Field, "Mental Health Programming in the Soviet Union," *American Journal of Orthopsychiatry,* 34:913–924 (1964).

2. Field, M. G., and J. Aronson, "Soviet Psychiatry: The Institutional Framework," *Journal of Nervous and Mental Diseases,* 138:306–322 (April 1964).

3. Field, M. G., "Soviet Psychiatry and Social Structure, Culture and Ideology: A Preliminary Assessment," *American Journal of Psychotherapy,* 21:230–243 (1967).

4. Field, M. G., "Psychiatry and Ideology: The Official Soviet View of Western Theories and Practices," *American Journal of Psychotherapy,* 22:602–615 (1968).

5. Jones, E., *The Life and Work of Sigmund Freud,* vol. II. New York: Basic Books, Inc., 1955.

6. Rickard, G., and H. Cohen, "Assessing the Emotional Development of Children," *Mental Hygiene,* 50:590–592 (1966).

7. Seely, J., *The Americanization of the Unconscious.* New York: International Science Press, 1967.

Index